VOLUME 529

SEPTEMBER 1993

THE ANNALS

of The American Academy *of* Political
and Social Science

RICHARD D. LAMBERT, *Editor*
ALAN W. HESTON, *Associate Editor*

RURAL AMERICA:
BLUEPRINT FOR TOMORROW

Special Editor of this Volume

WILLIAM E. GAHR

U.S. General Accounting Office
Washington, D.C.

 SAGE Periodicals Press *THOUSAND OAKS LONDON NEW DELHI*

THE ANNALS

© 1993 *by* The American Academy *of* Political *and* Social Science

Editorial Office: 3937 Chestnut Street, Philadelphia, PA 19104.

For information about membership* (individuals only) and subscriptions (institutions), address:

SAGE PUBLICATIONS, INC.
2455 Teller Road
Thousand Oaks, CA 91320

From India and South Asia, write to:
SAGE PUBLICATIONS INDIA Pvt. Ltd.
P.O. Box 4215
New Delhi 110 048
INDIA

From the UK, Europe, the Middle East and Africa, write to:
SAGE PUBLICATIONS LTD
6 Bonhill Street
London EC2A 4PU
UNITED KINGDOM

SAGE Production Staff: LINDA GRAY, LIANN LECH, and JANELLE LeMASTER
*Please note that members of The Academy receive THE ANNALS with their membership.

Library of Congress Catalog Card Number 92-62093
International Standard Serial Number ISSN 0002-7162
International Standard Book Number ISBN 0-8039-5111-6 (Vol. 529, 1993 paper)
International Standard Book Number ISBN 0-8039-5108-6 (Vol. 529, 1993 cloth)
Manufactured in the United States of America. First printing, September 1993.

The articles appearing in THE ANNALS are indexed in *Book Review Index, Public Affairs Information Service Bulletin, Social Sciences Index, Current Contents, General Periodicals Index, Academic Index, Pro-Views,* and *Combined Retrospective Index Sets.* They are also abstracted and indexed in *ABC Pol Sci, Historical Abstracts, Human Resources Abstracts, Social Sciences Citation Index, United States Political Science Documents, Social Work Research & Abstracts, Sage Urban Studies Abstracts, International Political Science Abstracts, America: History and Life, Sociological Abstracts, Managing Abstracts, Social Planning/Policy & Development Abstracts, Automatic Subject Citation Alert, Book Review Digest, Work Related Abstracts, Periodica Islamica,* and/or *Family Resources Database,* and are available on microfilm from University Microfilms, Ann Arbor, Michigan.

Information about membership rates, institutional subscriptions, and back issue prices may be found on the facing page.

Advertising. Current rates and specifications may be obtained by writing to THE ANNALS Advertising and Promotion Manager at the Thousand Oaks office (address above).

Claims. Claims for undelivered copies must be made no later than three months following month of publication. The publisher will supply missing copies when losses have been sustained in transit and when the reserve stock will permit.

Change of Address. Six weeks' advance notice must be given when notifying of change of address to ensure proper identification. Please specify name of journal. Send address changes to: THE ANNALS, c/o Sage Publications, Inc., 2455 Teller Road, Thousand Oaks, CA 91320.

Origin and Purpose. The Academy was organized December 14, 1889, to promote the progress of political and social science, especially through publications and meetings. The Academy does not take sides in controverted questions, but seeks to gather and present reliable information to assist the public in forming an intelligent and accurate judgment.

Meetings. The Academy occasionally holds a meeting in the spring extending over two days.

Publications. THE ANNALS is the bimonthly publication of The Academy. Each issue contains articles on some prominent social or political problem, written at the invitation of the editors. Also, monographs are published from time to time, numbers of which are distributed to pertinent professional organizations. These volumes constitute important reference works on the topics with which they deal, and they are extensively cited by authorities throughout the United States and abroad. The papers presented at the meetings of The Academy are included in THE ANNALS.

Membership. Each member of The Academy receives THE ANNALS and may attend the meetings of The Academy. Membership is open only to individuals. Annual dues: $42.00 for the regular paperbound edition (clothbound, $60.00). Add $9.00 per year for membership outside the U.S.A. Members may also purchase single issues of THE ANNALS for $13.00 each (clothbound, $18.00). Add $2.00 for shipping and handling on all prepaid orders.

Subscriptions. THE ANNALS (ISSN 0002-7162) is published six times annually—in January, March, May, July, September, and November. Institutions may subscribe to THE ANNALS at the annual rate: $132.00 (clothbound, $156.00). California institutions: $141.57 paperbound, $167.31 clothbound. Add $9.00 per year for subscriptions outside the U.S.A. Institutional rates for single issues: $24.00 each (clothbound, $29.00). California institutions: $25.74 paperbound, $31.10 clothbound.

Second class postage paid at Thousand Oaks, California, and additional offices.

Single issues of THE ANNALS may be obtained by individuals who are not members of The Academy for $17.00 each (clothbound, $26.00). California residents: $18.23 paperbound, $27.89 clothbound. Add $2.00 for shipping and handling on all prepaid orders. Single issues of THE ANNALS have proven to be excellent supplementary texts for classroom use. Direct inquiries regarding adoptions to THE ANNALS c/o Sage Publications (address below).

All correspondence concerning membership in The Academy, dues renewals, inquiries about membership status, and/or purchase of single issues of THE ANNALS should be sent to THE ANNALS c/o Sage Publications, Inc., 2455 Teller Road, Thousand Oaks, CA 91320. Telephone: (805) 499-0721; FAX/Order line: (805) 499-0871. *Please note that orders under $30 must be prepaid.* Sage affiliates in London and India will assist institutional subscribers abroad with regard to orders, claims, and inquiries for both subscriptions and single issues.

Printed on recycled, acid-free paper

THE ANNALS

of The American Academy *of* Political *and* Social Science

RICHARD D. LAMBERT, *Editor*
ALAN W. HESTON, *Associate Editor*

———————— **FORTHCOMING** ————————

INTERMINORITY AFFAIRS IN THE U.S.:
PLURALISM AT THE CROSSROADS
Special Editor: Peter I. Rose

Volume 530   November 1993

THE EUROPEAN COMMUNITY:
TO 1992 AND BEYOND
Special Editor: Pierre-Henri Laurent

Volume 531   January 1994

FOREIGN LANGUAGE POLICY:
AN AGENDA FOR CHANGE
Special Editor: Richard D. Lambert

Volume 532   March 1994

See page 3 for information on Academy membership and
purchase of single volumes of **The Annals.**

CONTENTS

BOOK DEPARTMENT CONTENTS

PREFACE

After reading these articles, I hope you are like the amazed teacher who asked his student, "How many seconds in the year?" and was given the answer, "Twelve: January 2nd, February 2nd. . . ." This volume is designed to kill some myths and stretch some views about the tussle that is occurring in rural America.

Put simply, rural America is shifting to a different paradigm, from geography to community. The rustic image of the rugged yeoman working the soil is fading. Rising is a new image of complex multiplex networks that link individuals into regional communities that target the world as a market for their services. This is not happening easily or painlessly, but it is happening.

Rurality used to be agriculture. Society used to be agriculture. Some 200 years ago, 95 percent of the jobs were rural. They were needed to provide basic sustenance and to support the 5 percent of the jobs that were filled by lawyers, doctors, politicians, newspaper editors, and other soft-service occupations. Now the percentages are reversed. Less than 5 percent of American jobs are needed in production agriculture to provide food for the 95 percent of the nation's people involved in industry, management, and services.

The growth of agricultural productivity has been utterly astounding. President Lincoln in the 1860s charged a few agriculture scientists to provide seeds and knowledge to America's farmers. The result has been a concerted knowledge machine that has conducted research, developed technology, and extended practice to millions of farmers. In the late 1700s, T. R. Malthus wondered if we could control science to sustain 1 billion people. Today, 200 years later, world agriculture provides for almost 6 billion people. To a great degree, it has been rural American agricultural enterprise and its worldwide technological extension that supports the added 5 billion people.

But the wealth and security from want that agriculture has provided has undermined rurality. The talent that typified the Grange, the development of community and conservation to improve production, has been eroded by the success of agriculture. Expanding metroplexes, extended roads and air routes, and instantaneous communication became possible because fewer jobs were needed to work the fields for food. Agriculture's success removed investment from rural communities and placed it into other ventures that eroded the very communities that nurtured agriculture.

Now the remaining rural base has awakened to reassert the underlying value of community, systems of symbiosis. Failing rural towns, fewer jobs, and out-migration of youths have forced what is left of rural America to rethink its mission. Two events have already occurred. One is that rural America no longer considers agriculture, forestry, or mining to be its primary economic mainstay. Second, energetic business, academic, and government

8

practitioners are experimenting with different links in order to draw on rural assets to promote new and better enterprises, risk takers, and jobs.

Innovations in both hard and soft technology are redefining rural values. While agricultural technology eroded community with its single-minded productivity, the emerging biotechnology is developing sustainable biosystems, a community of complex links with many players. Soft communication technology is reinvigorating the linkage of people from many enterprises. New community linkages are occurring via new societal images, new systems of governance, and new commercial operations. These are emerging from the pain of rural decay. With very few resources, practical people are reinventing the success that comes from sharing information and physical frameworks, competing vigorously, and linking public, private, and nonprofit resources.

Our roots are rural. Our success comes from cultivating the soil with much productivity. Productivity has encouraged change—and pain. Loss of rural communities has encouraged a new cultivation, a more encompassing tilling of complex systems of commerce, biotics, governance, and society. This redefinition of rurality into regional community systems is just beginning. At the General Accounting Office, we recently assembled a symposium of rural development specialists to explore the challenges facing rural America.[1] We found much frustration but also success. Rediscovering our rural heritage may well define our future social blueprint.

ORGANIZATION OF THIS VOLUME

The 14 papers in this volume are organized into four sections that deal with the changing philosophy of rurality, the emerging power of learning, agriculture's new mission, and real applications of frustration and success.

The philosophy of rurality includes contradictory elements. We are obviously drawn to what used to be rural, but we also know that a new day is dawning. Emery Castle describes the history of rural America and the reality of increasing interdependence between rural, urban, and global resources. In contemplating the wide diversity of rural assets, far beyond the traditional activities of farming, forestry, and the Department of Agriculture, Castle calls for a long-overdue review of federal programs in order to take advantage of adaptable and diverse rural enterprise. DeWitt John sees rural disadvantage spurring a more disciplined market that locates new enterprises with better information, stronger public-private links, but no new programs. Ronald Cooper questions the image of rurality and translates recent phenomena into larger patterns of regional development. Team Flora, Cornelia and Jan, challenges us to imagine a new social paradigm that places added value on diversity, resource mobilization, and network quality. Through constructive controversy instead of superficial harmony and by redeployment of risk as

1. U.S., General Accounting Office, *Rural Development: Rural America Faces Many Challenges*, GAO/RCED-93-35, Nov. 1992.

well as equity, the Floras see new community linkages developing between those with similar circumstances.

C. Brice Ratchford describes the marvelous engine of the University of Missouri as it transforms itself into a problem-solving enterprise modeled after rural agricultural extension. The University combined scholarship and the practical extension of science, engineering, business, and all departments of learning into a community entrepreneurial effort. This thirty-year odyssey, from 1960 to 1991, demonstrates the determined effort of Missouri leaders to use all the resources of the University system to help all the people and institutions of the state reach their goals.

Thomas Tate, a graduate of the University of Missouri, takes us into the future of learning systems. He uses examples from rural America to demonstrate how educational technology will allow anyone to shift dimensions of time, place, and pace to meet his or her own desire to understand. A new learning blueprint that is operational in the heartland is replacing the old structures of education.

Leo Mayer provides us with a history of energetic agricultural productivity, the resulting net flow of income from rural communities, and the turning point in the 1980s as rural communities recognized that production agriculture would not be a source of new jobs. Mayer points to increased community linkage and a transformation of land-grant universities into a total extension knowledge engine as the next steps for rural America. G. W. Bird and John Ikerd paint a new picture for agriculture in sustainable biosystems. This encompasses a new system of natural resources, communities, commerce, and technology, all ignited by the Food, Agriculture, Conservation, and Trade Act of 1990 and encouraged by a Department of Agriculture program called SARE. Instead of only food and fiber commodities, sustainable agriculture is expected to produce a wider variety of industrial feedstocks for industry, personalized nutrients to engineer health, bountiful ecosystems, and robust communities. Dennis Fisher, from the heartland of Texas, sees agriculture as being in a position to pull together a larger group of interests to redefine the rural American mission. He sees the necessity for the rural community to make its case before the American public; otherwise, rural assets will be ignored and unfulfilled.

Five articles describe the rich experiences of taking rural people, communities, and enterprises on the road to actual operation. Brian Kelley relates the four-year effort of the Southern Development Bancorporation in rural Arkansas to encourage 130 new enterprises with a $10 million investment. Kelley's unique tripod development organization, with for-profit, nonprofit, and public legs, is followed by a description by Ruth McWilliams, Ronald Saranich, and Jennifer Pratt of a dramatic shift in direction for the United States Forest Service. A series of legislative and administration efforts in the late 1980s and early 1990s focused the Forest Service on using the many forest assets for the benefit of the entire community, not just forest enterprises. H. Richard Anderson takes us on a tour of European enterprise development synergy between business, government, and academia. He contrasts this goal-directed cooperation with the United States' unique adversarial harmony, then adapts the Old World experience to a practical economic-development operation located in Michigan's removed Northern Peninsula. Anne Berblinger details the operation, frustration, and opportunity of the U.S. Economic Development Administration programs. Ted Bradshaw rounds out the volume by pulling together experiences, practices, and theories in achieving multicommunity development action.

The sum of these articles suggests that from the pain of rural decay is emerging some energetic and imaginative efforts to do more with less. This involves experiments in theory, design, and practice. Rurality still smacks of isolation, self-satisfaction, and rot, but a new image and operation are emerging from the experiments. Rural America is renewing itself and it looks like regional, sounds like new technology, tastes like community, feels like linkages, and smells like a new blueprint for success.

WILLIAM E. GAHR

Rural Diversity: An American Asset

By EMERY N. CASTLE

ABSTRACT: Rural America is an exceedingly diverse place, and this diversity constitutes a national asset. Diversity can be documented by an examination of any social or economic attribute one wishes to choose—educational attainment, per capita income, occupation, and ethnic background provide examples. This diversity shapes both the public policies applicable to the countryside and the opportunities of rural communities and rural people. Highly centralized public programs and policies, unless they provide for local adaptation, are unlikely to be successful. Many existing federal programs have outlived their usefulness. Federal entitlement programs continue to be enormously important to rural people and can be made even far more effective by recognizing rural differences. Not all rural areas will flourish in the future; the supply of rural places that would like to attract economic activity far exceeds the demand for such places. Exogenous forces that will improve the prospects for some rural areas include an increase in the number of people of retirement age and with a retirement income as well as growth of outdoor recreation and tourism activities. Entrepreneurship will continue to be of great importance as diverse rural places discover ways they can serve an increasingly urban and global society. The cost of distance and the benefits of space are key parameters in establishing the economic framework within which economic development will occur.

Emery N. Castle is professor emeritus, University Graduate Faculty of Economics, Oregon State University. He also is president emeritus and senior fellow emeritus of Resources for the Future, Inc., a Washington, D.C., public policy institute concerned with natural resources and environmental policy. His published work pertains to rural issues, natural resources and the environment, and education policy. Currently, he is chair of the National Rural Studies Committee, a multidisciplinary group of scholars funded by the W. K. Kellogg Foundation engaged in a comprehensive study of the relationship of higher education to rural America.

THREE major characteristics dominate the economic and political environment of rural America. One, which receives considerable attention in this article, is the enormous diversity of the countryside. This has significant implications both for economic development and for policy. A second is the strong interdependence between rural places and people, on the one hand, and the economic activity in metropolitan America and in the global marketplace, on the other. The third is the enduring myth that rural can be considered synonymous with agriculture and farming.

Enormous variation exists in the natural and human resources as well as in the social problems of rural America. This can be documented by a geographic comparison of any social or economic attribute deemed to be of importance—educational attainment, per capita income, occupation, or ethnic background, for example. Diverse conditions create diverse opportunities; they also place a premium on flexible and adaptable public policies and entrepreneurs. There is a great propensity in this nation to identify problems as they occur in individual circumstances, compare them under varying conditions, and then refer them to Washington for a comprehensive solution. This has not worked and will not work in rural America. There are a number of federal government activities important to the countryside, but rural problems are too diverse and complex for a highly centralized approach unless it is combined with a capacity to reflect local conditions and circumstances. It is the contention of this article that, rather than being an obstacle or hindrance, rural diversity creates opportunities and is an asset.

The interdependence between the rural, on the one hand, and the urban and international, on the other, can hardly be overemphasized. Even though it is useful and important to understand the particular circumstances of rural places, few of their problems can be addressed in isolation from the larger economic and social environment of which they are a part.[1] Rural areas engage in economic and social interchange with

NOTE: This article draws heavily on the experience of the National Rural Studies Committee (NRSC), which I chair. The NRSC is a multidisciplinary group made possible by a 1987 grant from the W. K. Kellogg Foundation. Its purpose is to focus academic work on the problems of rural communities and rural people. The committee has pursued its objectives in a number of ways. One of its major activities has been a series of five regional meetings that have combined the presentation of academic papers on major problems of rural America with an examination, in the field, of significant local problems. Academic disciplines represented on the NRSC include economics, sociology, geography, anthropology, regional science, and political science. Even though the work of the NRSC has greatly influenced this article, it should not be viewed as restating an NRSC consensus or position. Rather, it reflects one person's judgment about conditions in the countryside and what might be done about them.

1. Julian Wolpert and Michael N. Danielson, "The Rural Fringe in the New Metropolis," in National Rural Studies Committee Proceedings, ed. Emery Castle and Barbara Baldwin (Corvallis: Oregon State University, Western Rural Development Center, 1991), pp. 11-21; Edward Bergman, "Interdependent Development: Evidence and Policy," in ibid. (1989), pp. 29-45; David Holland, Bruce Weber, and Edward Waters, "Modeling Economic Linkages between Core and Periphery Regions: The Portland Oregon Trade Area" (Paper delivered at a meeting of the Western Agricultural Economics Association, Colorado Springs, July 1992), available from the Western Rural Development Center, Oregon State University.

other places. Migrants from rural places must learn to live and work elsewhere, a circumstance that has important implications for the design of rural education. And if firms are to be enticed to locate in rural areas, their needs should be understood. Global interdependencies are exceedingly important as well. In the early 1980s, the decline of rural manufacturing in many areas was linked directly to the growth of international competition. Rural economic vitality is seldom self-contained.

To be rural is not necessarily to farm. Informed people know that most rural people do not live on farms, even though they may not realize that those who live on farms constitute less than 10 percent of the rural population.[2] The issue is a deeper one, however. The historical role of agriculture and, to a lesser extent, forestry and other extractive industries in shaping the institutions and norms of rural areas is not universally appreciated. Unless it is appreciated, one cannot understand many rural institutions as they function today. There are few issues of greater importance for those who are concerned about adaptation and change by rural people and places. In some instances, these rural institutions and norms will assist adaptation, but often they become obstacles because they do not have the inherent capacity for adaptation. In other cases, the institutions may be capable of adaptation but are controlled by those who

2. Donald C. Dahmann and Laarni T. Dacquel, *Residents of Farms and Rural Areas: 1990*, Current Population Reports: Population Characteristics, ser. P-20, no. 457 (Washington, DC: Department of Agriculture and Department of Commerce, Mar. 1992).

do not place a high priority on accommodating change, often because they believe they are best served by the status quo. There are numerous illustrations of this phenomenon, ranging from the difficulty that water institutions have in accommodating instream water rights to the problems of land-grant universities in serving the total rural constituency as contrasted to mainstream agricultural interests.

RECENT ECONOMIC HISTORY
AND RURAL AMERICA

For the purpose of this article, three distinct eras in rural public policy can be identified. The first had the creation of economic opportunities in rural America as its objective. The Jeffersonian notion that the United States should be a nation of farms and small businesses was the dominant philosophy for this period. The early thrust of these policies was to encourage settlement and overcome space. As a general principle, the remote rural settler was not expected to pay the full incremental costs of mail service, rural roads, or other social services. Rural education often was recognized as being of great importance and became the focus of many rural communities. National educational programs, including the historic land-grant legislation of 1862 and 1890, came into existence during this era, which encompassed the period from the time of nationhood until the beginning of the present century (1776-1900).

The second era began shortly after the beginning of this century and continued until the time of the New Deal (1900-1932). At the beginning of the present century, rural space, natural resources, and, to a certain extent, rural people began to be seen in a different light from a national policy-making perspective. With the settlement of the frontier, there came the realization that the natural resource base was finite. Federal rural policies continued, but their emphasis shifted significantly. The fostering of economic opportunity in the countryside remained a public policy objective, but natural resource conservation also became an important concept in shaping rural programs. Conservation as a social movement rested on the philosophical base of utilitarianism. Natural resource use was emphasized, and resources were valued in terms of what they could contribute to economic activity and economic opportunity. A resource was a resource only if it had present or potential human use. Conservation called particular attention to potential future use, which, it was believed, had been neglected during the first era. This is in contrast to the attitude associated with environmentalism, which arose in the 1960s and 1970s and which ascribes importance to things in nature for their intrinsic value, not necessarily because they will serve a utilitarian purpose. The Forest Service came into existence during this era, as did the Bureau of Reclamation.

The third era began with the Great Depression. The federal government assumed increased responsibility for improving conditions in the countryside. It did so by advancing programs that supported agricultural commodity prices, provided rural credit, and encouraged resource conservation and development. Conservation continued to influence the natural resource policies of this era; as noted, environmentalism arose later. Natural resources continued to be viewed as sources of economic opportunity. The Soil Conservation Service was a New Deal program; the Bureau of Reclamation, which came into existence in the second era, received continued emphasis as a source of economic opportunity. Also, those programs begun by the New Deal, such as social security, which focused directly on individual welfare, eventually were to have an enormous impact on the countryside. In the beginning, however, social security had a greater urban than rural influence.

Clearly, conditions in the rural areas now are vastly different from what they were during the New Deal as well as in the earlier periods. Nevertheless, we live with an accumulation of policies and programs from all of these earlier eras. There are also numerous state and local efforts designed to affect economic activity in rural places. Some policies have been failures; some have been outstanding successes; but most have survived in one form or another. The results have been that U.S. agriculture has been and is exceedingly productive, and the lot of rural people generally has improved over time. There has also been an enormous out-migration of people and economic activity from the countryside. In addition, the extractive industries of farming, forestry, and mining have not always been kind to the natural environment, and rural poverty problems persist and are becoming more severe relative to urban poverty.

The late 1960s and most of the 1970s were good times for many who resided in the rural and nonmetropolitan areas. The international demand for agricultural products increased sharply, energy prices rose rapidly, and forest products were in demand in response to growing housing starts. Rural manufacturing was in favor because of low rural wages and new technologies that permitted decentralization. These developments masked many of the fundamental problems of rural America that had been developing since World War II.

If the problems of rural America were obscured during the 1970s, they were uncovered with a vengeance in the 1980s. International market developments and domestic policies combined to create havoc with a great deal of the rural economy. Macroeconomic policies were changed in fundamental ways early in the decade. Deregulation of many industries, including transportation, communication, and credit, proceeded forcefully. The quantity of money was managed to control inflation and interest rates increased dramatically. The 1980s was a decade of intense international competition as many other nations became more productive. Many goods produced in the rural areas came to be at a disadvantage in international markets, because of international competition and a strong dollar. Rural manufacturing, agricultural exports, and housing starts all suffered. The fundamental, major contemporary problems of rural America were not caused by the policies of the federal government during the 1980s, but the policies intensified rural distress and placed rural problems in bold relief.

RURAL ECONOMIC POLICIES FOR THE FUTURE

Rural development is not just rural economic development; rural studies are not just rural economic studies. Nevertheless, rural economic viability is of enormous importance to the social health of rural places. Many individual and community problems become much easier to solve if a good job can be had. In this section, rural economic public policies are discussed; the following section is concerned with individual entrepreneurship.

I believe that spatial considerations should be accorded greater attention in public policy generally. The particular problems and needs of rural areas should be given explicit attention as a part of this increased recognition of how geographic space should be used. The congestion, crime, and environmental problems of large metropolitan areas clearly would also qualify for special attention under such an orientation. This is not a call for a national rural policy. It is to argue that distance, population density, space, and diversity are important variables that should be considered when public policies are made.[3] With respect to rural affairs then:

1. The traditional space-using activities of rural America—farming and forestry, for example—are declining

3. For a similar analysis, see Emery N. Castle, "Rural Policy Needs Good Dose of Realism," *Forum for Applied Research and Public Policy* (in press).

sources of rural economic activity. Rural space needs to be managed to provide for a changing, urban, and internationally driven economy.[4] An attractive and environmentally healthy countryside will be an economic asset for the future of both rural and urban areas. Such a countryside can be provided only at a cost. Policies and institutions need to consider the spatial distribution of benefits as well as the assignment of costs in the creation and maintenance of this economic asset.

2. A strong case can be made that rural affairs should be made visible at the national level and that the major focal point for rural policies should not be in the Department of Agriculture. This is a recommendation to bring the spatial effects of all federal programs and policies into the open—for example, the effects of monetary and fiscal policy, international trade policy, deregulation, entitlement programs, and environmental policies. Such an approach would emphasize monitoring, information collection, analysis, and dissemination as well as program coordination.

3. A rigorous review of federal programs for rural America is long overdue. Federal farm programs benefit only a small percentage of rural residents. Much of the difficulty stems from the anachronistic, but often implicit, notion that agriculture and rurality are the same. Federal research and educational efforts are too narrowly oriented to be respon-

sive to total rural-area needs. Many programs should be eliminated, others reoriented; those remaining should be consolidated or better coordinated. The coordination of federal programs is usually weak at the state and local level. The result of this review of programs would be to drastically change the Department of Agriculture as we know it, if such programs are to be administered there.

4. The characteristics and needs of rural people and places should be reflected in the formulation and administration of federal entitlement programs.[5] This is of enormous importance. Too often, such programs are conceived and executed on the basis of an urban model. Not only may this be unfair or unworkable, but it may make some situations it is designed to address worse rather than better. For example, if payments for rural physicians under Medicare or Medicaid are set on the basis of existing differentials, the paucity of rural physicians may become worse.

5. Reforming rural education is no panacea for rural economic devel-

---

4. Ronald Oakerson, "Institutional Diversity and Rural Development in America: An Institutionalist's Approach to Rural Studies," in *National Rural Studies Committee Proceedings*, ed. Castle and Baldwin (1990), pp. 43-53.

5. James Hite has argued that too much attention is given to rural places relative to the needs of rural people. Hite, "Place versus People in Rural Development Policy," *Choices*, 7(1):36-37. He makes an important point to the effect that some public policies seem designed to bring about economic development in every hamlet in the nation. Clearly, this is unrealistic. If attention is directed to people, rather than places, according to Hite, they may be prepared and encouraged to reach their desired potential regardless of geographic location. I do not argue with this point of view. Even so, most of the geographic space is to be found in rural places, a proposition true by definition. How it is managed and who has access to it are important questions of public policy. See Oakerson, "Institutional Diversity."

opment, yet it is difficult to imagine a more important area of rural public policy. In the jargon of mathematical logic, it might be said to be a necessary condition even if it is not a sufficient one. Participation in many types of economic activity requires the use of contemporary technology for the collection, manipulation, and transmission of information. Rural education needs to prepare people to use this technology whether they migrate or whether they work in local firms that compete domestically and internationally. Entrepreneurship, as well as other occupations, requires the acquisition and synthesis of information. Surely, formal education adds to the efficiency of this process. In fact, Nobel laureate Theodore W. Schultz has written, "There are few economic propositions that are as valid empirically as is the proposition that the entrepreneurial ability of farmers is enhanced by their schooling."[6]

6. Finally, a strong dose of realism needs to be reflected in the rural economic policies of this pragmatic and optimistic nation. Not all rural areas will flourish in the future. The countryside will constantly change, largely in response to urban and international influences. Public policies should be formulated to help such areas adjust and adapt. Policies that tie rural areas to the way they were, the way they are now, or to any particular point in time will be counterproductive.

ENTREPRENEURSHIP IN
RURAL ECONOMIC DEVELOPMENT:
THE ROLE OF DIVERSITY

Despite the enormous diversity of rural America, some generalizations concerning economic opportunities can be drawn. In establishing a framework for such generalizations, it is necessary to make some assumptions about general economic activity in the United States. Large metropolitan areas will continue to exist, even though the rate of growth for the largest may well decline.[7] Nevertheless, some of the smaller metropolitan areas may experience considerable expansion. As this is written, Boise, Idaho, appears to be one such place. It is not anticipated that there will be a reversal of the longtime trend of more rapid growth of metropolitan centers, relative to more sparsely populated nonmetropolitan places.

The relatively sparse population of rural places provides a perspective from which the comparative economic advantage of such places can be judged. First, distance can be overcome only at a cost. Even though improvements in communication and transportation have reduced the cost of distance, it still imposes a cost in the conduct of economic activities. Some of the enthusiastic literature on communication technology would suggest otherwise, but to believe such a dubious contention is to ignore economic reality. The corollary to the above is that sparsely populated places have

6. Theodore W. Schultz, *Restoring Economic Equilibrium: Human Capital in a Modernizing Economy* (Cambridge, MA: Basil Blackwell, 1990), p. 6.

7. Edwin C. Mills, "Large Metropolitan Areas: Their Functions and Prospects," in *National Rural Studies Committee Proceedings*, ed. Castle and Baldwin (1993).

a comparative advantage in those activities that require space. The cost of space is minimized under such circumstances.

Even though the percentage of the rural population engaged in agriculture and forestry has declined, these industries occupy a great deal of the space of the countryside. Some types of outdoor recreation also require considerable space, although recreational space needs vary greatly by type of activity. Despite the lip service given to multiple use, one space-using activity often excludes or diminishes the use of the same space by another activity; many environmental conflicts attest to this.

Metropolitan growth stimulates suburban development. Residential development is often the cornerstone of the suburb, but the suburb then becomes the hub of additional activity and performs many of the functions of the traditional central city.[8] Rural places on the periphery of growing metropolitan areas typically have enjoyed good economic growth. Those rural areas that are not on the periphery of large places and that have performed the best during the past two decades are those that have benefited from outdoor recreation, retirement, and rural residences—the three Rs. Such developments are not possible in some places and often create problems, even though economic activity is stimulated. The jobs resulting from such development often pay low wages; income distribution within a community may become

more unequal; and community life may change for these as well as for other reasons. Nevertheless, these activities provide clues for other opportunities. Unique settings in sparsely populated places are attractive to many people. Even though distance can be overcome only at a cost, space of a certain kind may be an economic asset. Sparsely populated places may be able to accommodate some activities at a lower cost than if they were located near metropolitan areas. Waste disposal activities are a case in point. If the rural area becomes a dumping ground for urban waste, one place is being exploited at the expense of another. However, if urban waste is accommodated by a rural area in such a way that natural beauty is not diminished, the health of people is not affected, and the full cost associated with accommodating the waste is paid by those who generate the waste, a legitimate rural economic activity may be created.

Realistically, the economic prospects for rural areas vary enormously. Many exceedingly attractive rural communities exist. Some have excellent school systems and provide good social services. Many have relatively unspoiled natural beauty and are attractive places to live and work. Civic beautification is being pursued vigorously in many such places as well as in some that are often considered less attractive. Nevertheless, the supply of places that would like to attract additional economic activity far exceeds the demand for them, and this is not likely to change in the immediate future. In their zeal to attract industries to locate in their

8. Peirce Lewis, "The Urban Invasion of the Rural Northeast," in *National Rural Studies Committee Proceedings*, ed. Castle and Baldwin (1991), pp. 11-21.

communities, there is a great temptation for communities to engage in counterproductive competition.[9] Tax breaks are a favorite recruiting device.

Enter local entrepreneurship. Even though the location of a large business in a rural area always garners a headline, most jobs are provided by firms with payrolls of fewer than 100 employees.[10] Even so, small firms do not exist in isolation from large ones, metropolitan places, and global economics; they have direct or indirect linkages to larger organizations, systems, and networks. They often contract directly with large firms, which may acquire services that were once produced in-house.

The small firm necessarily must discover its niche. If that niche involves serving a larger firm in some specialized way, a very different situation exists for the small firm that seeks a more general market. Major economic activities emphasize mass production and consumption of increasingly homogeneous goods and services. Nevertheless, there are numerous specialized functions associated with such activities. Information about these specialized activities and how the small firm can best serve the larger constitutes a major advantage of being located near the large firm or firms. If the geographic distance is great, the small firm may need to address the problem of acquiring such information. When this problem is considered in the abstract,

the focus is often on the performance of the task required to create a good or a service; with modern communication technology, this often does not pose great difficulty. The more formidable problem may be that of discovering the original need or niche that the small rural firm can fill. The discovery process and the associated negotiation are not easily routinized. This is not necessarily an insurmountable obstacle, but the more geographically isolated small rural firm should give explicit attention to the problems and the costs of market creation and discovery.

There are reactions to these general trends. Rural diversity may be an asset to the rural entrepreneur on either the output or input side of the business. On the output side, enterprises that offer alternatives to that which is homogeneous and standardized may discover a previously unrealized demand for the good or service they provide. Even though such undertakings may not replace larger firms, they may well supplement or complement the offerings of such firms. For example, local breweries provide an alternative to a mass-produced, relatively homogeneous product. Even so, nationally known breweries are unlikely to be driven from the scene by such local entrepreneurs. It is, of course, possible that the unique local good or service will have broader appeal. Wal-Mart stores provide an example of a rural enterprise, originally serving one rural community, becoming a nationwide firm.

Rural uniqueness may apply to the input side of the business as well. Of course, a unique input may be translated into a unique output. It may

9. Edwin C. Mills, "The Determinant of Small Area Growth," *Lectures in Economics* (Oregon State University, University Graduate Faculty of Economics), lecture 1 (Oct. 1987).

10. *Statistical Abstract of the United States* (Washington, DC: Department of Commerce, Bureau of the Census, 1991), p. 532, tab. 871.

well be that Jack Daniel Whiskey can be produced at places other than Lynchburg, Tennessee, but the perception exists that the quality of that product is related to its location. Rural enterprises may receive an initial impetus from the characteristics of the rural labor force. For example, in the upper Midwest, where educational attainment is high, it may be possible to take advantage of the presence of people, especially women, who may be capable of performing at a high skill level. Other rural enterprises may be based on unskilled, low-wage labor. An advantage this provides may be of a temporary nature. Such enterprises have often proven vulnerable to even lower-wage labor from outside the United States.[11]

Sustainability, as a concept, is in great current favor. Although it has arisen out of concern about the natural environment, it is not surprising that the concept would be applied more broadly as, for example, in "sus-tainable rural communities" or "sustainable rural economies." One can hardly quarrel with the objective implied by such phrases. Nevertheless, the difficulty of reducing them to an operational policy should not be underestimated. The mix of economic goods and services provided by most rural communities varies with the passage of time. External markets change rapidly and, given a significant time period, often enormously. It is exceedingly difficult for a small entrepreneur or small geographic area to discover a good or a service for which it can be assured of a market far into the future. Sustainability is far more likely to be attained through adaptability.[12] Adaptability, in turn, will be advanced by providing for the health and education of local people, the conservation of the natural environment, flexible policies, and the preservation of that which makes the rural area unique in a fundamental sense. A highly specialized, rigidly organized enterprise may have difficulty responding to change; inherent differences may enhance adaptability. In an evolving society, rural diversity becomes a national asset.

11. For a discussion of rural labor markets, see Gene F. Summers, Francine Horton, and Christina Gringeri, "Rural Labor Market Changes in the U.S.," in *National Rural Studies Committee Proceedings*, ed. Castle and Baldwin (1990), pp. 61-79; Christina E. Gringeri, "The Nuts and Bolts of Subsidized Development: Industrial Workers in the Heartland," in ibid., pp. 81-88.

12. Edgar S. Dunn, *Economic and Social Development: A Process of Social Learning* (Baltimore, MD: Johns Hopkins University Press, 1971).

ANNALS, *AAPSS*, **529**, September 1993

Where Is Rural Policy Headed?

By DeWITT JOHN

ABSTRACT: New approaches to rural policy focus on (1) providing information and specialized expertise to rural communities along with traditional development finance and infrastructure programs; (2) building civic capacity to mobilize public and private resources for community development goals; and (3) new approaches to governance of the rural development process. These new governance strategies are similar to those now being used in other areas of public policy. Taken together, these approaches represent the beginnings of a fresh approach to rural development, and an alternative to seeking new policies and programs that are explicitly labeled "rural."

DeWitt John is director of the Center for Competitive, Sustainable Economies at the National Academy of Public Administration. Previously, he managed the State Policy Program at the Aspen Institute, a research unit on economic issues at the National Governors' Association, and the Governor's Policy Office in Colorado. He is the author of four books, including Civic Environmentalism *(1993) and, with Ron Ferguson,* A Rural Development Movement for a Competitive America *(1993). Mr. John has a doctorate in political science from the University of Chicago.*

IT is not news that most rural areas have lower wages, have almost as much poverty as inner cities, and are losing population. Nor is it news that traditional rural development policies are poorly funded and do not seem to be effective and that many state and federal programs are not well designed for rural conditions. But it is news that over the past several years, a movement has begun for a fresh approach to rural problems. This movement has had victories at the local level and sometimes at the state level, but its national profile is not high yet. For example, over thirty states have accepted an invitation from the federal government to form rural development councils, but the councils are too young to have had many results yet. Also, many states have launched rural initiatives, on their own or as a result of academies organized by the Council of Governors' Policy Advisers, but these efforts show more promise than broad impact on rural economies.

Rather than dwell on the old news of rural disadvantage or analyze the early results from new initiatives, this article takes a leap into the future and describes where we might want to go and where we might be heading. A decade from now, we might hope to see

— economic development programs that focus on information, expertise, and the capacity to mobilize resources, rather than on finance and physical infrastructure;
— an informed, disciplined market for industrial recruitment;
— an infrastructure of multi-community public-private development partnerships;
— traditional rural industries that are environmentally sound;
— work force programs that are integrated into business development initiatives;
— a stronger rural development movement but no new rural development policies or programs;
— a new approach to governance for rural development; and
— a new federal role in rural development, centering less on funding than on information.

This vision is fragmentary and impressionistic because the new rural development movement is so young. Analytically, the concepts that bring coherence to the foregoing eight pieces are information, expertise, civic capacity, and top-down support for bottom-up initiatives. To mobilize the political support for new rural strategies, we will need more evocative words. This article sketches each of the eight elements and concludes with comments about the old images that have guided rural policy for many years and new images that may bring political success in the future.

1. A NEW FOCUS FOR ECONOMIC DEVELOPMENT

Economic and community development policy is faddish. Think back: we experimented with research parks, incubators, entrepreneurship training, enterprise zones, export finance, small business development centers, and now industrial extension, flexible manufacturing networks, self-employment, and micro-enterprise. The Corporation for Enterprise Development report card and the directory of state incentives, published by the National Association of State Development Agencies, list dozens of programs.[1] In an ideal future for rural America, what might be said about these programs?

As the trends wash over us, we are making progress, and in particular we are moving toward programs that are more useful for rural places. In the early 1980s, the focus was on development finance and physical infrastructure. Now many of the newer ideas focus on bringing information and specialized expertise to small and medium-sized firms. This is the essence of industrial extension and flexible manufacturing networks. We are learning that development finance programs, for example, are usually successful to the extent that they provide borrowers with information about markets, technologies, and management along with cash, and with linkages to experts in technologies and markets as well as with financiers.[2]

This is particularly helpful for firms in rural places. Rural America

is diverse, but all rural communities are small and thus have fewer specialists. To get access to specialized information, one must often go outside the community. This is especially true for small and medium-sized enterprises in rural areas, and perhaps less so for branch plants of large corporations, because these corporations have their own internal information systems. In an economy based on information, the difficulty of gaining access to specialized information and expertise is a critical disadvantage of small places. So national and state policies that emphasize information and building links between people so that they can exchange specialized information are very beneficial for rural areas.

2. A SMART MARKET FOR RECRUITMENT

In some circles, it is not politically correct to speak positively about industrial recruitment. Recruitment is often a zero-sum game, a fruitless competition that subsidizes firms and weakens local tax bases without adding to the productivity of the national economy. However, recruitment is often the bottom line—the real action after the talking stops—especially in rural communities and in the South. What is the best that we might hope for with respect to recruitment?

We will never see an end to industrial recruitment, nor should we hope for it. The successful rural communities that I am familiar with do not stop recruiting; they just do other things, too.[3] Their efforts to improve

1. Corporation for Enterprise Development, *The 1991 Development Report Card for the States: A Tool for Public and Private Sector Decision-Makers* (Washington, DC: Corporation for Enterprise Development, 1991); National Association of State Development Agencies, National Council for Urban Economic Development, and the Urban Institute, *Directory of Incentives for Business Investment and Development in the United States: A State-by-State Guide* (Washington, DC: Urban Institute, 1983, 1986). See also Ernest J. Yarnella and William C. Green, eds., *The Politics of Industrial Recruitment* (Westport, CT: Greenwood Press, 1990).

2. See Deborah Markley with Katherine McKee, *Business Finance as a Tool for Development* (Washington, DC: Aspen Institute, 1992).

3. DeWitt John, Sandra Batie, and Kim Norris, *A Brighter Future for Rural America? Strategies for Communities and States* (Wash-

the competitiveness of existing firms and of their workers naturally attract new firms. The community welcomes these recruits, but it does not give everything away. Community leaders look at recruitment as an investment and weigh this investment against others.

Unfortunately, this is not enough. Recruitment is a market where communities and states are buying plants from industry. The market is not functioning well. It is one-sided, with one seller—the firm looking for a site—and lots of buyers—all of the states and communities competing for the plant. States and communities do not have good information, and they often pay higher prices than they should.

Better information could discipline and improve the efficiency of the market. Some kinds of plants are better than others to bring into a state or a community. The better ones pay better wages, stay longer, procure supplies locally, spin off new firms, and participate actively in civic affairs and local development efforts. We need tools to help us understand which plants are better, and to explain the differences to politicians and to the public. States and communities also need software packages to help local communities make dollar-and-cent estimates of the costs and the payoffs of individual deals with recruited firms.

We also need someone to monitor deals and publicize the costs and benefits. Federal agencies, states, and the private sector should establish a

nonprofit organization that might be called the Alliance for Smart Recruiting to play this role. Currently, people who follow recruitment closely may know about how much communities are paying for different kinds of plants, but this information is incomplete, unreliable, and not used widely. If such information were widely available, it would drive down the prices that communities pay, and it would help them see that there might be alternative investments that would pay off better.

States and the federal government could help improve the market for branch plants. More regulations are not the answer. Several federal programs already refuse to allow their funds to be used for recruitment, and this is not doing the job. Instead, a federal agency, or perhaps an impartial nonprofit agency funded by states, the federal government, and the private sector, could spot-check deals and publish reports with its estimates of how good the deals are and whether there were better alternative investments. States and localities could dispute these estimates if they wished but would nonetheless learn from them. Rural communities would benefit more than most, because they often lack professional staff and access to information; without these, they end up paying the most and buying the worst products in the market for branch plants.

3. A NETWORK OF COMMUNITY-BASED DEVELOPMENT ORGANIZATIONS

ington, DC: National Governors' Association, 1988), pp. 26-50.

There are already many exciting models of bottom-up efforts to revitalize rural communities. With proper support from the state and national level, there could be a nationwide network of organizations. We should expect a network, but no single model, because rural America is highly diverse.

From the perspective of development policy, there are at least four very different kinds of rural communities. Some live at close to Third World levels, with unpaved streets, few jobs, and tight control by outside corporations or narrow oligarchies. Here development means building basic infrastructure and democratic institutions. Other rural communities have incomes that are high by international standards but low by American standards, because they have an economic base of low-wage, routine manufacturing, and the supply of these jobs is disappearing as firms move their low-wage operations to Mexico, South Asia, and elsewhere. Here the agenda is to upgrade the industrial base.

A third group of rural communities depends on high-production, high-efficiency natural resource industries, including agriculture and sometimes mining. These towns enjoy relatively good standards of living, but in many places, the population is dropping. These areas must diversify or shrink. Finally, a very large part of rural America is being gentrified. As suburbia sprawls into the countryside, or as retirees and footloose professionals move to rural areas, these towns grow, but long-term residents may not share in the benefits of the growth.

For each of these kinds of rural areas, the vision of the future will be different. Consider the Southern Development Bancorporation in Arkansas, the Northern Michigan Initiatives Center, Coastal Enterprises in Maine, the Center for Self-Help in North Carolina, and the best regional councils and development districts. They have different funding and fit into different political and institutional settings.[4] There are some common themes: they combine development finance with close attention to the information and human needs of fledgling businesses; they seek to mobilize all of the resources in their communities, including women and minorities rather than just the usual suspects; and they are aggressively seeking ways to push their way into the policy arena, to make bottom-up development something very practical. Often, they operate at a multi-community level or even as important powers in state affairs.

4. A NEW AGENDA FOR RURAL NATURAL RESOURCE INDUSTRIES

Federal support for production agriculture and easy access to federal lands for mining, logging, and ranching were key parts of traditional rural development policy. A vision of a national rural strategy would be incomplete if it did not say something about these industries.

Without exception, these natural resource industries are under great stress as they try to respond to demands for environmental quality. The battle in the Pacific Northwest about timber and the spotted owl is

4. For short descriptions of these organizations, see Markley with McKee, *Business Finance as a Tool for Development.*

only one example. The ranching industry is under attack, as environmentalists protest that grazing has degraded public lands. In Florida, environmentalists want to "Say No" to the sugar industry, which is dumping phosphorus-laden waters into a national park and a national wildlife refuge. Rural electrical cooperatives and the federal power marketing authorities are under pressure to promote energy conservation instead of the use of more electricity and to change the way that federal dams are managed so as to restore natural flows to rivers. My favorite symbol of the standoff between environmentalists and traditionalists is the slogans about grazing on public lands. Some environmentalists demand that federal land be "Cattle Free in '93." The Wyoming Cattlemen's Association says, "Cows Galore in '94."

The pressure of environmental laws on rural industries and rural communities is truly enormous, and perhaps there will be a backlash. The new drinking-water standards are particularly difficult for small towns to handle. If there is a backlash, however, it is more likely to focus on environmental agencies than on the goal of a cleaner and more pleasant environment. Since Earth Day 1970, there has been a change in the attitude about environmental values. All public opinion polls say that the public strongly desires environmental cleanups and that the public would readily sacrifice jobs for environmental quality if necessary, especially if it is someone else's job, such as the job of a rancher or miner or logger.[5]

There is no way to continue with traditional ways of managing natural resources, no way to continue logging, farming, mining, grazing, or producing electricity without incorporating environmental considerations directly into the business plans of producers. After the battles, specialized information about environmental matters may become an important ingredient in natural resource industries. For example, agricultural co-ops may sell not just chemicals but also expertise to help farmers use fewer chemicals and to use them more efficiently. In addition, environmental restoration may become a growth industry, with construction firms dismantling roads they once built for loggers and rechanneling rivers that were once turned into ditches. The expertise in restoration that these firms will develop will become an important part of the economic base for the communities where they are based.

5. WORK FORCE PROGRAMS THAT ARE INTEGRATED INTO BUSINESS DEVELOPMENT

It is conventional wisdom that a nation's competitiveness depends on the skills of its work force. But the lack of highly skilled workers is usually not the critical constraint to economic development in rural areas. In the 1980s, many rural areas with highly skilled work forces did no better than those without skilled workers.[6] Thus

5. See, for example, Robert Cameron Mitchell, "Public Opinion and the Green Lobby: Poised for the 1990s?" in *Environmental Policy in the 1990s*, ed. Norman J. Vig and Michael E. Kraft (Washington, DC: CQ Press, 1990), pp. 81-99.

6. David McGranahan, "Introduction," in *Education and Rural Development: Strategies*

if a rural community invests in training its work force, the training may benefit the trainees, but there may be little payoff for the community.

This does not mean that investments in training or education should be reduced. Skilled workers and some employers are likely to consider good schools as the single most important indicator of a community's current and potential quality of life. Furthermore, training programs can be effective when they are tightly integrated into other business development activities. Indeed, for those rural communities lucky enough to be the home of an entrepreneurial community college or vocational school, these institutions might be central players in efforts to modernize local firms by improving their access to technology, information about markets, and management expertise as well as providing specialized training to upgrade the skills of workers in local firms.

6. A STRONGER RURAL MOVEMENT BUT NO NEW RURAL PROGRAMS

The rural-urban distinction has lost much of its value for categorizing state and federal economic development policies and programs. Certainly, systematic differences in rural and urban conditions still exist. One of the most important differences is the scarcity of specialized skills and information in rural communities. As generic policies move to emphasize

access to expertise and knowledge, however, there is less of a need to differentiate between rural and urban programs.

Furthermore, as explained earlier, rural communities are highly diverse. The most persuasive argument for distinctive rural programs and policies is that generic programs do not fit well in rural communities. But rural communities are so diverse that generic rural programs might not fit much better. Indeed, one can make a strong case that generic programs do not fit well in inner cities or suburbs either, because of the diversity of those communities as well.

It is difficult to make the case that rural communities have any major categories of need that urban communities do not, and vice versa. Along with colleagues, I have searched for good examples to justify the need for distinctive rural policies and programs. For the most part, however, the answer appears to be that rural and urban communities tend to have the same types of needs. They can be served by the same policies and programs if those policies and programs are designed and implemented with appropriate flexibility and adequate funding.

What is important, then, especially for rural areas, are the ways that policies and programs can accommodate the diversity of local conditions. Over the next decade, we might expect that many advocates for economic development on behalf of rural constituencies will want to shift their emphases away from asking for development policies that are specifically rural. They may, for example,

for the 1990s (Washington, DC: Department of Agriculture, Economic Research Service, 1991), p. 7.

focus more on the importance for rural communities of state and local policies traditionally regarded as urban. In addition, they need to insist that regulations, operating procedures, eligibility rules, and funding formulas governing state and federal policies and programs are flexible enough to accommodate a variety of rural—as well as urban—conditions. In the current situation of highly fragmented programs—there are over 580 separate federal grant programs, for example—it is especially important to find ways to collaborate across program lines, to simplify access to different funding pools, and to allow resources to be transferred from one program to another when local conditions require it.

This emphasis on flexible but broadly appropriate generic policies that foster competitiveness and opportunity for both rural and urban communities is quite different from the traditional approach to rural development. For mostly historical reasons, communities for some time will continue working in political coalitions along rural and urban lines. But political victory, as well as success in implementing programs, may lie with efforts that steer away from the traditional strategy of asking that rural areas get their fair share and instead focus on flexibility.

7. A NEW APPROACH TO GOVERNANCE

It may seem quixotic to stake the future of rural policy on flexibility and an end to fragmentation. The political facts of life in Washington, D.C.—and also in many state capitals —are that legislative authority is fragmented into many different committee and subcommittee jurisdictions and that organized interests mirror and reinforce this fragmentation. For example, there are strong lobbies and clear paths to congressional action on wheat prices or on low-income rural housing, and only weak lobbies and complex paths for broad rural development legislation.[7]

Nonetheless, there are many signs of dissatisfaction with this fragmentation. In many fields of domestic policy, including human services, environmental policy, and surface transportation, there are active efforts among insiders—policy experts, program managers, and frontline workers—who assert that there is a mismatch between the goals of public policy and the programs that government operates to achieve these goals. This dissatisfaction is leading to efforts to transcend program and professional boundaries. The impetus for holistic approaches takes many forms, such as the current interest in monitoring outcomes rather than outputs and in involving staff workers and customers of government programs to help define goals and shape the design of public initiatives. Another example is the proliferation of non-

7. For extensive discussions of the failure to mobilize broad rural constituencies, see James T. Bonnen, "U.S. Perspective on the Interest Group Base of Rural Policy: People, Agriculture, and the Environment" (Paper prepared for the Rural Economic Policy Program, Aspen Institute, 1990); William P. Browne, *Form without Substance, Past over Present: The Institutional Failure of U.S. Rural Policy* (Washington, DC: Rural Economic Policy Program, Aspen Institute, 1992).

profit, public-private partnerships for many of the tasks of government, ranging from setting goals and designing initiatives to delivering services.[8]

At the local level, we know that some rural communities find opportunities for achieving their goals even while their neighbors see only problems. Although the evidence is not entirely clear, we suspect that the reason for many success stories lies in the superior ability to forge a consensus on community goals and to mobilize public and private resources to achieve these goals. We are even learning something about the technology of local success; it includes individuals who are spark plugs, forums where people can meet, and techniques for assessing community strengths and opportunities, for setting objectives and monitoring progress.

We are also developing new ways of spanning boundaries and mobilizing resources at the state and substate level. Here are three examples of trends that are just starting and that might emerge full-blown.

The first example comprises efforts to frame development policies at the level of substate regions. Some economists tell us that around the nation, the rise of the global economy is leading to an erosion of national economic boundaries and making regional agglomerations more important. In urban areas around the world, "citistates" are emerging that

include concentrations of firms in closely related industries, universities and research institutes with expertise in technologies that are important to these firms, a highly skilled labor force, and public policies that encourage these firms in a variety of ways. Citistates may become the central geographic and political building block of the global economy.[9] Many urban areas in the United States are attempting to organize at the level of metropolitan areas, and there are some signs, such as the federal Intermodal Surface Transportation Efficiency Act of 1991, of federal support for addressing issues that cut across program and policy boundaries at the regional level.

For rural areas, the key question is how to relate to citistates—or whether it is possible to organize rural regions into something like independent citistates. There may be examples of such independent rural conglomerations in other countries, such as the North Jutland area of Denmark, and perhaps small-scale clusters in the United States.[10] Several states with large rural areas, including Nebraska and Minnesota among others, are confronting this issue directly by trying to develop a regional capacity to frame and deliver development initiatives in rural

8. See, for example, Lisbeth Schorr, *Within Our Reach: Breaking the Cycle of Disadvantage* (New York: Anchor Books, 1988). See also U.S., General Accounting Office, *Integrating Human Services: Linking At-Risk Families with Services More Successful than System Reform Efforts*, HRD-92-108 (Washington, DC: Government Printing Office, 1992).

9. See Michael E. Porter, *The Competitive Advantage of Nations* (New York: Free Press, 1990), p. 622; Stuart Rosenfeld with Philip Shapira and J. Trent Williams, *Smart Firms in Small Towns* (Washington, DC: Aspen Institute, 1992); Neal Peirce, *Citistates* (forthcoming).

10. See Stuart A. Rosenfeld, *Competitive Manufacturing: New Strategies for Regional Development* (New Brunswick, NJ: Rutgers University Center for Urban Policy Research, 1992), chap. 5.

areas. Perhaps these efforts will eventually evolve in the direction of what one might call locally designed block grants, where the federal and state roles set overall goals and audit performance, leaving discretion at the regional level to focus resources on the biggest opportunities and the biggest problems.

Another way to cut across programmatic lines is to focus on industrial sectors, like textiles, commercial aviation, or the recycling industry. This need not involve national sectoral planning. Instead, decentralized approaches, such as working through trade associations, industrial extension, flexible manufacturing networks, and other vehicles, may help mobilize resources and coalitions to tackle the multidimensional task of modernizing small and medium-sized firms.

The new State Rural Development Councils are another promising vehicle far too young to be called a success but full of potential when they get past an organizational phase. If they work well, they may help to orchestrate collaborative rural strategies and may also function as a forum where representatives of separate programs and interests can meet to bargain and strike deals.[11]

8. A NEW FEDERAL ROLE

Also slowly emerging is a new role for the federal government in rural development and perhaps also in other domestic policy areas. If indeed

citistates are to be a key to economic competitiveness, and if we need more collaborative approaches to mobilizing public and private resources, the role of the federal government will shift. Traditionally, the most important federal role in economic development has been to provide funding. I would guess that currently states spend about $1 billion on economic and community development programs and that the federal government spends about $5 billion.[12] Only a guess is possible because there are no solid figures. Local governments probably spend more, but here the figures are even more elusive.

Perhaps, as suggested by new Office of Management and Budget Associate Director Alice Rivlin, the balance between federal and state funding on development should be reversed. She has advocated a major swap of functions between the state and federal levels. The federal government would pick up the responsibility and the bills for welfare and social service programs and would reduce its spending on development

---

11. Beryl Radin, "Rural Development Councils: An Intergovernmental Coordination Experiment," *Publius: The Journal of Federalism*, 22:111-27 (Summer 1992).

12. The $1 billion figure for state programs is an estimate of the total budgets of state economic development agencies in 1987 from DeWitt John, *Shifting Responsibilities: Federalism in Economic Development* (Washington, DC: National Governors' Association, 1988), p. 4. I know of no more recent estimate. The $5 billion figure covers function 450 of the federal budget, which includes a variety of economic and community development programs, including Community Development Block Grants, the Economic Development Administration, and the Small Business Administration, among others. By adding other programs, such as subsidies for rural electrical cooperatives and farm price supports, the General Accounting Office recently estimated total federal spending for rural development to be as high as $30 billion.

as well as other functions. States would cut back their spending on welfare and social services and would have more funds to invest in development.

Even if such a swap were to take place, there would still be a continuing role for the federal government in rural development. The role, however, would be less that of financier and initiator and more that of a switching station for information and provider of specialized information. Federal leadership in disciplining the market for industrial recruitment through gathering data and marshaling information could be an example of such a new approach.

GOALS AND IMAGES

These eight points would represent a radical alteration of rural development policy. It is far from clear that they could reverse the decline of a large number of rural communities, but they might help significantly. Even if they would constitute less than a zero-defect regime, failing to guarantee universal rural prosperity and opportunity, events do seem to be moving in this general direction.

These eight points certainly are not politics-as-usual. If they are to represent the future, they will have to be framed in terms that can evoke the enthusiastic support of rural citizens and interests. The images that have animated rural advocates in the past are those of a prosperous production agriculture, stable and friendly small towns, and an end to grinding rural poverty. These goals still have tremendous emotional power. But to these images we might add new goals and new images that center on the themes of opportunity, choice, or bottom-up development.

In his inaugural address, President Clinton invited Americans to join in "reinventing America." His campaign book, *Putting People First*, speaks of specific new federal programs like community development banks and apprenticeship programs but also of "a shift from top-down bureaucracy to entrepreneurial government that empowers citizens and communities to change our country from the bottom up."[13]

Such a vision might be translated into goals for rural residents, communities, and businesses. For example, we might say that residents of rural areas should be rural residents by choice. Many rural Americans are now trapped in low-wage, low-skill jobs or in areas of chronic poverty. Our vision for rural America might include opportunities for rural children and rural workers to get the education and skills they need to compete in an international labor market. The goal of rural policy would then be to provide skills and opportunities to individuals.

Rural communities might also have choices. We know that there are no iron laws of economics that say that specific communities are doomed to shrink and die or to prosper.[14] For an individual community, the future depends in significant

13. Bill Clinton and Al Gore, *Putting People First: How We Can All Change America* (New York: Times Books, 1992), p. 24.

14. See John, Batie, and Norris, *Brighter Future for Rural America?* pp. 85-95 for a literature review, which concludes that studies that try to explain why some communities grow while others languish almost always have a large margin of unexplained variation.

measure on how it is able to deploy its financial, physical, intellectual, and civic assets. Even in areas that are losing population, where the economic base is shrinking, or where increased productivity means that fewer workers are needed, there are vibrant, prosperous towns. These towns escape generalizations about buffalo commons or the inevitable decline of population on the Great Plains, because development depends not only on economic and technological factors but also on the social and political capacity to organize resources. The goal of rural policy might be to help rural communities mobilize their internal resources for bottom-up development and then to respond effectively to bottom-up initiatives.

Like workers, rural businesses must be world-class if they are to prosper. Government has less responsibility to provide a safety net for businesses than for individuals, however. Businesses will therefore have fewer choices. The goal of rural policy might be to ensure that the public services on which businesses depend are available in an effective manner in rural areas.

Could this vision of the goals of rural policy animate a powerful rural development movement? Is it sufficiently broad to encompass the diverse objectives of poor rural communities, rapidly growing tourist towns, farm towns, and centers of low-wage manufacturing?

The New Economic Regionalism:
A Rural Policy Framework

By RONALD S. COOPER

ABSTRACT: A conceptual framework is presented that clarifies issues involved in the rural policy debate. A new economic regionalism is emerging in which rural areas develop only as integral parts of larger regional economies. Advances in technology and new forms of economic competition that transcend both industrial and national boundaries have created a new regional dimension to the development process. The economic hardships and future opportunities of rural areas are better understood as the focus moves from rural economic development to the new regional development framework.

Ronald S. Cooper is a consulting economist specializing in technological change and its role in industrial competition and regional development. During the past six years, he has worked extensively in the areas of rural development and technology program assessment. His current research activities include the empirical measurement of technological modernization activity in U.S. manufacturing, the analysis of determinants of rural area growth, and the economic effects of state technology programs. His research focuses heavily on the implications for current public policy.

THE national debate on rural development policy has made little progress not only because of the competing political and economic interests involved but also because it has been conducted within the conceptual confines of an obsolete economic development paradigm. The old paradigm focuses attention on the unique hardships and bleak prospects of rural areas, but it fails to shed light on the underlying causes or on current opportunities for development. A new conceptual framework is needed: a new economic development paradigm that encompasses the global restructuring of economic activity, incorporates the underlying transformation of business competition, and places the focus on the development of integrated economic regions. The current economic problems of rural areas reflect the emergence of a new economic regionalism. The relevance of the national rural policy debate hinges on the extent to which this new regionalism and its implications for rural areas are understood.

RURAL ECONOMIC DEVELOPMENT: CAUGHT IN A PARADIGM TRANSITION

Rural America is in trouble. Hit hard by the recession of the early 1980s, rural areas in the United States have since lagged behind urban areas in employment growth, suffering declining relative incomes, higher poverty rates, and net out-migration. The restructuring of traditionally rural industries has caused widespread dislocation, yet rural America remains vulnerable to further distress, being dependent on low-wage industries to employ a work force of lower than average skill.

Fueled by these hardships and given substance by the experiences of states during the past decade, the ongoing public debate has been over what, if anything, the public sector should do. Does the federal government have a responsibility to rural America? If so, what is the best way to achieve rural development? What is it about rural areas that makes them so vulnerable to downswings and sluggish in the upswing? What kind of economic assistance is most effective? Should we even be trying to alter the natural course of events?

Refuge in the details

These questions have been answered by a steady barrage of statistical and anecdotal evidence of rural plight. The trends and profiles of rural America have painted a picture of forsaken economies—casualties of the current economic transitional period. We now know, in considerable detail, the economic, social, demographic, cultural, and environmental composition of rural America. Defined and described with such rigor, rural America has come to acquire an identity and autonomy akin to sovereignty. It is the "other America."

But the flood of descriptive information has not helped clarify the nature of rural areas or the underlying causes of their hardships. Like its subject matter, the rural development debate is itself in trouble and in transition. The problem is that current rural area dislocations reflect a transformation in the nature of economic development. The effect of this has been the obsolescence of our understanding of the process of economic development in rural areas. A new set of ideas is needed. Evidence of the need for a new paradigm is visible in the growing difficulties and confusions in the rural development debate and in the consequent aversion of practitioners and policymakers to seek explanations of underlying causes.

Growing confusion

One form of evidence is the difficulty in agreeing on a definition of "rural." Although most of us feel we know what we mean when we say "rural," when we are pressed to define it for policy debates or academic research, there is considerable flexibility. Definitions vary from the totally rural to the not-so-rural, depending on the degree of urbanization within the area, adjacency to a metropolitan area, population density, and industry mix. In addition, the standards tend to vary from state to state. Perhaps the most reasonable standardized measure proposed to date, and one that might now be applicable worldwide, is the "McDonald's criterion": an area is truly rural only if it is still without a McDonald's restaurant. In much of the policy debate, rurality usually assumes simply a sectoral definition—farmland, natural resource areas, and so forth —depending on the interests being represented.

Related to this definitional difficulty is the scarcity of analysis of underlying causes. To be effective, rural policy and programs need to understand how rural economies are changing and why. "Why" has never been a popular word in Washington or in state or regional program offices. But aversion to addressing the whys of rural development has created an embarrassingly unproductive debate over the policy options.

Experimentation over explanation

Evidence of a pending paradigm shift, or the need for one, is also found in the behavior of rural development practitioners. Over the last ten years, rural development leaders have exploited the potentials of state governments as laboratories for designing and testing new development approaches.[1] Successful experiments have been celebrated, and, often before the impacts are understood, the project is transmitted across the country for the purpose of replication. This third wave of local development experiment knowledge has washed over the country's rural communities with a dual message: (1) development must come from within, building on an area's local capacities, indigenous industries, and so on; and (2) area leaders may, if they wish, select from a smorgasbord of rural development success stories—the best practices in rural development.

Here we see the emergence of a best-practices syndrome, where practitioners rush from one success

1. Many of the lessons learned and the new directions currently being taken were discussed at the June 1992 symposium sponsored by the General Accounting Office. See U.S., General Accounting Office, *Rural Development: Rural America Faces Many Challenges*, GAO/RCED-93-35, Nov. 1992.

story to the next, taking with them new ideas to be transplanted but little knowledge of the transferability of the ideas. A popular best-practice success story in current circulation is that of the flexible manufacturing networks of small rural firms found in several industrial districts of northern Italy. These "Third Italy" regions, as they have been called, are celebrated as examples of how rural area economies of small manufacturers can thrive in today's global economy. These regions have reportedly raised their income and profitability through regional specialization, the division of production processes among specialized firms, and the organization of networks that foster interfirm communication and cooperation on, for example, research and development, training, and export and legal services.

While providing useful and inspiring messages for rural development efforts in the United States, the Third Italy examples should not necessarily be presented as systems to emulate. For every specific example of a potentially useful practice—for example, a new form of small-firm cooperation—closer inspection reveals reasons why the practice may not be transferable to rural areas in other industrialized countries. For example, much of the production in the Third Italy districts is in skilled, traditional craft industries with specific world market niches. Also, much of the success of the small-firm cooperation can be attributed to personal ties between the predominantly family-run community businesses. While such cooperation may succeed in es-

tablished rural regions in the United States, it may not in areas that need to introduce new industries if they are to survive.

Furthermore, some empirical studies have shown that small firms in these regions have not performed as well as large firms in terms of labor productivity, exports, or technology innovation. Evidence suggests that small-firm growth is closely tied to subcontracting activities of large corporations; that wage, unionization, and women participation rates may be relatively low; and that geographic clustering often occurs among small firms at the same stage of production within a single industrial sector, suggesting features of less balanced, externally driven local economies.[2]

However, reliable comprehensive information on the underlying economies of these and other best-practice examples is not available. Most of the attention to date has focused on describing the appealing features of such examples and searching for other, similar examples. Alongside this hunt for inspiring rural success stories has grown a supportive theory that sees diversity—one size does not fit all—as the principal feature of economic development in the new era. It holds that development is, by its nature, a local, indigenous, and heterogeneous process and that the best policy is therefore to provide support

2. A. Amin, "Flexible Specialization and Small Firms in Italy: Myths and Realities," in *Farewell to Flexibility?* ed. A Pollert (Cambridge, MA: Basil Blackwell, 1991); G. Rey, "Small Firms: A Profile of Their Evolution, 1981-1985," in *Small Firms and Industrial Districts in Italy*, ed. E. Goodman (London: Routledge, 1989).

for spontaneous or experimental, bottom-up development initiatives.

The variety of definitions of "rural," the emergence of a nontheory of development diversity, and the elusiveness of explanations of regional economic success are all symptoms of the need for a new framework, or paradigm, of the development process. The rural policy debate and even the rural development experiments themselves are constrained by development concepts and theories that are rapidly becoming obsolete. The very concept of rurality has become less useful, and even arbitrary, within the economic development context.[3] Elements of a new paradigm are emerging, however. The following section traces the outlines of this paradigm shift.

ECONOMIC DEVELOPMENT AS A COMPLEX REGIONAL PHENOMENON

Economic development occurs on a regional basis. The location of economic activity is determined by the characteristics of geographic areas and the dynamics of competition to which enterprises are subject. Development occurs as economic activities in an area become linked and pro-

gressively more complex. Over time, the businesses, economic infrastructure, social institutions, and cultural features of an area may become integrated so as to define it as a development region. In fact, development regions and economic development itself are distinguished precisely by the complexity of this integration. Development regions are demarcated economically (economics being broadly defined) and often do not coincide with the political boundaries of counties, states, or nations. They can be distinguished within states and can exist within larger regions encompassing several states.

The role of rural areas in development has changed over time. In the past, development regions were often entirely rural. As recently as the early 1900s, the United States economy still retained enough of an agrarian base that many rural areas constituted economic development regions unto themselves. The development of towns and transportation infrastructure followed the pattern of location of land-based production. But industrialization has dramatically peripheralized the role of rural areas in the development process. Most rural areas now constitute specialized components of larger regional economies, supplying a particular industry and/or factor of production.

Rural areas continue to play an important role in regional development, but now their development problems and prospects can be understood only when viewing them as integral parts of larger regional economies. Many of the obstacles to understanding the changes in rural

3. As the old development paradigm becomes outmoded and loses its explanatory power, its concepts appear detached and arbitrary. Also, as real-world economic development acquires the new regional dynamic, the old paradigm tends to generate anomalies. When exceptions appear to outweigh the rule, analytical efforts are frustrated and ignored. For the seminal description of the nature of paradigm shifts, see Thomas S. Kuhn, *The Structure of Scientific Revolutions* (Chicago: University of Chicago Press, 1970).

economies and formulating clear rural policy lie in analyzing rural America as if it were an autonomous, identifiable economic entity, with its own particular economic dynamics. As an analytical concept, then, the term "rural development" is somewhat misleading. I will therefore refer to "regional development" and "rural area development."

This point must be conditioned by defining what we mean by "economic development." As noted, it is defined in part by its complexity. Simple concepts such as growth of an industry or of an area's income and employment do not capture features we typically associate with development such as job quality and stability, health and safety, and education. As a policy goal, economic development can be broadly defined as the creation of high-quality jobs, the presence of a stable community, and the improvement of the standard of living and quality of life in a region. This can occur with expansion or it can involve a restructuring of activities.

Thus, true, integrated economic development does not occur in rural areas per se; it occurs in regions that contain rural areas. Rural development—as development that is unique to rural areas—is essentially either enclave economy development—branch plant—or a subsistence system of production.[4] A defining characteristic of enclave or subsistence economies is that local capacities—such as work force skills,

4. Enclave economies, as they have been defined in the economic development literature, are based on production operations of, typically, branch plants with few local backward or forward linkages.

technological knowledge, and so on—are not developed or improved.

As noted previously, the location decisions of businesses and the consequent regionalization of economic activity is determined not only by the characteristics of geographic areas but also by the dynamics of competition to which business enterprises are subject. The following section outlines ways in which business competitive dynamics are changing and the implications of this for rural area development.

THE NEW GLOBAL ECONOMIC PRODUCTION SYSTEM

As noted elsewhere in this volume, much of the relative decline of rural area economies since the 1930s has been due to successful adoption of labor-saving technology in agriculture and mining. During the past several decades, we have seen a restructuring of rural areas away from resource-based industries, toward manufacturing, services, and retail trade. Much of the growth that occurred in rural manufacturing was due to branch plants seeking lower costs of production. Rural areas have provided lower property costs, low-skilled low-wage work forces, and often attractive tax breaks and other incentives. These were what many manufacturing operations were looking for as they competed in relatively stable industries on the basis of production costs.

Advances in information and communications technologies over the past two decades, however, have catalyzed business activities, transforming the very basis on which firms compete, the organizational structure of firms, and the sectoral structure of the economy. As the dust settles, the basic features of the new competition are emerging, bringing a sobering image of rural area economies as well as suggesting new opportunities.

The evolution of technology-push competition

Since the industrial revolution, competition between firms in capitalist economies has been based on technological change. The focus of the competition, that is, the role of technology, is changing, however. Under the earlier forms of competition, firms competed primarily on the basis of production cost. Competitive battles were fought by reducing the labor involved in the production of existing products in existing industries. The development of this competition involved the continual division of labor as Adam Smith described, the scientific time-motion analysis of Fredrick Taylor, and the introduction of mass production techniques à la Henry Ford. Economies of scale dominated and led to the formation of large, vertically integrated corporations that could reap the benefits of market power in mature but stable industries.

This traditional form of competition has been disrupted by the inevitable evolution of technology. As the pace of technological change continued to build through the past century, it reached a point where, in the past two decades, it was able to expand into new areas, restructuring the competitive process itself. The acceleration of technological change has

shortened product life cycles, placing ever more emphasis on innovation and new product design and less on production cost reduction. The effect has been to shift the economy generally toward the front end of the product curve as fewer industries survive long enough to make it into their mature phase.

Also, new information technologies that integrate production and design processes—for example, computer-aided design, engineering, and manufacturing; local area networks—are leading firms to compete by means of improved response time to markets, product quality, and productive flexibility. They are changing the very nature of the products produced. Microcomputer and software products, for example, require, and generally include, specialized support services. Such products are becoming indistinguishable from their related services.

This new competition does not simply take advantage of change; it is based on change. It involves a shift of emphasis from process to product innovation and has been triggered by the catalytic innovations of the electronics industry. The new information and communications technologies are enabling, and thereby forcing, firms to compete on the basis of technology and change.

Integrated production systems

These changes in the forms of industrial competition have transcended traditional industrial boundaries, producing structural change at the level of the firm, the industry, and the economy as a whole. The emphasis on innovation, flexibility, and responsiveness to markets has caused firms to become more fully integrated internally, increasing their efficiency and flexibility by pooling internal capacities and functions to strengthen interdepartmental communication.

At the same time, firms are becoming more specialized in their output —reducing vertical integration to focus on core activities and capacities. As markets and industries become ever more ephemeral, business enterprises are restructuring to be less dependent on specific products while becoming more dependent on relations with other firms and external economies of scale and scope. Thus we see the divesting of up- and downstream operations and, in their place, the formation of networks and strategic alliances between firms. This enables greater flexibility at the industry level, paralleling the organizational flexibility at the firm level and the technical flexibility on the shop floor.

In addition to the replacement of intra-firm vertical integration with new interfirm relationships, there is yet another new dimension of industrial integration rapidly emerging. The acceleration of technological innovation in most industries has made it necessary for the producers and users of capital equipment to develop and maintain close working relationships. While this is widespread among firms in innovative Japanese industries, where equipment vendors supply extended maintenance and support services to their customers, it occurs much less fre-

quently among American manufacturers. It is becoming clear that this ongoing relationship, with its continuous informational feedback, is crucial to competitiveness in the new era.

Thus the new forms of competition, which involve a new multilayered flexibility and interindustry integration, are restructuring the economy toward what can be called integrated production systems. In these production systems, specialized firms act within networks and form strategic alliances to meet specific market demands. These alliances operate within a context of rapidly shifting markets and industry boundaries. They are based increasingly on firms' basic production and design capabilities and less on their industry- and product-specific expertise.

Integrated production systems are predicated on the new developments in information technology, which catalyzed the new technology-push competition, enabling and enforcing the formation of flexible networks and production alliances. The new production systems are emerging at the same time that competitive barriers to industry entry and exit are overcome through innovation, resulting in a blurring of traditional industry boundaries and product definitions.[5]

For example, the growing use of contracting-out for information processing and other services is blurring

5. The measurement and monitoring of this economic restructuring is frustrated by the need to introduce new industry, product, and occupational categories. Evidence can perhaps be seen in the mounting difficulty in fitting the new activities into existing categories. But because reclassification is not performed regularly, the trends are not visible.

the distinction between products and services and making the usual classifications of service and manufacturing sectors outdated.[6] These changes have not only increased the complexity and integration of relations between businesses, but they have also made the business-customer relationship much more complex, bringing the human element more directly into product design.

Economic supranationalism

The new technology-push competition, along with the attendant economic restructuring, is not only breaking down sectoral boundaries; it is also transcending geopolitical boundaries. Firms are able and forced to conduct business in global markets either as multinational corporations or as members of transnational alliances. Innovation and the rapid creation and destruction of industries have provided more opportunities for penetration into foreign economies.

Under the old technological competition, large business concerns have been able to use national boundaries as barriers to foreign competition, restricting the globalization of industries to their advantage. The new competition, with its impact on firm and industry structure, has engendered new forms of transnational interfirm alliances designed to overcome the political-economic advantages of the home market. These new alliances, or "relationship-enterprises" as they have been called, give

member firms the advantage of local market access and knowledge around the globe. Therefore, associated with the integrated production systems and caused by the new technology-push competition is a new economic supranationalism.[7] Just as the impact of technology-push competition on sectoral restructuring results in the formation of integrated production systems, its effect on spatial restructuring is the new economic supranationalism.

NEW ECONOMIC REGIONALISM

The integrated-production-system and economic-supranationalism dimensions of the restructuring are accompanied by a greater mobility of capital and resources and involve the transcending of the existing sectoral and spatial boundaries of competition. Does this mean that regional boundaries are no longer important? To the contrary, as these barriers are dismantled, new economic regions form and regional location takes on a new importance.

Under the old competition, regional characteristics have determined growth and business location precisely because of the immobility of capital and labor. The emphasis has been on the natural resources of a region and the related industrial specialization of its economic development. In the context of the old competition, the regional role in development was passive and static. Regional patterns of development were determined by initial natural

---

6. Cf. the unbundling of service and other noncore activities by large manufacturing firms. This applies to low-tech services as well as high-tech.

7. "Supra-" is used rather than "trans-" to emphasize the characteristic of transcending rather than merely crossing boundaries.

endowments, history, inertia, and economic barriers to entry and exit.

Under the new competition and economic supranationalism, each investment decision involves a location decision. The added mobility and flexibility of capital means that a range of locations globally can, and therefore must, be considered for each investment. As a result, location decisions and the consequent regional distribution of development take on a more rational and intentional, and less arbitrary and historical, pattern.

Location decisions and patterns become more economic, broadly defined, in two ways. First, as business decisions increasingly involve a location consideration, regional development and its boundaries will reflect the competitive needs of business. Second, since competition is no longer conducted solely on the basis of the cost of homogeneous products but on the basis of the quality, differentiation, and innovation of the product, the locational interest is broadened to include a wider range of a region's characteristics. With competitiveness hinging on access to a quality work force, location decisions reflect not only natural resource endowments and wage differentials but also political, social, cultural, and economic resources—that is, the community.

One of the most important features of business location in the new era of competition is its effect on the sectoral linkages of the enterprise. Economies of agglomeration have been widely recognized as contributing to the clustering of business activities and, indeed, to the very formation of metropolitan economies. Under the new competition, agglomeration benefits are increasing in complexity and importance. In addition to the traditional competitive advantages gained from the face-to-face contact, interaction between innovative enterprises, and lower infrastructure costs, the new agglomeration efficiencies include greater access to networks and participation in production alliances.

Therefore, the evolution of competitive dynamics has led to the emergence of a new economic regionalism wherein regional location gains importance in investment decision making and regional development is determined by a wider range of regional characteristics and, most important, by its capacities for change such as work force quality, productive flexibility, and network or alliance capabilities. The new economic regionalism is, therefore, a product of both the sectoral and the spatial dimensions of the new technology-push competition (Figure 1).

The concept of the new economic regionalism is useful in that it helps steer analysis, and policy implementation and design, to identify appropriate regional economies. Development regions are currently defined in many ways, ranging from government jurisdiction, such as census data collection regions or state or county groupings, to economic areas, such as labor market or dominant industry areas, to ecological areas, such as the 10 ecoregions recently defined for California. But using these regional definitions only obscures the new development patterns. The framework of the new eco-

FIGURE 1
THE NEW GLOBAL PRODUCTION SYSTEM

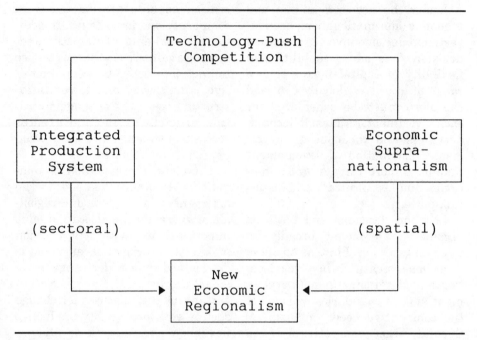

nomic regionalism leads one to look for new forms of regional development as they begin to be defined by the new competitive forces. Specifically, it focuses attention on integrated regional economies structured on network linkages and focuses less on the old sector-specific, periphery-core dualism of enclave and resource extraction economies. Most generally, it directs attention to the connection between the changes in business organization and regional patterns of economic development.

This is not to say that the traditional dualism no longer exists. It does, and it still dominates the economic profile of rural areas. But these older economic structures are based on relatively simple, direct,

backward-and-forward investment linkages.[8] The emerging patterns of regional development involve an added dimension of new dynamic linkages based on the use of technical and economic information.

Examples of emerging forms of economic clustering that reflect the new economic regionalism are the high-tech growth zones sprouting up in suburban or exurban areas across the country. These zones are based on, among others, the computer,

8. Beginning with Albert Hirschman, *The Strategy of Economic Development* (New Haven, CT: Yale University Press, 1958), the concept of linkages has been widely used and debated in the economic development literature. See also *Quarterly Journal of Economics* (1976).

laser, medical device, software, and biotechnology industries.[9] They are typically clustered around a research university that attracts both large corporations and entrepreneurs. Other necessary ingredients seem to be supportive state and local governments acting in concert with business leaders to design policies that encourage the development. Many of the firms that are attracted to these growth corridors are foreign, reflecting the supranational dimension of investment location decision making. These growth zones may indicate the pattern of future regional development: integrated regions comprising interlinked pockets of industrial specialization.

The other advantage of the new economic regionalism framework is that it can help raise the debate above the limitations of the best-practices syndrome. Focusing on context-dependent examples without developing an underlying analytical framework has led to misleading generalizations and policy lessons. An example is the conclusion of some analysts, based on several examples of successful small-firm manufacturing districts, that the global economy is restructuring toward smaller firm size to better meet the flexibility demands of the new competition.[10] This

greatly oversimplifies the underlying changes in industry and firm organization, and it leads one to overlook the complex new role of small firms in the competitive process and the degree of integration needed among small firms in regional development.

Starting from a more comprehensive analytical framework, such as that outlined here, however, leads to a focus on the new competitive dynamics, to the recognition that large firms also benefit from restructuring and networking, and to the realization that small firms in rural areas face a new set of disadvantages in addition to new possibilities.

IMPLICATIONS FOR
NATIONAL RURAL POLICY

The United States does not have an explicit national rural policy. The many federal and state programs that in some way influence rural development tend to be unrelated elements of industry-specific programs, such as farm programs; general local development funds that are not targeted for rural development, such as block grant programs; or land-use programs and regulations that do not have development as their primary objective, such as those of the Inte-

9. Ceramics Corridor in Corning, NY, for example, is based on ceramics and electronics packaging activities; Medical Alley in Minneapolis-St. Paul makes medical instruments and health care products; Boomtown Boise, in Idaho, specializes in semiconductor chips and laser printers; and Laser Lane in Orlando, FL, and Optics Valley in Tucson, AZ, are hosts to the laser and electro-optics industries. *Business Week* (19 Oct. 1992) identifies 15 such "hot spots."

10. One of the many examples of this in the literature is Michael Best, *The New Competi-*

tion: Institutions of Industrial Restructuring (Cambridge: Polity Press, 1990). A profile of the small-scale flexible manufacturing networks in the Third Italy leads Best to develop a relatively static view of the new competitive dynamics. Best sees small flexible manufacturers as better adapted to the new forms of competition and therefore predicts continued downsizing. For a critical review of his book and citations of empirical evidence contradicting his generalizations, see the review by Kathy O'Donnell in *International Review of Applied Economics*, 7(1) 1993.

rior Department and the Environmental Protection Agency. In other words, while a complex array of programs and policies affect rural area development, they have developed without the guidance of an explicit rural policy. Furthermore, the most proactive of these programs, the industry programs, are structured on an economy of the past.

As public debate builds about whether federal programs should be radically restructured, and about what if anything the government should do to address the growing economic hardships of rural communities, it becomes increasingly clear that there is very little common ground. Participants disagree not only on the nature of the solutions, but also on the nature of the problems and even on the very meaning of rural development. The conceptual framework presented in this article is intended to help structure and clarify the issues of the debate. By focusing on the underlying economic forces at work, the patterns of rural decline can be understood, and it becomes easier to identify and anticipate the potential strengths and opportunities of rural areas within the new production system.

There are several direct implications of the foregoing analysis for rural policy. First, to be effective, development policy must target the appropriate geographic area. For any particular rural area, development programs need to identify, and work within the context of, the appropriate development region that encompasses the targeted rural area. They need to take into account the new patterns of integration in regional economies. This applies to the structure of assistance programs, to the boundaries of federal program service areas, and to local development initiatives.

Second, the success of regional development hinges on the capacity for change. Public policies and programs should therefore target their efforts to help areas improve this capacity, emphasizing education, continual work force training, and technological modernization and innovation. This means that policy targeting rural areas should work to improve the integration of regional economies by fostering communications, manufacturing, and technology networks. With the new interest in Washington in assisting the development and dissemination of new technologies, including environmental technologies, there are opportunities for new alliances between the manufacturing technology extension programs at both federal and state levels and rural development programs and institutions.

Third, certain public sector responsibilities and interests need to be uncoupled from economic development objectives. As the new competition develops, the grounds for public sector intervention need to be clarified. This is especially true in light of the heavy historical involvement of the government in rural industries. While the new dynamics of competition may tend to create a greater overlapping of public and private interests in some areas—for example, the contribution of community and a high-quality work force to competitiveness and profitability—private enterprises will face new competitive pressures to ignore the interests of employees, their communities, and the environment. A realistic analysis of the new competition and its new economic regionalism should be used to distinguish the areas of potential conflicts of interest and thereby identify the appropriate public sector role. In addition to the traditional areas of conflict—environmental quality and conservation, health and safety standards, worker benefits— there is the public interest in maintaining the aesthetic and cultural qualities of rural areas—assistance to small farms might be justified on these grounds alone—as well as concerns regarding the geographic distribution of growth, with an eye toward reducing urban congestion and taking advantage of possible efficiencies of dispersion.

Entrepreneurial Social Infrastructure: A Necessary Ingredient

By CORNELIA BUTLER FLORA and JAN L. FLORA

ABSTRACT: Local communities are faced with increasing responsibilities to provide for their own well-being and development. With fewer resources, communities need more successful ways of uniting people and resources. Entrepreneurial social infrastructure (ESI) is a necessary ingredient for successfully linking physical resources and leadership for community development. ESI includes three elements: symbolic diversity, resource mobilization, and quality of networks. Instead of fostering perverse conflict or superficial harmony, symbolic diversity inspires communities to engage in constructive controversy to arrive at workable community decisions by focusing on community processes, depersonalization of politics, and broadening of community boundaries. Resource mobilization involves generating some surplus within the community beyond basic subsistence with relative equity in resource and risk distribution, investment by residents of their own private capital locally, and collective investment in the community (willingness of residents to tax themselves). Quality networks include establishing linkages with others in similar circumstances and developing vertical networks to provide diverse sources—both within and outside the community—of experience and knowledge.

Cornelia Butler Flora and Jan L. Flora have taught sociology at Kansas State University and served with the Ford Foundation in Latin America. C. Flora is currently head of the Sociology Department and J. Flora is professor of agricultural economics and sociology at Virginia Polytechnic Institute and State University. They both recently authored Rural Communities: Legacy and Change, *and C. Flora recently edited* Rural Policies for the 1990s *and* Sustainable Agriculture in Temperate Zones.

NOTE: This material is based upon work supported by the Cooperative State Research Service, U.S. Department of Agriculture, under Project No. 92-37401-8286.

R URAL development provides unique challenges. Rural communities, by definition, have low population density and are spatially isolated. These circumstances make provision of physical infrastructure more difficult and more expensive, often requiring federal investment. Federal dollars, either directly or indirectly, funded the canals, railroads, highways, postal services, electricity lines, and telecommunications networks that link rural areas to the rest of the country and the world. Federal funds were also crucial in the construction of rural hospitals and water and sewer systems, providing a basis for sanitation and health care.

With the current fiscal crisis of the federal government, such subsidies are rapidly decreasing or being eliminated. The state and, increasingly, local governments are having to assume the responsibility for physical infrastructure. Most localities, however, have neither access to the capital needed nor the political will to raise it. Thus a series of economic and physical prerequisites to development are often lacking in rural areas. Much attention to rural development in the past has focused on the provision of this infrastructure as the basis for economic growth.

The major economic restructuring that has taken place in the last decades has made it clear that physical infrastructure is not enough. There has been increasing concern, particularly in the private sector, that the individual leadership skills needed to build community are also in short supply in rural areas, as out-migration has resulted in an exodus of educated young people. Low population density has meant that, even with the same proportion of leaders as in urban areas, many rural areas lack a critical mass for concerted action and lack access to specific expertise, either hired locally or acquired from the outside.[1] Thus a large number of leadership training activities have been undertaken, spurred often by organizations in the private sector, such as the Kellogg Foundation and chambers of commerce. These are often implemented by public sector groups, such as the Cooperative Extension Service and community colleges, which attempt to fill the gap in human capital necessary for community development to take place.

It is our contention that both physical infrastructure and leadership training are necessary components of community development but are not sufficient, either separately or in combination. Our 15 years of research on rural communities in the United States suggests that a third component, social infrastructure, is the key to linking individual leadership to physical infrastructure and to facilitating community development.

Social infrastructure is the group-level, interactive aspect of organizations or institutions. As social infrastructure resides in symbols and interactions, not in individuals or things, it is less tangible and thus more difficult to measure than either physical infrastructure or human capital (which includes individual leadership capacity, as well as other

1. Ronald J. Hustedde, "Developing Leadership to Address Rural Problems," in *Rural Community Economic Development*, ed. Norman Waltzer (New York: Praeger, 1991), pp. 111-23.

knowledge and skills gained from formal and informal training and education).[2] Yet our research suggests that it is crucial that entrepreneurial social infrastructure be present before individual leadership can be executed and physical infrastructure successfully deployed.

Our awareness of social infrastructure came gradually in the course of our research. At first, we, like those who focus on leadership training, thought the problem was at the individual level—the lack of persons with the vision and skills to galvanize a community to action. But we found that key individuals who had spurred action in one community were totally ineffective when they moved to another, seemingly similar, community and attempted similar action. For instance, an innovative

2. Swanson conceptualizes social infrastructure as having three parts: (1) social institutions, including local government, social service institutions, voluntary and civic organizations, and the like; (2) human resources, which include attributes of inhabitants such as their technical expertise, organizational skills, educational levels, and even social structure—class, race, ethnicity, gender, and so on; and (3) characteristics of social networks, including innovativeness, ability to mobilize resources within the community, ability to link up with outside expertise and information, and so on. Louis Swanson, "Rural Social Infrastructure," in *Foundations of Rural Development Policy*, ed. J. Norman Reid et al. (Boulder, CO: Westview Press, 1992). We have defined social infrastructure more narrowly, limiting it to specifically collective or explicitly interactive elements. Since human resources, or what the economists call human capital, are properties of individuals—although a product of collective human endeavor—we have omitted them from our definition, which includes group-level or collective aspects of social institutions, such as communities or organizations.

newspaper publisher who played a major leadership role in bringing economic development activities to one rural community in Kansas encountered outright rejection of his leadership in the community where he subsequently became publisher of the local newspaper. The communities were similar in their size, physical infrastructure, and economic base. One could, however, point to significant differences in community-level social infrastructure, particularly in terms of such things as the character of linkages with the outside, acceptance of outsiders in leadership positions, and willingness to commit local resources to development projects.

Entrepreneurial social infrastructure has three major dimensions: symbolic diversity, resource mobilization, and quality of linkages. The configurations of these three dimensions that are associated with progressive community change will be outlined later in this article.

As we have developed our understanding of these dimensions in the course of our research, both our work and that of colleagues suggest that these aspects of social infrastructure are not fixed for a particular community but can be developed and changed. Mary Emery, working with communities in northern Idaho, found that, by changing specific aspects of social infrastructure, communities that had previously not engaged in development activities were able to bring about concrete economic change through community-based activities.

Thus our ability to accurately assess the various dimensions of social infrastructure not only improves our research but helps the practice of community development as well. Understanding and measuring social infrastructure contribute to our understanding of the development process in rural communities and also contribute to that development if used as a basis for purposive community action, what sociologists refer to as collective agency.

Conceptualizing the community as a system is the key to our ability to analyze it effectively. When we analyze a system, we are forced to confront what sociologists call the mosaic fallacy, the false assumption that a system is simply the sum of its parts. Interaction between the parts yields a different organism on a different level. By simply summing, we cannot understand reality. While we need to look at the parts of a system, social or biological, we need the overall system view as well.

Analysis of social infrastructure directs community analysis to consideration of interactions. What happens to community residents and what happens to the local economy are mediated by social structure.

How can we build communities able to deal creatively with systems, externalities, and ambiguity? It is not enough to call for more money or more physical infrastructure. At this time of financial crisis, such solutions will not happen—even if they would work. As more responsibility is placed on localities to solve their challenges of maintenance and development, we need to examine what type of social infrastructure is most propitious for economic development at the community level.

In the course of our studies of rural communities, we observed a series of qualities in the communities that produced entrepreneurial rural communities. These communities were able to optimize multiple goals, rather than maximize any particular end. In addressing the challenge of optimizing multiple goals, which will include balancing what is best for people, the economy, and the environment, we need to rethink our own institutional framework. We cannot totally remove the people from the environment, and we cannot pursue short-term profitability to the exclusion of other objectives. Entrepreneurial social infrastructure is an important mechanism of institutional analysis as a basis for change.

The distressing aspect of our community research is how little entrepreneurial social infrastructure exists. The hopeful aspect of the research is that communities that try to develop it are able to do so.

We will now discuss the three components of entrepreneurial social infrastructure: symbolic diversity, resource mobilization, and quality of linkages.

SYMBOLIC DIVERSITY

Symbolic diversity is a collective or community-level orientation toward inclusiveness rather than exclusiveness. Rather than fostering rancorous conflict or superficial harmony, symbolic diversity inspires communities to engage in constructive controversy in order to arrive at workable community decisions by focusing on community processes, depersonalization of politics, and broadening of community boundaries.

In order to understand the importance of symbolic diversity—and the reasons for its infrequent occurrence in rural communities—it is necessary to examine the character of rural communities in which there is intense and frequent interaction between community members, that is, rural communities characterized by a high density of acquaintanceship. High density of acquaintanceship can be seen as an important aspect of feeling part of a community.

Blockages to symbolic diversity: Density of acquaintanceship

Density of acquaintanceship is defined as the extent to which community members interact with one another on a regular, informal, and relatively personal basis. High density of acquaintanceship, according to Freudenburg, is associated with small population size, long length of residence, anticipated continuing residence, low diversity, and high segregation, both social and physical, of people who are different from each other.[3]

Blockages to symbolic diversity: Role homogeneity

High density of acquaintanceship in turn leads to role homogeneity. Role homogeneity refers to the extent

to which community members interact with one another across a wide variety of settings—not only at work but also at school events, in civic organizations, and at the local grocery store. Because people see one another across a range of roles, they develop relationships with one another based on the whole person. Rural communities, in part because of their smaller size, offer environments where people see each other often doing different things.

Acceptance of controversy

The first characteristic of symbolic diversity is willingness to accept controversy. Because of role homogeneity, rural communities tend to suppress controversy. One risks too many relationships when one disagrees in public on the need for a new landfill. For example, one may fear that the people who take the opposite point of view would stop shopping in one's store, that one's spouse would lose the promotion at the workplace, that one would feel uncomfortable singing in the church choir led by the person who expressed a different point of view, that youngsters would drop out of one's Little League team, that one would no longer be included on the bowling team, and that one's daughter would be embarrassed by one's behavior because she is dating

3. William R. Freudenburg, "The Density of Acquaintanceship: An Overlooked Variable in Community Research?" *American Journal of Sociology*, 92:27-63 (July 1986).

4. Role homogeneity and high density of acquaintanceship can also exist in ethnic or minority neighborhoods in urban areas. Rural communities that are undergoing rapid growth or that serve as bedroom communities for larger urban centers may not have those characteristics.

the son of the principal landfill advocate. To voice an opinion in many situations means risking all such relationships, public and private.

Nonetheless, some level of controversy is necessary in order to make informed and democratic choices. In order for people to weigh the advantages and disadvantages of alternatives, there must be debate in the community. Controversy is the opposite of conflict, not the opposite of absence of disagreement.

Absence of controversy is as dangerous for communities as is conflict. Important issues that are not addressed early may later break out in rancorous conflict. Then people do not speak to each other for years and years. Not only is such a situation not pleasant, but it is also not productive. It drains resources from useful collective activity.

Role homogeneity that is compounded by a high density of acquaintanceship tends to result in the suppression of controversy, because of the fear that, by disagreeing with someone in one setting, one may jeopardize one's relationship with that person—or his or her relatives—in another setting, perhaps one even more central to one's well-being in the community. That then becomes translated into communitywide norms suggesting that it is inappropriate— "not nice"—to generate controversy; hence controversial issues tend to be avoided. Thus most rural communities characterized by even a moderate level of density of acquaintanceship will tend to avoid controversy.

Acceptance of controversy means that disagreements do not become moral issues but are recognized as different ways to see the world. In communities where controversy is accepted, people can disagree with each other and still respect each other. People address problems and do not become defensive. Acceptance of controversy allows early identification of problems, before subgroups become wedded to particular solutions. Acceptance of controversy is the first characteristic of an entrepreneurial symbolic social infrastructure.

Depersonalization of politics

Acceptance of controversy allows for the emergence of the second characteristic of symbolic diversity, the depersonalization of institutional politics. Under this condition, those who disagree with a particular position are seen as doing so not out of their evil nature but because of honest differences as to alternative solutions. One can be a leader or assume responsibility without fear of losing friends. One can discuss issues, lay out different arguments, and still view the person with another viewpoint as a moral human being.

One does not start off a critique of someone by saying, "Only an idiot could have conceived of looking at this in that way." Such words are the personalization of a political stance. When local politics are personalized, no one cares to assume leadership in the community. It seems better to criticize the character of a community leader than participate in a positive way. Community citizens do not care or dare to risk everything. As a result, they do not put themselves in the position of being personally crucified if they enter the public arena. The fact that politics are highly personalized in most communities means that the incumbents are seldom challenged—and when they are, it is because of perceived flaws in character, not because the challenger truly hopes to improve the community's well-being.

Focus on process

The third characteristic of symbolic diversity is a focus on process rather than on winning. In communities with entrepreneurial social infrastructure, the various interests are given the same emphasis. The sports analogy of life as a competitive game is rejected. In a game there are clear rules. There is a playing field with immutable boundaries and measurable slope. There is the starting whistle and the final gun. The big play puts the ball over the goal line. There are always clearly labeled winners and losers. That sports analogy gives too much emphasis to short-term heroics, the quarterly-profit view of success.

An analogy of child rearing is more apt, because of its focus on process rather than final score. Parenthood is never over. Just when you think you have done a good job, they stay out all night or get a *D* on an algebra test—or move home again. Child rearing is a process that has ups and downs but no precisely defined wins and losses. What makes us good parents is attention to the process, not fixation on a predetermined outcome. We do not necessarily win if our kid makes it through Harvard with all *A*s and is class president; that is not what parenting is about. Parenting is having a decent human being who can then contribute with you in the larger society. The same is true of communities. While communities with entrepreneurial social infrastructure celebrate successes, that celebration itself becomes part of the process of community building, not a prize for winning.

Broad definition and permeable boundaries

A fourth characteristic of symbolic diversity lies in defining the group widely and drawing boundaries loosely. Expanding who "we" are, with fewer and fewer "theys," allows institutions to have allies, not adversaries. In a world where group boundaries are being tightened—with disastrous and violent results—making boundaries more permeable and expanding group membership are imperative. The more we can be inclusive, the more we are then able to cope with the new set of parameters in which we must function.

RESOURCE
MOBILIZATION

The second dimension of entrepreneurial social infrastructure is resource mobilization. Given the current fiscal crisis that has hit the national and state levels of government and industry, communities must be ever more dependent on their own resources if development is to occur. Yet the economic restructuring facing rural America has led to decreasing incomes and a decreasing tax base in many areas.

Relative equality
in distribution
of resources

Surplus must be relatively equitably distributed if innovation is to occur. It is difficult for communities without any surplus at all to be innovative. Innovation is truly stymied if resources are concentrated in the hands of a few. With resource concentration, protecting one's own resources becomes more important than expanding them for the entire community.

There is often more surplus than we know, not as visible fat but covered up by traditional organizational structures. Rearrangement of resources can provide the flexibility to do new things. But without entrepreneurial social infrastructure, such rearrangement is too threatening to most members of the organization. There is a saying that necessity is the mother of invention. In fact, however, people with great necessity often cannot be very inventive—the risk is too great. Surplus allows people to risk a little bit. Entrepreneurial social infrastructure allocates resources for risk. We have found in communities where resources are relatively concentrated in a few hands, either internal or external to the community, such as mining or mill towns, there is much less entrepreneurial activity, either on the individual or community level.

For communities, it is important to risk collectively, rather than forcing risk on just a few individuals. Resources must be defined broadly. The resources that communities have include not only money but also positions, space, communication, and equipment. Risk means the real possibility that one may lose. Entrepreneurial social infrastructure is facilitated when there are enough resources so that the community can still keep going if it loses on a particular investment.

Willingness to
invest collectively

Resource mobilization in communities with entrepreneurial social infrastructure includes willingness of the community to tax itself for activities that cannot or will not be provided through the private sector. We spend money differently individually from the way we do collectively. We often spend money individually—on clothes, entertainment, home furnishings, and so on—without its significantly affecting the quality of community life. But an equal amount of money, combined with a similar amount of money from each taxpayer in the community and spent on upgrading schools or an antiquated sewer system, can have an important impact on community quality of life. Entrepreneurial communities are willing to tax themselves, either through new taxes or through reallocation, to ensure that certain physical infrastructure and human capital are available to the community. That willingness is part of entrepreneurial social infrastructure.

Willingness to invest private capital locally

The third resource-related characteristic of entrepreneurial social infrastructure is willingness to invest private resources locally. Enterprises in entrepreneurial communities are able to obtain both debt and equity capital locally. Individuals in entrepreneurial communities are also willing to contribute nonmoney capital, in the form of physical and human resources, to enterprises that are anticipated to benefit the community. Such capital may then be used to leverage outside capital and investment, but the initial self-investment means a greater degree of local control and flexibility.

Since locally generated enterprises are often risky, it is preferable that people contribute no more than they are willing to lose. One community we studied raised $500,000 from community members for two locally controlled industrial enterprises. The firms failed and people lost their money, but because the funds had been collected widely from within the community, the losses did not stifle future entrepreneurial efforts on behalf of the community.

QUALITY OF NETWORKS

The final dimension of entrepreneurial social infrastructure in rural communities is quality of networks. Networks, formal and informal, within the community and with the outside, facilitate the flow of resources, particularly information. In the information age, broad linkages are important. Effective social infrastructure cultivates those networks.

Network diversity

The first characteristic of networks in entrepreneurial social infrastructure is diversity. Voices are heard that are different from those of traditional elites. The process of decision making is opened up. Leadership is spread broadly, including both men and women, different ethnic groups, different races, different classes, and different clienteles. Network diversity allows communities to be more innovative in setting the development agenda. This diversity of leadership and of approaches is uncomfortable for many community and economic development professionals, who are used to educating people to be more like themselves. The very uncertainty of the future means that communities have to be aware that solutions must respond to groups of people who are increasingly more diverse and who have different pressures on them.

Communities that have deliberately expanded decision-making structures to include women, African Americans, Hispanics, workers, and youths have made strides in economic as well as community development.

Horizontal networks

The second network characteristic that increases quality is the formation of horizontal networks. Communities tend to learn best from those most like themselves. We call this horizontal networking lateral learning. Lateral learning is important in technology generation and transfer and in organizational innovation as well.

People learn more from people like themselves than they do from experts. Communities that are entrepreneurial form groups to visit other communities where they have heard that something important is going on that they wish to emulate. They are also visited by other communities, with those visits serving as both learning for the visitors and consultancies for the communities visited. After visits to similar ventures in other communities, citizens of Oberlin, Kansas, put together a hometown carnival, a feedlot, and a dairy. The community-built playground in Blacksburg, Virginia, was the result of a community member's having seen a similar activity in another town. Horizontal networks result in innovative thinking: "If they can do it there, then we can do it here."

Vertical networks

The final network characteristic is the development of vertical networks with two-way flows of information. Entrepreneurial communities cannot depend on only their own resources if development is to occur. They must link themselves to private and public resources outside the community to gather information, credit, materials, and technical assistance. They must also link to specific groups within the community. Vertical networks link different system levels. Entrepreneurial communities are centrally located in the interstices between systems.

In a nationwide survey of recent grass-roots economic development efforts in rural communities, we found that while leaders of those efforts felt the greatest obstacle to success was money (too little and too expensive), the in-depth case studies that complemented the survey revealed that management and social organization were in even shorter supply.[5] Appropriately chosen expertise from the outside, via vertical networks, can ameliorate problems of both inadequate funding and inadequate management.

CONCLUSION

Communities that have entrepreneurial social infrastructure can begin to deal with the complex, messy, unreliable-indicator problems of development and change. They focus not on immediate short-term solutions but on the process of empowering people for the long term.

Such communities meet resistance from within and from the outside. Desperate people do not always want process; they want the formula for success: 3 ways to lose weight, 6 steps to stop smoking and improve your sex life, 14 steps to total happiness. Process is more than that. Process is when the person seeking a solution is a part of deciding how to

5. Jan L. Flora et al., *From the Grassroots: Case Studies of Rural Self Development Efforts,* Agriculture and Rural Economy Division Staff Report (Washington, DC: Department of Agriculture, Economic Research Service, forthcoming).

find it. The empowering part of entrepreneurial social infrastructure is that it is a new way of conceptualizing how knowledge is generated and transmitted.

Entrepreneurial social infrastructure means that communities begin to look at making slots rather than fitting into slots. Communities with entrepreneurial social infrastructure do not say, "Gee, if only someone would build a factory" and then complain because the factory pollutes. Entrepreneurial communities are proactive in identifying problems and alternative ways to solve them. Entrepreneurial social infrastructure means communities begin to look at risk, both collectively and individually, in a different way. Willingness to risk means entrepreneurial communities are able to look more systematically at where the risk occurs and how it can be rationalized in terms of where communities want to be in the future. Entrepreneurial communities are willing to risk the semblance of cohesion to attempt to set collective visions of the community's future.

Entrepreneurial communities grapple with the organizational aspects of resolving what seem to be insoluble dilemmas. Must the problem be framed only in dichotomous terms, as in the conflict over saving either spotted owls or jobs? Or can communities phrase their problems in nonpolemical ways that allow for controversy, for discussion of multiple alternatives? Through the process of social interaction in entrepreneurial communities, leaders can facilitate change through information gathering, through participation, and by listening as well as talking.

Rural communities will change as we enter the twenty-first century. But only if communities work to develop entrepreneurial social infrastructures can they participate in that change in a positive, proactive way that utilizes the leadership potential of their citizens and the physical infrastructure that they have built.

ANNALS, *AAPSS*, **529**, September 1993

Knowledge in Action:
The University of Missouri's
Extension Network

By C. BRICE RATCHFORD

ABSTRACT: This article reviews how the University of Missouri organized in the 1970s to be a readily available knowledge resource to all the citizens and institutions of the state. The goal was to enhance individual and institutional capacity to solve problems and achieve goals, including economic development. To accomplish this mission, the University placed many academic activities in a single unit, the Extension Division. Leadership for the Extension Division was part of the central University administrative staff. A critical decision was that the outreach work would be part of the regular academic program and that extension personnel would be part of the regular faculty. Every school and college of the four-campus system came to be involved in some way in the extension mission. The two major thrusts are the traditional continuing education of professionals and problem solving. In addition to campus-based faculty with continuing and ad hoc extension assignments, there is a field staff of some 400 persons located in offices in every county. The program has been rated as effective, particularly in rural areas where there is a dearth of expertise and organizations.

C. Brice Ratchford earned a professorship in agricultural economics at North Carolina State University before moving to Missouri in 1959 to head the Cooperative Extension Service. He was named dean in 1960 of the newly created Extension Division. In 1965 he became vice president of extension for the University system. From 1970 to 1977 he served as president of the University. Until retirement in 1991, he taught and did research as a professor of agricultural economics and was involved in the University's international programs in Peru, Tunisia, Liberia, and Kenya.

THE University of Missouri is both a land-grant and a state university. It is comprehensive, with degrees offered in all major disciplines and professions. It is also classified as a research university, offering the Ph.D. in most disciplines. Research is part of the responsibility of essentially all faculty members; in addition, the University has a number of organized special-purpose research programs, the largest being the Agricultural Experiment Station.

Prior to 1960, the University had two very different extension services; this continues to be the pattern in most state and land-grant universities. The first, the Cooperative Extension Service, was created by the Smith-Lever Act, which became law in 1914. It provided the third dimension to the land-grant universities' mission, teaching and research having been created earlier—teaching in 1862 by the Morrill Act, and agricultural research in 1888 by the Hatch Act. The Smith-Lever Act authorized federal funding for the land-grant colleges to extend to the people of the nation practical information on agriculture, home economics, and related subjects. These funds had to be matched.

Subsequently, the University of Missouri and all other land-grant universities developed an institution that included specialists located at the university in the several program areas in agriculture and home economics, and a staff of generalists located in every county. Programs were limited to agriculture and home economics broadly defined and were directed to farmers and rural residents. The mission was broadened over time to include marketing and rural development as well as several initiatives directed to urban areas.

The second extension organization was General Extension. Its activities were confined largely to credit courses off campus; high school and college courses through correspondence; and also conferences and short courses on campus. It had one specialist in the School of Journalism to work with high school publications, four persons specializing in community development, and two specialists who provided training to fire fighters in small towns and rural communities.

The two extension services had contrasting philosophical underpinnings. Cooperative Extension used full-time personnel compensated with state and federal funds. All assistance was free, and meetings and individual consultation were the primary educational methods. While the service was designed to transfer technology, it achieved this mission through introducing technology to help solve problems and achieve goals. This approach was much more effective than selling technology per se and is the reason why Cooperative Extension has been highly successful when compared to other technology-transfer programs.

General Extension operated differently. It employed persons for specific tasks such as teaching a course in a small town out in the state for one semester. The price was negotiated, and if the person was a University employee, he or she received extra compensation. The programs were supported primarily through student fees. There was little if any problem-solving mission involved in the General Extension operations.

The Governing Board of the University approved the recommendation of President Elmer Ellis that effective 1 July 1960 the University would have a single extension program. The scope of extension was defined as all credit courses conducted off campus and all noncredit work on and off campus. The reason given for the reorganization was to make the total University knowledge resource-base available to the entire state for the purpose of enhancing individual and institutional development.

Cooperative Extension in Missouri, and in most other states, had been part of the College of Agriculture. The new plan called for the leader to be a dean who would report directly to the president of the University. In 1965, the title of the leader was changed to vice president.

IMPLEMENTING THE PLAN

Implementing the policy was a vexing assignment. It was facilitated by the fact that the University had some flexible resources in 1960. At that time and still to this day, there was no earmarking of state appropriations to the University. The president of the University, with the approval of the Governing Board, allocated the money to the several units and programs. Further, all income generated from fees and sales of services and federal programs was retained by the University, and

state government exercised no control over its use. In many states, all funds from nonstate sources must be reappropriated. For these reasons, funding was not a constraint in early years.

A real constraint was the fact that on-campus enrollment was increasing by leaps and bounds and there was a severe national shortage of qualified professors. The faculty was understandably reluctant to even consider taking on any additional responsibility. The most serious hindrance was a pervasive attitude, even in the College of Agriculture, that extension work was of low quality and low academic level and hence should not be a part of the mission of a research university. This was a long-standing attitude and was responsible for the section in the Smith-Lever Act that prohibited the use of any federal funds and the mandatory matching funds to support the teaching of courses for academic credit. It was also this attitude that caused both Cooperative and General Extension to be organized as a type of institute apart from the regular academic program. In some states, extension resembled another university with a limited mission.

The single most important decision made as the plan was implemented was that extension would be part of the regular academic program of the University of Missouri. Several specific policies were stated to carry out this decision. First, extension would not do any work in a field where the University did not have an academic program. The prime example was architecture. Second, any fac-

62 THE ANNALS OF THE AMERICAN ACADEMY

ulty member employed on a continuing appointment to do extension work on a full-time or part-time basis would be a regular member of the academic department and have the privileges and responsibilities of other members of that faculty. Third, persons employed on an ad hoc basis would be approved by the department chair. Fourth, approval would be given by the appropriate academic department for the location, content, and instructors for all credit courses offered off campus and all noncredit courses and conferences.

These policies were faithfully adhered to and were important in countering the criticism that extension was outside the regular academic program. Incidentally, several other universities, the most notable being the University of Wisconsin, were reorganizing extension at about the same time. Wisconsin opted to make extension another campus of the statewide system. To a degree, the University of West Virginia and later the University of Maryland followed the same pattern. The proponents of that approach argued that it was necessary for flexibility and to secure tenure for extension appointees. These different approaches were widely debated, and University of Missouri spokespersons became the leading proponents for making extension a part of the regular mission of every department. Missouri demonstrated that the fears of the proponents of a separate institution were unfounded, and the University of Wisconsin has since abolished the other-campus approach in favor of making extension a part of the

mission of the regular academic units.

Concurrent with the development and implementation of the previously mentioned policies, procedures were developed and implemented to eradicate the differences in the practices of Cooperative and General Extension. Some of the more important were (1) employing regular faculty to do extension work on a continuing basis (often these persons also had some combination of resident teaching and research responsibilities); (2) charging fees—what the market would bear—for all program areas when cost-effective and appropriate; however, no program was mandated to pay its way; (3) vigorously seeking soft money to support in part all programs; and (4) adopting uniform policies on extra compensation and consulting.

SCHOOLS AND COLLEGES
BEGIN RESPONDING

There was no line of schools and departments or even individuals waiting for the new opportunity; that had to be sold. This effort was strongly supported by President Ellis and the Board of Curators. The College of Education was the first to respond, and that was because of its strong ties to the public schools and the fact that all teachers had to periodically take credit courses to maintain a license to teach. The College of Medicine was eager for a mechanism to provide continuing education to all classes of medical personnel throughout the state, particularly in rural areas, and quickly jumped on the bandwagon. The School of Social Work accepted the responsibility for community development that was very aggressive statewide.

Several persons felt very strongly that the University should have a continuing-education program for local government officials and employees. This belief was based on the work of the Institute of Local Government at the University of North Carolina at Chapel Hill. Governmental institutions were very similar in North Carolina and Missouri, but the officials in North Carolina were well trained and operated in a more sophisticated manner. The only readily apparent difference was the Institute of Local Government, which had consistently provided training and consultation starting in the mid-1930s. Three events occurred that helped make such a program a reality almost simultaneously. First, the Kansas City Trusts and Foundations made a grant to support for five years an M.S. program in Kansas City in public administration for public employees. Two full-time faculty members were employed by the College of Business and Public Administration in Columbia to reside in Kansas City and lead the program. Second, the Business College decided that it would give leadership to a statewide program and subsequently recruited a leader. Third, Lawrence Roos, the newly elected supervisor in St. Louis County, asked that the University employ a person to be placed on the St. Louis County staff to work with the many units of local government in that county, and the University responded positively. This act had far-

ranging consequences as this was the first person placed in a Cooperative Extension Service Office who had training and background in fields other than agriculture or home economics.

The Economics Department had a respected professor in labor economics who had an interest in an education program for the leadership of organized labor. He sold the department on sponsoring the program and subsequently was important in promoting the idea of employing a full-time person to lead the effort.

The University had two engineering colleges, one in Columbia and the other at Rolla. The latter was established in 1870 pursuant to the passage of the Land Grant College Act. Both were poorly located with respect to engineering activities in the state; each concentrated on undergraduate education and had no outreach efforts. Both got new deans in July 1961 who were energetic and ambitious. In short order, each of the schools had a large number of credit courses at the graduate level in St. Louis and Kansas City and were offering conferences and noncredit courses throughout the state.

The College of Business and Public Administration at Columbia had for many years offered credit courses in Kansas City leading to an MBA. The College was initially unhappy that the program was placed under the extension umbrella. It soon realized, however, that extension had the capacity to facilitate and strengthen the program; it subsequently broadened its credit courses and initiated a noncredit program throughout the state.

While the College of Arts and Science in general was unresponsive, the Departments of Sociology, Anthropology, Archaeology, Music, and Geography showed interest in participating. No one had a pattern or plan for such departments. Once faced with the challenge, the faculties created ideas that received support.

By 1963 the University was still far from its goal of having every academic unit involved in extension work, but it had gone far enough that the term "University Extension" had some meaning. The changes on campus had resulted in no significant changes for over 400 professional Cooperative Extension workers located in the 114 county offices. In general, the workers supported the broader concept and gladly helped arrange and promote the credit and noncredit courses in their area. They began monitoring examinations for the correspondence courses. A few individuals tried to organized courses, and most experienced frustration at the limited capacity of the campus to respond.

PROGRESS ACCELERATES

Between 1963 and 1966, several unrelated events resulted in dramatic change in the entire extension effort. In 1963, the state decided to create a University system with major campuses in St. Louis and Kansas City. An entirely new campus was to be built in St. Louis, and a financially troubled private university—the University of Kansas City—was taken over in Kansas City. The School of Mines at Rolla became a separate campus and not just another school of the Columbia campus. The plan for extension that was being implemented at Columbia became applicable to the other campuses.

Beginning in 1970, the Congress appropriated funds to the 1890 land-grant colleges for research and extension. While the funds went directly to the colleges, the legislation mandated a single coordinated program. For extension, Lincoln University became, in effect, another campus, and the letterhead and logos were shared by both the University of Missouri system and Lincoln University.

The urban campuses provided some unexpected benefits for extension. The Cooperative Extension Service had well-staffed offices in the metropolitan areas, but the programs and staff expertise were essentially the same as in most rural areas, namely, agriculture (albeit horticulture), home economics, and 4-H. Extension was asked to open the St. Louis campus using the same mechanics it had developed for offering credit courses off campus. Dr. James Bugg was the first head of that campus and had as a major objective building an urban campus following the land-grant mission of access to practical university programs and assistance to the community through problem-solving research and extension activities. He built bridges to the existing Cooperative Extension staff. The same person, Virgil Sapp, served as both dean of extension on the campus and as regional director for the Cooperative Extension Service. Bugg and Sapp proceeded to rapidly change personnel and build programs really suited to the needs of a metropolitan area. Of course, a faculty residing in the community broadened the resource base for extension. The same approach was used in Kansas City but, while effective, never worked as well as in St. Louis for a variety of reasons.

NEW FEDERAL PROGRAMS PROVIDE ASSISTANCE

Some of the initiatives started during the Kennedy-Johnson years provided motivation and support for new and different extension programs. One that actually provided few funds but had significant long-range impact on University Extension was the State Technical Service Act passed by the Congress in 1965. The bill was sponsored by the U.S. Department of Commerce and promised to do for business and industry what Cooperative Extension had done for agriculture. The Engineering and Business Schools seized on the opportunity. The schools employed faculty to provide leadership and serve as knowledge resources to the program. The decision was made to add business and industry specialists to the field staff. The Colleges took the lead in recruiting the staff and provided preservice and in-service training as well as continuous backup. The field staff completely changed the philosophy of extension programs in the schools. Before the advent of the field staff, the schools sometimes responded to requests, often in the formal manner of a meeting or noncredit course. There was no follow-up. The field staff continued to organize noncredit courses, but these were designed to meet the needs of a specific group and there was usually some follow-up. More important, the field staff sought out firms with problems and opportunities and followed up on a one-on-one basis.

Title I of the Higher Education Act of 1965 started out as a tool to provide institutional support to General Extension as the Smith-Lever Act had for Cooperative Extension. When finally passed, it provided assistance for problem solving, primarily in urban areas. It is difficult today to identify what specifically remains of the effort. For the University of Missouri, it did broaden the involvement of faculty in extension and help build an extension program for urban areas.

The Economic Opportunity Act (War on Poverty) had a strong continuing impact on the University and extension. The war was slow getting off the ground in rural areas. Governor Dalton asked University Extension to lend a hand. The community development specialists, with assistance from the traditional field staff, quickly had the entire state organized into community action agencies with approved programs. Intensive training was provided for board members and staff of the new agencies. The Colleges of Education and Home Economics helped develop and implement the Head Start program and provided training for the new staffs. In most parts of the state, the traditional field staff developed components focusing on agriculture, home economics, and youths. They were very different, however, from the traditional programs, which were directed to the white middle and upper classes. The new programs were directed to blacks and poor whites. Another truly significant change was the recruitment of the staff from the target clientele. Cooperative Extension gained responsibility for and continues to support with Smith-Lever funds the nutrition program with low-income families and the urban gardening program. The latter assisted inner-city youths in their use of abandoned lots for vegetable and flower gardens. The greatest impact was in changing attitudes on whom extension should seek to serve.

COUNTY PROGRAMMING
CHANGED TO
AREA PROGRAMMING

The most significant step in completely changing the makeup of extension occurred in 1965, when counties were abandoned as the main programming units in favor of 20 regions. While there were over 400 Cooperative Extension field staff, there was little flexibility when agriculture, home economics, and 4-H had to be covered in 114 counties and the city of St. Louis. The new regions consisted of 3 to 10 counties and on average had a pool of 20 positions each. All staff were converted over time from generalists to specialists. Every person with a specialist title was tied to a regular academic department, which participated in employment, evaluation, and salary adjustments and which were fully responsible for staff training.

The typical staffing pattern for a region included several specialists in agriculture, home economics, and 4-H. Each also had at least one community development, one business and industry, and one continuing-education specialist. The job of the continuing-education specialist was to promote programs in fields not covered by the other specialists. Some areas chose to add specialists in local government, communications, health education, as well as other fields.

For the next 30 years, the University followed a consistent policy for extension, and by the late 1980s, every college in the four-campus system had an outreach program that had activities on and off campus. The field staff comprised persons with widely varying backgrounds and academic training, and they all had ties to a regular academic department.

The Extension Division became quite entrepreneurial over time, and its efforts were very successful. Incidentally, the same was happening in the other functions of the University, particularly in research. Fees for services became a more significant part of the total budget. The extension service did, however, resist the temptation to mount activities simply because they promised to make money. Large and small foundations were approached for funds. Contracts were executed with a number of federal and state agencies for carrying out specific educational programs. The administration aggressively pursued the nonformula funds available under the Smith-Lever Act. The service even mounted a significant long-range program of solicitation of unrestricted gifts and bequests to provide core support. In order to be successful in securing such funds and in using the funds effectively, the service had to create great flexibility in personnel management. Some of the more important changes included use of part-time and adjunct employees, para-professionals, and so on.

EXTENSION AND ECONOMIC DEVELOPMENT

It was always tacitly assumed that the Cooperative Extension Service along with the Agricultural Experiment Station were tools for economic development. In one sense, they exceeded all expectations as they played a major role in the creation of a large, efficient, and dynamic U.S. food system. The major beneficiaries, however, were quite different from those originally anticipated. The big winners were the consumers and employment in the farm input and food processing and marketing industries. By the mid-1950s, it was becoming apparent that many farmers and rural communities were being left behind by the technological and organizational revolution.

In 1957, the U.S. Department of Agriculture (USDA) announced a pilot program in rural development. The effort was led by True D. Morse, Under Secretary of Agriculture for Ezra Taft Benson. The states with extensive rural areas were invited to name one to three counties to serve as pilot projects. All USDA agencies were to participate, with extension in the lead. Very modest funding was provided for increased extension work.

Except for a few counties where serendipity played a role, little happened. Taney County, Missouri, is an example. It has turned into the new country music capital of the world. In retrospect, however, not much should have been expected. Extension and the related agricultural agencies primarily intensified existing programs, which in a general sense had contributed to the problem. Also all of the agricultural agencies were directed to individuals as farmers or citizens and not to group or collective action.

The Kennedy-Johnson administrations greatly expanded the rural development effort, with the Farmers Home Administration in the lead. Large sums of money were available for rural housing, water systems, and even community facilities, including golf courses. Real successes continued to be few and largely serendipitous. While not evident at the time, some of the infrastructure that was built has subsequently been a major contributor to development. The development of the southern part of Columbia, Missouri, is a case in point. The building of a rural water district overcame the problem of a lack of a dependable, safe water supply. Efforts were primarily within the agricultural establishment, sans the farm organizations. Within the establishment, policy and group action have generally been the prerogative of the farm organizations, which have never shown any interest in rural development.

All efforts in rural development have been frustrated by lack of agreement on what rural development is and the inability of anyone to write a prescription for the development of a specific area. On the other hand, it was accepted that some characteristics and attitudes must exist before there was even a possibility for development.

In 1987, the Extension Division designated economic development as one of its seven major program initiatives. While the entire staff contributed time when needed, leadership in the field came from the community development and business and industry specialists who made it their number one goal. These workers had developed access to a large number of faculty on the campuses and had become experts in bringing in the right consultants at the right time.

The campuses, usually with some financial assistance from external sources, have organized multidisciplinary programs that have economic development as an explicit mission. The two major units on the Rolla campus are the technology-transfer unit and the engineering management program. There are several economic development units on the Columbia campus. The Rural Innovation Institute, which is financed by the Kellogg Foundation, strengthens the traditional community development approaches. Among its tools are a referral service for communities and a rural health initiative that makes wide use of electronic communications media. The office of Social and Economic Data Analysis, with leadership from the Rural Sociology Department, provides the data base necessary for rural development. The School of Business gives leadership to the Small Business Development Center, funded in part by the Small Business Administration. The Business School also provides leadership to the Trade Area Assistance Program, which is funded by the U.S. Department of Commerce. A multidisciplinary effort that is labeled "Career Options" is funded by the USDA and state government and provides

counseling to workers, including farmers, who have lost jobs due to plant closings and bankruptcies. All of these programs operate statewide and interact on a continuous basis with the staff located in the field offices.

The St. Louis and Kansas City campuses have economic development initiatives that are limited primarily to their respective metropolitan areas. The Schools of Business provide leadership, but a number of disciplines contribute their expertise.

Given the uncertainty about the keys to unlocking economic development, it is not surprising that, frequently, several programs that do not have development as an explicit goal do in fact provide the key in a specific location. As examples, local government specialists have provided assistance in zoning and government reorganization; the food scientists have assisted in the creation of new employment opportunities; and the chemists have helped solve pollution problems that threatened the existence of some firms.

Seldom does the University directly create economic development except in a community where a campus is located, but it has made itself available statewide to assist individuals, firms, and communities achieve economic development. The impact is most significant in rural areas where there is a dearth of expertise and the problems at least seem smaller in scope and hence more comprehensible.

GENERALIZATIONS

The University of Missouri has demonstrated that it is possible for a university to make its total resources available to help the people and institutions of the state achieve their goals. It is not easy, however. The following conditions were necessary for the University of Missouri efforts to succeed:

1. Outreach must be stated and accepted as a primary mission of the University.

2. There must be strong support for the mission from the Governing Board and the top administration. The five University presidents serving from 1960 to 1991 vigorously supported the program. They were Ellis, Weaver, Ratchford, Olson, and Magrath.

3. There must be a single office with the responsibility for the planning and coordination of the many initiatives. The office must be a part of central administration. Naming any one school as leader will effectively deter other colleges from participating.

4. The program must have core support in hard money. In some of the most important program areas, the payoff is in the long term and the beneficiaries unknown. Prime examples of the latter are the beneficiaries of economic development and reorganized local government.

5. The program should be an extension of the regular academic departments and the personnel part of the regular faculty. True, this approach does present some difficulties. The two major ones are securing a multidisciplinary approach and securing tenure and promotion for extension personnel. With persistence, these can be overcome, and this arrangement is much preferable in the long run to some organization such as a center or institute that appears to bypass the problems. Basically, it boils down to this: when the regular departments own the program, they become its advocates; otherwise the programs become competitive and hence adversaries.

6. In all programs except where the potential participants are clearly identified—attorneys, M.D.'s, and so on—a field staff is needed, preferably living in the geographic area served. The staff members are more than salespersons. They assist in articulating problems to which education can contribute to solutions, in tailoring the educational efforts to a specific situation, and in providing follow-up and continuity. When they are part of a community, there is automatically strong accountability.

7. The basic approach should be problem solving. While a new technology is frequently the answer, people are interested in solving problems and not in technology per se.

8. Funding from a host of external sources must be aggressively pursued, and positive results shown from their subsequent expenditure.

Securing institutional change has a cost, and no organization is without its weaknesses. There are two identifiable costs. The first is the creation of a large bureaucracy to plan and manage the Extension Division. Some type of organizational structure is necessary, as are some policies and regulations, and today the overhead cost is under intense scrutiny. Some even ask if the bureaucracy is impeding the accomplishment of the basic mission. The second cost is the loss of some support from county govern- ments as a consequence of multi- county programming; this has led to some strengthening in recent years of county-based programming.

There are other costs that are real but difficult to quantify. A success- ful Extension Division is highly visi- ble and will upset some people. The service finds itself constantly on the defensive in state executive offices and legislative halls. Some of these complaints feed back to the Univer- sity administration, and the mission and policies must be constantly re- justified.

Some farm organization leaders have never been happy with the deci- sion to take Cooperative Extension out of the College of Agriculture. The issue is power and not service. These leaders, even after thirty years, want to pull the Extension Division apart and place Cooperative Extension in the College of Agriculture. This con- tinuing struggle has a cost.

Learning Networks: Looking to 2010

By THOMAS G. TATE

ABSTRACT: Proposed learning network technology offers some alternatives to the way we currently carry out education and training. High schools, state land-grant universities, libraries, community learning centers, public information terminals in public buildings will all be affected by new innovations in information technology. Reinventing and conversion of our traditional educational institutions are feasible and plausible as a result of development in new learning network technologies. We are becoming a nation of community learning centers that cater to formal and informal training and educational needs. These learning centers will be used by a full range of learners: K-12 students during the regular school hours; students in after-school programs during the afternoon and early evening hours; and adults in labor, management, and the professions all during the day and night. This network of community learning centers will be linked by the new National Research and Education Network. Satellite as well as land-based educational networks will be involved. Information terminals at schools, libraries, community learning centers, public buildings, homes, farms, and firms will have access to and be linked by learning networks.

Thomas G. Tate is National Program Leader for the Communication and Information Technology Staff of the U.S. Department of Agriculture's Extension Service in Washington, D.C. He has been providing leadership to national and state information technology initiatives for more than 24 years. He has degrees from the Massachusetts Institute of Technology and the University of Missouri.

CRIME in our city streets, declining farm prices, drug use and abuse, teenage pregnancy, decline in rural employment, obsolete industrial workers, home-bound senior citizens, soaring health costs, displaced military personnel, the handicapped—what do all of these challenges have in common? The answer is that in the year 2010 learning network technology will have a positive impact on them all.

We are living at an incredible crossroads in this world. How quickly everything is changing and turning over. The rules, the issues, the problems we are working on, and the tools that we have to work with all seem to be changing at an accelerated rate. Not only are we setting up demonstration farms in this country, but we are helping our new partners in the former Soviet Union to do the same.

We are recruiting teams of U.S. agricultural producers and advisers to go into Eastern Europe to help build a new understanding of market systems and democratic processes. We are beginning to exchange information with those new partners through telecommunication links.

Within our country, our primary and secondary school systems need revitalization. Our nation's small and intermediate-sized industrial and manufacturing firms have fallen behind many of their international competitors. Both arenas need modernizing.

HOW DO WE PREPARE FOR THE TWENTY-FIRST CENTURY?

What is the best way for us to prepare for the twenty-first century? One alternative is to begin living as though we were already there. For example, many residents in rural America now have access to the same knowledge bases, experts, seminars, presentations, and course offerings as their urban cousins. Some may argue that they have better access, depending on the policy of the state they live in.

THE SHOW-ME NETWORK: SATELLITE DOWN-LINKS

In Missouri, high schools and junior high schools are now equipped with satellite down-link dishes that allow learners to participate in video teleconferences that are broadcast on the Missouri satellite network. Students who live in a small community that cannot justify having a calculus or physics teacher for the 4 students who are ready to learn can participate in the statewide high school video classroom in their own community. Students in schools throughout the state participate in the Missouri video learning network. The Missouri group also produces a guide to educational programs available via satellite. Their magazine and satellite program guide is called *Education SATLINK*.

How was Missouri able to afford this system? A modest 10 percent tax on the rental of videotapes in each video store in the state is earmarked for financing the state's video learning network. The taxpayers have been very accepting of this tax and feel good about the benefits that come to the state.[1]

---

1. For more information on the Missouri effort, contact Educational Satellite Network, 2100 I-70 Drive S.W., Columbia, MO 65201.

Learning centers for retraining adults

In addition to the formal class work that students are able to accomplish, the community school is now positioned to be a round-the-clock learning center that can be used to retrain and reskill displaced military personnel, to upgrade the knowledge and skills of industrial and manufacturing workers and managers, as well as for continuing education for professionals.

Information transfer between learners and teachers

With the addition of the National Research and Education Network (NREN) hookups that are on the way, learners, teachers, tutors, and coaches will be able to interact with each other.[2] Teachers and learners can transfer work in progress, mark papers, and engage in other learner-teacher feedback electronically via personal telecomputers connected to NREN. Then-Senator Al Gore sponsored the legislation to support the NREN. Perhaps the Clinton administration will support the expansion of the NREN for use by learners nationwide. Long-distance and local telephone companies, cable companies, and wireless communication firms will each provide appropriate telecommunication components, pieces of the patchwork quilt to support local learner access to national information resources.

2. The NREN and other civic networks will evolve into the National Information Infrastructure (NII). For more information on NREN and NII, contact CIT-ES-USDA, Room 3322, Washington, DC 20250-0900.

AN AGRICULTURAL LEARNING NETWORK

The nation's leading land-grant universities have joined to establish and operate a new agricultural information and instructional service called AG*SAT. By combining satellite, audio-video, and computer technologies, AG*SAT affiliates are able to share academic instruction, Cooperative Extension programming, and agricultural research information. Ultimately, all land-grant institutions will have the opportunity to participate in AG*SAT.

Learners are able to go to a Cooperative Extension service learning center in their community. Local citizens are encouraged to participate in the educational programs that are downlinked by the local receiving dish. Farms, ranches, homes, schools, and firms with a satellite signal receiving dish may also receive AG*SAT educational programming.

How does AG*SAT work? All AG*SAT institutions develop educational programming based on their strengths. Rather than reinventing the educational wheels, the member institutions plan programs that will have national applicability and increase the impact of shrinking funds available for educational programming. The Cooperative Extension system then alerts the educational community through its electronic program guide, which can be subscribed to on the NREN. Subscribers receive an electronic-mail version of the Satellite Calendar each time it is updated.

AG*SAT learners do not have to be passive viewer-listeners. AG*SAT learners may call in their concerns or questions via an 800 number, à la Larry King, or communicate their concern or question by electronic mail to the site that is originating the program.[3]

DISTANCE EDUCATION: PLACE SHIFTING

"Distance education" is a term that is creeping into our vocabulary. It simply means learning methods where the learner does not have to be eyeball to eyeball with the knowledge provider. The Missouri learning network and AG*SAT are good examples of one type of distance education, satellite video teleconferencing. Similar interactive video classrooms can also be established through land-based cable. Telephone companies are investing now to link learners via telephone lines that will permit the learners to have two-way audiovisual interaction with a teacher who may be miles away from their learning location. These examples provide an important advantage to learners, place shifting. Place shifting is making the learning experience available to the learner at a place where the learner can participate.

DISTANCE EDUCATION: TIME SHIFTING

Another important element of distance education is time shifting. Time shifting is packaging the learning tool in such a way that the learner can access it at a time that is convenient to him or her. Current learning tools that have this characteristic are

3. For more information on AG*SAT, contact AG*SAT, Box 83111, Lincoln, NE 68501.

books, films, audiotapes, videotapes, videodiscs, compact discs, computer programs, and so forth. When the NREN is fully operational, the current learning tools will be retrievable from resource centers for use in schools, learning centers, farms, ranches, business firms, and homes. If the learner has a personal computer at home or in the workplace that is connected to the network, he or she will retrieve them from providers who will be available on the network 24 hours a day. Currently, Compuserve and Prodigy are two examples of commercial network providers that make learning tools available to remote personal computers connected over the telephone lines by modem.

PUBLIC INFORMATION TERMINALS

The federal government has tested the use of public information terminals that make federal information available to the public in public places, such as shopping malls and post offices. The U.S. Department of Agriculture, the U.S. Postal Service, the Veterans Administration, and the Social Security Administration are considering the possibility of public information kiosks that locally store a wide variety of information about the programs that these organizations offer. Applications range from changing one's postal delivery address to finding out how to control the pest attacking one's crops. These kiosks are a good example of time shifting and place shifting. These public information terminals will be connected to a national network that will be used to keep users, viewers, and listeners up to date on the latest information. Local input can be provided that will permit these public information terminals to serve as local community bulletin boards. These terminals will be equipped with printers to permit output to be taken away by the taxpayer. The terminals will provide audio, video, and textual information in response to buttons pushed on a control panel.

These public information terminals will be important assets to the community. For those individuals who do not yet have access to the public networks through their computer at home, school, or workplace, the public information terminal will ensure that information technology does not provide the technologically literate with unfair access to information. Publicly accessible information terminals are important to equality, ensuring that people can enter, on foot or by wheelchair, a library or post office and have open access to public information.

LEARNING AT ONE'S OWN PACE: PACE SHIFTING

Imagine having your own personal portable television for your own entertainment as well as educational needs. Imagine being able to learn about whatever you want whenever you want from your own battery-operated interactive audiovisual compact disc player. Imagine being able to carry a national library collection with you wherever you go, being able to ask questions and get answers on the screen as text, still photographs, or audiovisual presentations. Imag-

ine learning new skills, wherever you want, 24 hours a day. Imagine being able to use this learning tool whether your first language is English or Spanish. It is hoped that everyone in the United States, urban or rural, will take this for granted in 2010 as a birthright. In the meantime, national consumer electronics companies are producing edutainment—education cum entertainment—products such as those just described.

NATIONAL LIBRARY IN YOUR POCKET

New developments in information storage technology are creating new opportunities. Compact discs, popular throughout the world for distributing high-quality music entertainment, are now being used to store large quantities of data and information for retrieval onto display screens by learners. The CD-ROM (compact disc read-only memory) provides personal-computer users with convenient storage and retrieval of specialized collections of data and information.

The Grolier Encyclopedia company has just released *The New Grolier Multimedia Encyclopedia* on compact disc. It features all 21 volumes of the *Academic American Encyclopedia* on a single CD-ROM, with articles on everything from covered wagons to lunar landers. A host of new features makes the urge to explore virtually irresistible. The on-disc encyclopedia includes color photographs, illustrations, sounds, and motion sequences. Famous speeches, music, and more can be listened to. This development turns the personal computer into a multimedia learning center. There are now more than 1000 CD-ROM titles that have been released.

INTERACTIVE TELEVISION

How about those who do not know nor ever want to know how to use a personal computer? The latest development, compact disc interactive (CDI), will make them want to trade in their home audio compact disc player. The CDI players being introduced in 1993 provide educators and learners with a new set of options. The CDI player is connected to a television. The audio comes out of the speaker of the television—or it could be routed to come through a home entertainment center. A remote control unit is used to move the selector to items that appear on the television screen, similar to a jukebox selection panel. After two or three answers or options are selected from the screen, the action begins. The action is a learning sequence that demands the learner's involvement in order to progress. A dynamic mix of music, audio, and still and motion photography guide the learner to a knowledge destination that he or she determines. It is an interactive electronic game that teaches, not preaches.

Initially, the CDI product is being introduced with course options that range from learning how to play musical instruments to improving one's golf game. For the younger set, Sesame Street characters teach logic, letters, and numbers. There are tours of museums in Italy, Mexico, and the United States. Bell Atlantic is testing CDI as an alternative to the traditional Yellow Pages. If you want to build your own learning program, you can send your next roll of Kodak film to Kodak, and they will return your latest photo session to you on a compact disc that you can present to learners via the television screen. Portable units that are battery-operated will be introduced over the next couple of years.

In the test labs, these products have held adults and youths, rural and urban, spellbound and learning for hours. They are being introduced into the U.S. marketplace in the 1993-94 season.

EXTENSION COMMUNITY LEARNING CENTERS

Increasingly, institutions in the community are beginning to take on a more proactive role in providing self-improvement opportunities. Cooperative Extension offices located in public buildings such as courthouses and post offices are increasingly sharing their learning resource technology with other groups in the community. Computers in the local Extension centers are beginning to be connected to national networks that provide on-line retrieval access to knowledge and expertise stored in computers in the next county, state, or nation. Conference rooms in Cooperative Extension offices that are connected to satellite or land-based cable systems are being made available to a wide variety of groups throughout the community. This trend needs to spread to other institutions in the community that have facilities that could be shared as learning centers rather than sit idle or underused.

REINVENTING THE
LAND-GRANT INSTITUTION

The problems of our society have become too complex to be solved solely by the resources available in our colleges of agriculture, natural resources, and home economics. The learning resources of every department of the college and university are needed to solve the problems of formal and informal learners.

For many years, two land-grant institutions, the University of Missouri and the Massachusetts Institute of Technology, have made all of their subject matter departments available to business, industry, and labor clientele. Missouri has made its experts available through its Business, Industry, and Labor Extension Program, and the Institute through its Industrial Liaison Program. These models have been emulated by land-grant universities in other states. Perhaps it is time to accelerate these programs nationally.

Information and learning technology can broaden our access to the learning resource base of all subject matter departments, yet give us the power to narrow our focus to the specific problem and objective of the learner. If local citizens can understand and effectively tell the story, I believe that future national decision makers will allocate the resources necessary to permit the total land-grant university to work on improving schools and firms as well as farms. Industrial and educational units need the benefits of the learning systems that have made American agriculture the envy of the world.

BECOMING A
LEARNING NETWORK

U.S. institutions are becoming a part of a learning network for firms, schools, families, and farms. The institutions and the individuals within them carry out multiple responsibilities as teachers, researchers, information providers, and problem solvers. We need to find new methods of breaking the linear teaching period of the traditional classroom location. Most learners are at the teachable moment at times and places other than where learning experiences tend to be offered. Most learners learn at a pace that is different from that of even other learners who are most like themselves. Can we convert our land-grant classrooms into interactive centers for learning and problem solving? Time shifting, place shifting, pace shifting: can information technology help us master these concepts? Can we become a connected network of learners, information providers, and problem solvers? Can we access and share learning resources across institutional, state, and national boundaries?

How can your own community begin to enjoy the benefits of these seemingly futuristic developments?

Learning institutions in your community are beginning to plan and implement some of these advanced learning technologies. In every state, the state land-grant university has established a major NREN terminal at the university's computer center. In most states, the outreach division of the university, the local county Extension offices, are becoming the first point in the community to have access to the learning resources on the NREN. To learn more about how to help with this effort, contact your local county Cooperative Extension office or Extension computer coordinator at your state's land-grant university.

Some communities have launched after-school programs that give young learners an opportunity to have semi-structured free time on computers in the school's learning centers. In many instances, these after-school programs are being supervised by volunteers. The volunteers are often parents or friends of students; they bring their professional skills and excitement to the learners in an informal atmosphere. The learners proceed at their own pace and often develop projects that are highly creative and lead to an improved interest in learning. The local 4-H club in many communities provides the program with structure, educational materials, and a supply of volunteers from the local community.

In some communities, volunteers are making their firms' computer training centers available to students' computer clubs on an after-school basis. In other communities, local firms are providing computers to school learning centers in exchange for grocery sales receipts collected by the students. Your local school board and local Cooperative Extension office are good contact points for getting involved in this movement.

COMMUNITY MOBILIZATION

If the computers in your community schools and libraries are not yet connected to the NREN, you may be the catalyst that can get the ball rolling. Why not identify others in your community who use information technology in their day-to-day work? You could contact them and organize a group that has a common vision to upgrade the tools that learners have access to in your local community. This action will strengthen your community. You will be empowering others to learn new ways of learning. You will help provide options for people to retrain themselves for new and different employment possibilities.

To help mobilize the resources needed for this educational transformation, you can contact your local chamber of commerce and its members for support. You can help them envision how these tools can strengthen the state and local work force and thereby the state and local economy.

Your local Cooperative Extension office is connected, or is in the process of being connected, to the NREN. Office staff can guide you to the experts in your community or state who will identify an individual who can provide advice and counsel on taking these steps toward the future. Close to 1000 local Cooperative Extension centers are now equipped with satellite down-link capability to bring education to learners in your community from providers all over the nation and around the world. The local Cooperative Extension center can also connect you to a network of more than 500,000 volunteers who are interested in advancing learning by young and old in rural and urban communities.

Help your elected officials understand how they can be part of the solution, not part of the problem. Tell them about the distance learning in Missouri. Make your community a member of the growing national network of community learning centers. It is your choice. Get involved.

ANNALS, *AAPSS*, **529**, September 1993

Agricultural Change and Rural America

By LEO V. MAYER

ABSTRACT: Rural America is known worldwide for its productive farms and agricultural abundance. Less well-known are the rural businesses that service America's farms, supplying inputs, buying output, and providing consumer goods to rural families. Even less well-known are the 70,000 small and medium-sized industrial firms that are located in rural communities. These businesses have slowly increased in number over the past half century as the farm population has dropped by two-thirds, the rural nonfarm population has grown slightly, and the national population has almost doubled. This article examines the role of agricultural change in rural decline and recommends two possibilities for expanding economic activity in rural communities.

Leo Mayer is an economic counselor in Alexandria, Virginia. Previously, he was a faculty member at Iowa State University. In Washington, D.C., he has worked for the Council of Economic Advisers, the Library of Congress, the U.S. Trade Representative, the Department of Agriculture, and the General Accounting Office.

T. W. Schultz, a Nobel laureate in agriculture, once described the movement of several million people from America's farms as "the greatest peaceful migration in the history of mankind." While largely accurate in terms of numbers, it left out the fact that most traveled only a short distance. This aspect comes out as one studies rural population trends, which show that America's total rural population changed little from 1910 to 1970 even though the farm population declined dramatically over this period. What occurred was a shift of persons from farms to rural towns and communities, with the result that small-town population increases generally offset farm population decreases.

The movement of people from farms to rural towns began in earnest circa World War II. Labor shortages associated with the war effort encouraged farm mechanization, freeing many farm workers for off-farm jobs. Many joined what was then an expanding farm service sector—businesses that were selling new, technologically superior inputs to farmers, inputs that caused a sharp rise in farm output, creating surplus supplies and lowering farm prices, especially real farm prices. As farm returns declined, government programs cut back planted acreages of crops, reducing labor needs and freeing up even more people to leave the farm.

Nationally, the massive migration of people from farms to towns was hardly noticeable. The enormity of rural America, with its thousands of small towns, allowed a few dozen farm families to migrate in each county each year almost imperceptibly. Spread out over several decades, the impact was relatively small in any given year, further softening the impact and lessening the visibility.

With the migration obscured by space and softened by time, most urban Americans were more impressed with the stability of rural America than with the ongoing change. Rural stability was reflected in the serenity of small towns, the unchanging nature of farmsteads even as science revolutionized food production, and the abundance of food and fiber supplies through all types of economic adversity—inflation and deflation, high interest rates and low interest rates, high and low exchange rates, oscillating employment rates, and rising and falling land values. Farmers and farm output seemed almost insulated from these macro cycles, capable of meeting almost any adversity—a reassuring trend to urban food and fiber consumers.

In reality, behind the facade of rural stability was an onslaught of new technology that imposed constant change on farm families.[1] The appearance of stability came from the enormous size of rural America— natural disasters like drought affected only small parts of the country at any one time—and from widespread personal sacrifice that resulted in low levels of farm debt in

1. A well-known agricultural economist of that era, Willard Cochrane of the University of Minnesota, labeled the economic pressure on farmers an agricultural treadmill. See Willard W. Cochrane, *The City Man's Guide to the Farm Problem* (Minneapolis: University of Minnesota Press, 1965), p. 66.

TABLE 1
INDICES OF FARM PRODUCTIVITY IN THE UNITED STATES, 1870-1990

Year	Farm Output	Farm Inputs	Productivity
	(1977 = 100)		
1870	14	38	36
1880	22	51	43
1890	25	60	42
1900	33	70	47
1910	36	84	43
1920	42	95	44
1930	43	98	44
1940	50	97	52
1950	62	101	61
1960	76	98	78
1970	84	97	87
1980	104	103	101
1985	118	92	128
1990	119	88	135

SOURCE: U.S., Department of Agriculture, *Agricultural Statistics*, 1989; idem, *Agricultural Outlook*, May 1992.

relation to assets, a condition that created an unusual ability to withstand national economic cycles.

Both the fiscal attitudes and the rising productivity that eventually made America the best-fed nation in the world began during the Great Depression of the 1930s. They were buttressed by the onset of World War II, which made increased food production a national priority. Postwar farm policies continued to support farm income, making more capital available for the purchase of new farm machines and, thereby, more labor available for other parts of the economy. Both excess labor and abundant farm output became a chronic plague on commodity markets.[2]

2. A well-known agricultural journalist of that era wrote a book entitled *An Embarrassment of Plenty* in which he detailed the evolution of the American farm from subsistence levels of food output to commercial methods of food production that created chronic surpluses.

The impact of war, farm mechanization, and scientific improvement show up in overall measures of farm productivity like those in Table 1. Farms and farm productivity had changed little between 1880 and 1930. Then farm productivity began to rise rapidly, outdistancing a rapid rate of both population and income growth. Surpluses began to accumulate, depressing farm markets, lowering farm incomes, and forcing less efficient farm operators off the farm and into nonfarm jobs. When rural road systems began linking rural consumers to urban shopping centers in the 1950s, rural towns began to see growing numbers of abandoned business sites. An economic malaise spread across rural areas.

See Lauren Soth, *An Embarrassment of Plenty: Agriculture in Affluent America* (New York: Thomas Y. Crowell, 1965).

TABLE 2
**POPULATION OF THE UNITED STATES,
FARM, RURAL, AND TOTAL, 1880-1990 (in Millions)**

Year	Population		
	Farm	Rural	Total
1990	4.6	67.0	246.1
1980	6.1	59.5	226.5
1970	9.7	53.6	203.2
1960	13.4	54.1	179.3
1950	23.0	54.5	151.3
1940	30.5	57.5	132.1
1930	30.5	54.0	123.2
1920	32.0	51.8	106.0
1910	32.1	50.2	92.2
1900	28.9	46.0	76.2
1890	24.8	40.9	63.0
1880	22.0	36.1	50.2

SOURCE: U.S., Department of Commerce, *Residents of Farm and Rural Areas: 1990*, Current Population Reports, ser. P-20, no. 457, Mar. 1992.

Rural decline continued throughout the 1950s and 1960s. Then came a sudden explosion of farm exports in the 1970s that raised farm income and caused small towns to blossom. The new Golden Age was short-lived, however, and evaporated almost as quickly as it had come. After farm trade prospects faded in the 1980s, a report published by the U.S. Department of Agriculture noted that "between 1985 and 1986, 632,000 people moved out of nonmetro areas . . . greater than the average of either the 1950s or 1960s, and a turnaround from the 1970s when nonmetro areas netted over 350,000 persons per year."[3]

3. The Department of Agriculture report went on to note that "slow population growth and outmigration, though indicating decline in the performance of rural economies, do not necessarily mean that the remaining population is impoverished or that communities lack essential services and facilities. In fact, in some areas, those who stay behind may have improved income and wealth positions and the

The severity of the rural situation led the Congress to triple federal farm subsidies in the 1985 farm bill. Severe drought in 1988 and 1989 brought more federal payments for disaster programs. As farm income began to recover, high migration rates subsided, and the 1990 population census recorded a net increase in rural population during the 1980s (Table 2).

PAST AS PROLOGUE

For the average person who works and lives in rural America, empty farmsteads and community deterioration have been facts of life for most of their lifetimes. It would be difficult for them to envision economic growth

communities may have an oversupply, rather than a lack, of public facilities." U.S., Department of Agriculture, Economic Research Service, *Rural Economic Development in the 1980s: Prospects for the Future*, Rural Development Research Report no. 69 (Sept. 1988), p. ix.

and expansion for their rural town or community. They remain in slowly disintegrating rural settings because of a preference for the freedoms that rural living provides—freedom from traffic jams, air pollution, and population congestion—and the absence of ill humor that these factors generate in urban settings. Most do not miss visits to art museums, professional sporting events, ethnic restaurants, and the other special amenities of urban life. Many would like greater economic opportunity, but not if it means accepting the ills of cities.[4]

One should stress, however, that despite their misgivings about urban life, most rural residents understand the value of more economic activity and recognize that it can provide the taxes necessary for better schools, modern hospitals, and professionally staffed retirement homes. Some simply do not want to bear the up-front costs of economic development, such as the higher real estate taxes required for improving local infrastructure. Others demur because they are unconvinced that development projects will succeed. In essence, most rural residents want more economic activity, but few are willing to bear the risk of starting new economic endeavors.

The reluctance to invest in community growth and expansion does

4. The right to choose where to live is a strongly held value. A national survey conducted by the Roper Organization for the National Rural Electric Cooperative Association found that 63 percent of those surveyed thought the American dream "was the freedom to live where you want to." See U.S., General Accounting Office, *Rural Development: Rural America Faces Many Challenges*, GAO/RCED-93-35, Nov. 1992.

not extend to agricultural growth and expansion. Experience with farmers' adopting new, output-expanding and structurally changing technology has been positive, despite the economic and social costs of family relocations, school reorganizations, and business closures. The social costs of farm change fell on those who left, creating only a temporary disruption in the harmony and stability of those who stayed behind. Those who remained witnessed a long string of successes with new farming technology, in sharp contrast to their experience with new off-farm enterprises.

The positive manner in which new agricultural technologies are viewed in rural America is not as widely shared in urban America. Like the nation's nineteenth-century success with rapid economic development that eventually came under question, the successful adoption of new agricultural technology has run into economic, social, and environmental limitations. Groundwater contamination, pesticide residues, pollution of waterways, erosion of fragile cropland, and food-safety questions relating to the use of growth hormones have all become national concerns. While generating less apprehension in rural America, where they are viewed with a degree of skepticism, some of these concerns, like groundwater contamination, touch tender nerves among farm families dependent on rural wells for drinking water. Others, such as protection of wetlands and the environmental impacts of modern agricultural technology, seem of dubious merit to many rural residents. As additional examples of this type of conflict arise, however, they tend to complicate investment in new agricultural technology, investment that had once been seen as risk free.

Thus an examination of the climate for economic growth and expansion in rural America leads to two separate conclusions. One is that the population and institutions of rural America remain supportive of the existing structure of economic activity on farms, dismissing much of the national concern over environmental impact as unwarranted. The second is that these same populations and institutions are less supportive of strong measures to gain a share of the new jobs and new economic activity that are generated by the national economy each year. It cannot be said that there is no interest in industrial development in rural areas. There is. But experience suggests that the strong financial and technical support that exists for investing in new, on-the-farm enterprises does not exist for investing in new, off-the-farm enterprises. America's land-grant universities, for example, have not been pressured by rural constituencies to transfer their technological knowledge and procedures to the expansion of a rural industrial base. Nothing equivalent to the "engine of growth" that technological advance has represented for farming has been developed by land-grant universities for rural industries. Nor have rural financial institutions offered financing for new industrial enterprises with the same enthusiasm that was true of their investments in agricultural technology. As a result, rural areas have continued to decline as larger and larger machines and

newer and newer farm technology have made the nation's farmland more and more productive, requiring fewer acres for food production and fewer families to operate the farms that remain.

BEHIND RURAL DECLINE

The impact of agricultural change on rural communities can be illustrated with a diagram like Figure 1. It describes the flows of income through a rural community. Income in a rural community arises from three main sources: farm production, agricultural supply and marketing firms, and businesses providing consumer goods and services. Farm production generates output that is sold to processing firms in urban areas, causing income to flow back into a rural community. Income flows out of the rural community when local agricultural supply firms purchase farm inputs from urban manufacturers for sale to farmers. The level of transactions determines the flows of income into and out of the community. The difference between the two income flows determines the amount of income left over for purchasing consumer goods from local retail businesses or for savings and investment. Purchases by local consumer-goods businesses also result in a flow of payments to urban manufacturers, but this is minor in comparison to the other income flows out of the community.

Why have changing farm practices had such a negative effect on rural towns? The reason is that most changes in farming practices have increased the flow of income out of

FIGURE 1
ECONOMY OF A TYPICAL RURAL COMMUNITY

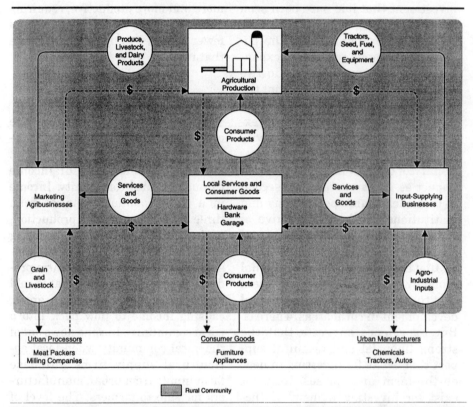

SOURCE: Leo V. Mayer, "Why the Rapid Change in Our Rural Areas?" *Iowa Farm Science*, 24(4):7 (Oct. 1969).

rural communities without a commensurate flow of income into the rural community. The case of commercial fertilizer serves as an example. Beginning in the 1930s, farmers began to buy more and more commercial fertilizer to apply to their crops. As fertilizer businesses in small towns purchased larger supplies from urban businesses, more and more funds flowed from the rural community to urban processors. Although more fertilizer raised crop output, the larger quantities of commodities sold caused prices to fall, an effect of an inelastic demand. Lower commodity prices more than offset the larger quantity sold, resulting in less revenue flowing into rural communities, leaving rural consumers with less income to spend and rural businesses with fewer sales.

There is an additional twist to this matter that explains why it has continued for nearly half a century. Not every farmer in the community had less income just because the total flow of income into the community was lower. Progressive farmers gained by buying new machines, planting more acres of new, higher-yielding seed varieties, and applying more fertilizer per acre, thus increasing their output by more than the decline in prices. The total revenue of these farmers increased, raising family incomes and improving their living standards. For less expansion-minded farmers, however, the outcome was more like that for the whole community. With stable acreages and yields, lower prices reduced the value of their marketings. As their cash receipts shrank, most survived by not replacing machines as depreciation occurred or by cutting other costs wherever possible. Nonetheless, the pressure to leave farming gradually increased. The outcome for these farmers and for rural communities in general was negative, in sharp contrast to the outcome for progressive farmers and the agribusinesses that supplied them with new technologies. As might be expected, the desire for more industrial development, with its potential to create jobs and drive up local wage rates and other production costs, likewise varies among these different groups.

RURAL GROWTH AND EXPANSION

After more than half a century of decline in rural America, the task of turning rural areas toward a path of growth and expansion will not be an easy one. New investment will be required to initiate more economic activity, thereby adding jobs and new sources of income. Once under way, the process can become self-sustaining as new entrepreneurs start up new businesses, more and more workers are added to payrolls, new homes are built to house them, and the community tax base broadens to support schools, libraries, hospitals, and retirement homes.

To set in motion what appears to be a rather simple investment process turns out to be anything but simple in rural communities. Isolated by space, lacking adequate markets, burdened by high infrastructure costs, the process is complex, involving unique restraints at nearly every step. Would-be entrepreneurs in rural communities often run into public bodies that lack a growth orientation, the amenities necessary to attract qualified workers, or the capacity to provide additional electric power, modern telephone systems, or water, sewer, and other basic items like modern highways and high-speed communication systems. To add this infrastructure is costly and requires public investment that the entrepreneur does not control and that the community is often reluctant to make. These types of deficiencies, over and above higher costs for transportation to and from urban centers, place most rural towns at a disadvantage when investment decisions are made by businesspersons located in urban areas, even though land and labor costs are lower in rural communities.

Even for businesspersons already located in rural communities, the problems are substantial. New productive enterprises must fit into a rural mold and still compete with urban enterprises for investment dollars. Identifying markets that are far away is difficult; locating venture capital to fund new enterprises can be equally difficult. The absence of technical assistance to help solve start-up problems is another problem. In urban settings, technical assistance to solve nearly any problem is readily available; in a rural area it is not. While farmers have access to substantial technical assistance for starting up new farming enterprises through the land-grant universities, a rural businessperson who undertakes a new enterprise is pretty much left to his or her own devices.

This isolation exists even when the activity is closely related to agriculture. An example often cited is the development of anaerobic digesters that turn animal waste into fuel for powering electrical generators. Farmers successful in developing this technology and selling electrical power to power companies indicate that they have received little or no assistance from their land-grant university. While the agricultural colleges of these universities have long pushed supplemental enterprises as additional sources of income, they appear to have shown little interest in helping farmers perfect this particular farm-related enterprise. One must wonder why when almost all of the agricultural universities have departments of mechanical and electrical engineering and some even have engineering extension services.

The seeming lack of interest among these institutions in assisting rural nonfarm entrepreneurs appears to be a major roadblock to expanded rural industrialization. Without the availability of publicly funded technical assistance, more risk is involved in starting up new enterprises. New business starts tend to be limited to those affiliated with large corporations that can provide this type of assistance. Unless this sort of assistance is provided in the future, rural areas will continue to decline as labor-saving technology requires fewer and fewer families for food production.

There is one other line of argument often heard on this issue that must be addressed directly. It goes like this: why not reverse the forces that have created rural decline over the past half century, return agricultural production to a more labor-intensive structure, commit more resources to food production, and allow food prices to rise in order to pay the added costs? Such an approach was followed in the European Community until recently, when the budget and trade implications eroded its practicality. A similar outcome would almost certainly ensue from such an approach in the United States.

The argument is useful, however, because it draws attention to the massive savings of food dollars that agricultural development has brought to the nation. Had some portion of those savings been invested in generating new industrial enterprises for rural areas, the agricultural success story would have been even more impressive. To date, neither the efforts of the federal government nor those of the land-grant universities have achieved the broader goal. The question that remains is whether this can be changed for the future.

REVERSING RURAL DECLINE

Past efforts to assist rural towns and communities were largely indirect— a by-product of government farm programs directed at agricultural producers. Those programs concentrated on increasing total income flows to rural communities by raising and stabilizing the prices of farm commodities. To the extent that the programs were successful, farm families had more income to spend. Whether they spent it in their rural towns and communities was up to them. Judging by the gradual decline in most rural communities, much of the added income went elsewhere.

There is one caveat to this general conclusion. The 1970s illustrated that a large enough increase in farm income holds the potential to reverse rural declines. As exports rose in the early 1970s, rural towns enjoyed an economic revival. Farmers planted more crops, purchased more tons of fertilizer, sold more bushels of grain, and earned the highest incomes of their lifetimes. Most were unprepared for the economic downturn that struck in the 1980s, when world commodity trade shrank and food-buying countries shifted toward purchases of processed and retail-ready food products. With U.S. farmers and U.S. farm policy focusing almost solely on bulk commodities, the growing demand was filled by other countries, leaving many expansion-minded farmers with falling incomes and heavy debt burdens.

The severity of the rural economic downturn in the early 1980s may have formed a turning point between traditional agricultural development patterns in rural America and newer, broader-based systems of rural development. The growing disparity between rural and urban economies received an undue amount of attention, as the national news media exposed extreme examples of rural decline. As the urban economy experienced an extended surge of economic activity in the late 1980s, it eased the excess labor problem in rural and urban areas, reducing unemployment, raising the average wage scale, and improving the living standard for most families.

Unfortunately, the economic expansion of the 1980s turned into a decline as the 1990s arrived, withdrawing many of these economic benefits. As industry after industry saw profits fall, cost-cutting measures were imposed, causing rural affiliates to feel the sting of recession and job loss. Out of this crisis came a new recognition about rural development: it requires more than simply enticing large industrial enterprises to locate affiliates in rural settings. That kind of economic development fits the terms of an old cliché—easy come, easy go—and leaves behind economic pain and suffering.

There was also some broadening of the focus of rural development efforts as regional economies began to replace counties and even states as the foci of developmental policies. This points up a new paradigm that already is evolving in rural America, with private financing replacing government financial assistance. Combined with the fact that the farm population decline is gradually ending and the rural population is increasing, rural America may be on the verge of a renaissance. The questions that remain include, Do we want to speed up the process of energizing this new paradigm? Do we want to reshape it into a different format? Or do we want to allow market forces to shape it for us? And what about the ties to urban problems? Is it in the joint interest of urban and rural areas to slow the agglomeration of population in metropolitan areas? One can argue that both central cities and rural areas are becoming unattractive areas to live, for very different reasons.

TWO USEFUL STEPS

Past federal assistance for rural development has been targeted to several specific needs of rural America. Rural infrastructure has received extensive funding, with new water and sewer systems installed in many rural towns and communities. Rural communication systems have received similar kinds of injections of federal assistance, through rural telephone cooperatives. There has also been a heavy focus on developing rural community leadership through programs of the Cooperative Extension Service.

While these targeted programs have helped solve individual community problems, they have not been an adequate catalyst to turn most rural communities toward a path of growth and development. To offset the decline in rural communities associated with further efficiencies in farming, new jobs must be added by adding new enterprises.

Early in this century, the federal government gave farmers the authority to form marketing and supply co-ops. This allowed farmers to join together and build businesses that were impossible before this legislation was enacted. New legislation could now take the next step and allow rural communities, or groups within a rural community, to join together and establish businesses without concern over collusion, price fixing, or other issues that restrain joint action.

Such a step might offset the impact that steps like deregulation of the nation's banking system in 1979 had on rural communities. Deregulation allowed rural banks the option of moving excess funds to urban financial institutions as opposed to investing them in the local community. Many rural banks began to invest in urban financial instruments to gain a higher return on their funds. As local interest rates rose to competitive levels, rural investment was discouraged. Establishing a financing mechanism outside the local banking system might encourage local savings to be invested in local projects.

Second, and finally, the provision of technical assistance to rural communities should become a major responsibility of the educational systems in rural areas. Land-grant universities and community colleges have a significant opportunity to be of greater service to their rural constituencies. Each land-grant university should consider forming a universitywide outreach service to create new technology and extend assistance to communities that have engineering, industrial, or financial problems associated with new business enterprises.

The concept could be built on the model established by the agricultural extension service. That model was appropriate for its time; now the needs are different. The principles remain the same, but the clientele comprises rural communities rather than farmers. Through such a change in focus, these institutions could broaden the land-grant concept beyond their colleges of agriculture, drawing the full potential of the other colleges to concentrate on the problems of rural communities. The benefits of a broader focus for these educational institutions would accumulate throughout the next century, improving the welfare of generations yet to come.

Sustainable Agriculture:
A Twenty-First-Century System

By G. W. BIRD and JOHN IKERD

ABSTRACT: U.S. agriculture has been very productive during the past fifty years. A number of unexpected consequences, however, are believed to be detrimental to the long-term interests of our nation's agriculture and natural resources. In response to this issue, the Food, Agriculture, Conservation and Trade Act of 1990 mandates that the U.S. Department of Agriculture conduct research and education programs on alternative agricultural systems. These must be productive, economically viable, and environmentally sound; they must conserve natural resources, make optional use of on-farm resources, and enhance the quality of life for farmers and ranchers, members of rural communities, and society as a whole. The Sustainable Agriculture Research and Education (SARE) Program has evolved as an important initiative for development and promotion of alternative agricultural practices and production systems. This article describes sustainable agriculture and its role in the development of a philosophy for identification of research, education, and policy initiatives for twenty-first-century U.S. agriculture.

George W. Bird is director of the Sustainable Agriculture Research and Education Program at the U.S. Department of Agriculture. He is also professor of nematology at Michigan State University, East Lansing.

John Ikerd is professor of agricultural economics and director of sustainable agriculture at the University of Missouri, Columbia.

NOTE: This article is based, in part, on four presentations made at the USDA Agriculture Outlook '93 Conference, held in Washington, D.C., on 2 December 1992, and a 1991 report of the SARE Sustainable Agriculture Quality of Life Task Force.

U.S. agriculture became increasingly productive during the past fifty years as it adopted the structure and technologies of the industrial agribusiness system of farming. The structural attributes of the industrial agribusiness farm model include

— centralized management;
— emphasis on specialization;
— the number of hired-worker days exceeding the number of on-farm work days by owners;
— separation of management and labor;
— use of technology to minimize labor inputs;
— heavy reliance on purchased inputs;
— technology designed to minimize real-time, in-field decision making; and
— emphasis on standardized farming practices.[1]

The evolution of U.S. agriculture, however, has resulted in a number of important unexpected consequences. These include a decrease in the number of farms and ranches, an increase in farm and ranch size, major dependence on purchased off-farm inputs, an increase in risks associated with environmental quality and human health issues, relatively little reliance on local rural communities, and limited direct contact between rural people and people in urban and suburban environments. It is now perceived by a significant component of the agricultural community that the industrial agribusiness model is having important long-term impacts that are detrimental to the natural resource base upon which agriculture depends and to overall quality of life for society as a whole. Although these trends have been known for several decades, it has only been during the past ten years that they have become widely recognized. This was catalyzed, in part, by concerns related to the restructuring of U.S. agriculture during the mid-1980s and to a renewed awareness of the finite limits of the quality and quantity of our natural resources.

Today, approximately 15 percent of our agricultural enterprises are responsible for 85 percent of the food, feed, and fiber produced on U.S. farms. Although the vast majority of these operations fit the industrial agribusiness model, they may be classified as corporate farms, family farms, or part-time farms. Part-time farms currently represent 55-65 percent of the operating units. During the past ten years, there has been a significant increase in the number of farms using the practices of organic agriculture, and a new category of sustainable-agriculture farming has emerged as an alternative system.

In 1984, the late Robert Rodale proposed three phases for the evolution of U.S. agriculture: discovery of the natural resources upon which our agriculture is based, utilization of these resources for high-production initiatives, and development of a partnership with nature for sustainable food, feed, and fiber production in an environmentally sound and socially acceptable manner.[2] During the past decade, a coalition of envi-

1. After Marty Strange, *Family Farming: A New Economic Vision* (Lincoln: University of Nebraska Press, 1988).

2. Robert Rodale, *Our Next Frontier* (Emmaus, PA: Rodale Press, 1984).

ronmental advocates, organic farmers, and ecologists have worked with Congress and the U.S. Department of Agriculture (USDA) to obtain funding for research and education programs in alternative agriculture. In 1987, Bob Rodale provided leadership for this initiative, and Congress appropriated resources for the Low Input Sustainable Agriculture (LISA) Program. The Food, Agriculture, Conservation, and Trade Act of 1990 (the 1990 farm bill) expanded the program, and today it is known as the Sustainable Agriculture Research and Education (SARE) Program. A 1992 General Accounting Office report indicated that LISA and SARE have served as a catalyst for building new coalitions between, on the one hand, farmers and ranchers and, on the other, representatives of nonprofit private organizations, agribusiness, government, and academia and for the development of a new vision of U.S. agriculture for the twenty-first century.[3]

In the 1990 farm bill, Congress defined sustainable agriculture as "an integrated system of plant and animal production practices having a site-specific application that will, over the long-term: satisfy human food and fiber needs; enhance environmental quality and the natural resource base upon which the agriculture economy depends; make the most efficient use of non-renewable resources and integrate where appropriate, natural biological cycles and control; sustain the economic viabil-

ity of farm operations; and enhance the quality of life for farmers and society as a whole."[4] Numerous individuals representing widely diverse sectors of U.S. agriculture indicate that this definition represents a long-term goal for U.S. agriculture. How to convert this goal into practical realities, however, is a major challenge.

THE CURRENT STATE OF
SUSTAINABLE AGRICULTURE

In 1991, SARE commissioned the Task Force on Sustainable Agriculture and Quality of Life, and in 1992 it sponsored a forum on this topic at the USDA Agriculture Outlook '93 Conference. The results of these activities are used in the present article as a basis for describing the current state of sustainable agriculture and identifying the potential structural attributes of a twenty-first-century family farm. These are used in developing a philosophy for identification of future research, education, and policy initiatives for U.S. agriculture.

A farmer's perspective

In his presentation at the Agriculture Outlook '93 Conference, Tom Frantzen, president of the Practical Farmers of Iowa (PFI), indicated that if our natural resources were under sound long-term management, the issue of agricultural sustainability would be irrelevant.[5] He stressed the

3. U.S., General Accounting Office, *Sustainable Agriculture: Program Management, Accomplishments, and Opportunities*, GAO/RCED-92-233, 1992.

4. Food, Agriculture, Conservation, and Trade Act of 1990, Pub. L. 101-624, § 1603.

5. This subsection of the present article is abstracted from a presentation by Tom Frantzen, president of Practical Farmers of Iowa, New Hampton, to the USDA Agriculture

need for a comprehensive ecological approach to future U.S. farming systems. Frantzen cited Savory and his book on holistic resource management and gave special emphasis to the impacts of agriculture on water cycles, mineral cycles, and energy. He related these to communities of species and their interrelationships and stressed that nothing exists in a vacuum.

PFI is a private, nonprofit organization of farmers. Members of PFI are learning to judge the merits of farming practices by their ability to coincide with good water and mineral cycling, efficient use of solar energy, and the existence of stable and complex communities of plants, animals, microorganisms, and people. A founder of PFI, Dick Thompson, has received national recognition for development of ridge tillage row crop farming without herbicides. This system leaves the soil covered to prevent erosion and improves water infiltration. Livestock manure and crop rotation are part of the system. In recent years, PFI has worked in cooperation with Iowa State University and has pioneered the concept of strip intercropping on ridges in a manner that captures more sunlight and boosts corn and small-grain yields. PFI is actively promoting a concept of intensive grazing management known as planned grazing. The sustainable farming practices under development by PFI farmers require a skilled and well-educated farm population.

An agribusiness perspective

Ray Eid represented agribusiness at the Agriculture Outlook '93 Conference. He indicated that a meaningful partnership between the public and private sector is the backbone upon which a sustainable agriculture must be built.[6] He stressed that today's global population of 5.4 billion is forecast to grow to 8 billion by the year 2020, and that the world's food supply must double in the next thirty years to meet this growth and provide an appropriate diet. At the same time, weeds, insects, and plant diseases are all competing with humans for food resources, and the public is becoming increasingly concerned about agrichemicals.

Agrichemicals are among the major tools that have enabled farmers to give Americans an abundant, inexpensive, and safe food supply. Today the public is asking more of agribusiness. Essentially, it wants agribusiness to make sure that quality of life and environmentally sound practices are intrinsic parts of our agricultural system. Society wants us to ensure that agriculture is sustainable, that it nourishes us today and safeguards the land for future generations.

The Du Pont Agricultural Products Division takes a holistic view of sustainable agriculture in which agriculture is productive, socially acceptable, economically viable, and

6. This subsection is abstracted from a presentation by Ray Eid, consultant to the vice president, Du Pont-Ag Chemicals, Wilmington, DE, to the USDA Agriculture Outlook '93 Conference.

Outlook '93 Conference, Washington, DC, 2 Dec. 1992.

environmentally sound. These four components work and thrive together to achieve a balanced and sustainable system at the farm, national, and global levels. The role of science and technology is to produce technologies to help farmers balance production, economics, quality of life, and the environment, including cultural practices, crop varieties, natural enemies, diagnostics, biotechnology, agrichemicals, and biological and expert systems.

Du Pont believes that agrichemicals, such as the sulfonylurea herbicides, are vital to achieving a sustainable agriculture. Du Pont also believes, however, that partnerships are vital in achieving a sustainable agriculture through better uses of science and technology. Two years ago, Du Pont developed the Environmental Respect Award, the first national program that recognizes agricultural dealers for operating their business in a way that protects the environment but also establishes new, higher standards for storing and handling pesticides. This year, Du Pont began the No-Till Neighbors Program to provide a forum for farmers to teach other farmers about residue management and conservation tillage. Recently, in cooperation with the USDA, the Environmental Protection Agency, and several research and environmental institutions, Du Pont launched a major on-farm demonstration and education project in sustainable agriculture at its Remington Farms on the eastern shore of Maryland. These are examples of the commitment of Du Pont to develop successful partnerships with other stakeholders in the agricultural systems to work together for the common good of agriculture, society, and the world at large.

A social scientist's perspective

According to Dr. Cornelia Flora, quality of life related to sustainable agriculture is not just the sum of levels of contentment of individual farm family members but the product of interaction between various enterprises of the production unit.[7] Whether the farm involves an individual, a farm family, or a corporation, quality of life is the product of the interactions between producers, the input networks on which they depend, the output networks that distribute their products, and byproducts such as waste and pollution. Understanding the interactions that affect quality of life involves focusing on human values, economics, and political power. Values and power determine what is defined as quality of life and by whom.

It is possible that quality of life in a sustainable production system could be defined as a highly profitable corporate farm that minimizes toxic inputs and takes measures to reduce risks to the environment. The soil could be maintained and enriched, and the few permanent employees could be well paid and content. But unless the implications for rural communities are enhanced, the

7. This subsection is abstracted from a presentation by Dr. Cornelia Flora, professor of rural sociology, Virginia Polytechnic Institute and State University, Blacksburg, to the USDA Agriculture Outlook '93 Conference.

system will not be sustainable. The impacts of alternative production systems on the community, defined in terms of interactions between people in the locality, must be considered. Corporate farm operators are less likely to buy locally than are locally owned production units. Less local buying reduces local commercial interactions and results in fewer farm residents to provide leadership for local community development.

Distribution of power at the local level is an important consideration. Unequally distributed resources are likely to lead to differentiated class structures. This differentiation brings with it little hope of social mobility for individuals who have relatively few resources, while individuals with the majority of the resources maintain their privilege by protecting opportunities for private consumption through minimizing local collective investment in schools and health care facilities. Control of access to processing and marketing facilities is also an important consideration. Unless integrated into vertical networks, it is impossible to produce a product different from that required by the processor.

Quality of life opens a wide range of considerations far beyond environmentally sound farming practices. But if more sustainable systems of farming are to be introduced and adopted, quality-of-life issues must be considered. Quality of life goes beyond the farm family and community to economic structures and policies, and it encompasses the powers that have major overall impacts on our lives.

A public policy perspective

The primary public mandate for U.S. agriculture throughout this century has been to support the process of industrial development.[8] The industrialization process required additional labor to run the factories and discretionary consumer income to buy the things that factories produce. At the turn of the century, a large proportion of the U.S. work force was engaged in farming and a large proportion of consumers' incomes was spent on food and fiber.

Agriculture had to be made more efficient to reduce agriculture's claim on consumers' incomes and to free farmers and their families to work in the factories and offices of an industrial economy. Government programs for agriculture, including publicly funded research and education, were focused on increased agricultural productivity in support of the public mandate for industrialization. The mandate for publicly funded research and education was to develop new technologies that could increase productivity by substituting mechanization and commercial inputs for farm labor and for management provided by farmers.

Agriculture has fulfilled its public mandate for the twentieth century. Workers have been provided for factories and offices. Expenditures on food have dropped. A century ago, the

8. This section is abstracted from a presentation by Dr. John Ikerd, professor of agricultural economics, University of Missouri, Columbia, to the USDA Agriculture Outlook '93 Conference.

1890 U.S. census indicated that approximately 22 million people, 40 percent of the population, lived on farms. A hundred years later, only 4.6 million people, less than 2 percent of the total U.S. population, live on farms. Food production probably claimed close to 50 percent of the nation's resources in 1890, with resources used in transportation and marketing added to those in farm production. A hundred years later, food costs amount to less than 12 percent of average consumers' income.

Farmers receive only about 20 cents of each dollar spent for food. The rest goes to marketing firms. In addition, farmers net only about half of what they gross, or 10 cents of each dollar that consumers spend on food. The other 10 cents pays for purchased inputs including rent, hired labor, and interest on borrowed money. The farmer's share of total consumer expenditures, including food and all other items, is less than 1.5 percent.

There is relatively little left to be squeezed out of farm-level food costs to benefit either society or farmers. Farm profits over the past several decades have been created primarily through adoption of new cost-cutting technologies. But, as the gap between increasing input costs and decreasing prices narrows, the cycle of declining profits, technology adoption, rising profits, production expansion, falling prices, and the return to falling profits has become even more vicious.

Society appears to be giving agriculture a new and broader mandate than that of the past. The mandate is to develop food and fiber systems that are efficient and productive but also ecologically sound, economically viable, and socially supportive. Public policies of the future must consider the quality of life of the people who farm and live in rural communities as well as of society as a whole as consumers and occupants of the natural environment.

SUSTAINABLE AGRICULTURE
AND QUALITY OF LIFE

The Sustainable Agriculture Quality of Life Task Force was formed as part of a national SARE project in 1991. The task force included scientists from the disciplines of sociology, economics, community development, and agronomy. The group also included a farmer, two private consultants, and two representatives of private, nonprofit organizations.

*People, agriculture,
and the environment*

According to the SARE quality-of-life task force, agricultural production systems are complex and dynamic.[9] Sustainability requires an

9. This section is abstracted from U.S., Department of Agriculture, Sustainable Agriculture Research and Education Program, Sustainable Agriculture Quality of Life Task Force, *Sustainable Agriculture and Quality of Life* (1992). Members of the Sustainable Agriculture Quality of Life Task Force include Fred Kirschenmann (Northern Plains Sustainable Agriculture Society, Windsor, ND); Jerry Wade (University of Missouri-Columbia); Jerry Dewitt (Iowa State University, Ames); Oran Hestermann (Michigan State University, East Lansing); Marty Strange (Center for Rural Affairs, Walthill, NE); Jackie Langston (Research Triangle Park, NC); Cornelia Flora (Virginia Polytechnic Institute and State Uni-

approach to decision making that treats farms, families, and communities as components of shared ecological systems. It is generally accepted that the best way to protect the environment associated with agriculture is to have people who understand and care for the environment living on the land or in associated local rural communities. Similarly, soil conservation requires that people who are willing and able to care for farmland live on that land.

Wendell Berry has written extensively about the connections between people, quality of life, and sustainable agriculture.[10] In his recent book of essays, *What Are People For?*, it was stated that "if agriculture is to remain productive, it must preserve the land and the fertility and ecological health of the land; the land, that is, must be used well. A further requirement, therefore, is that if the land is to be used well, the people who use it must know it well, must be highly motivated to use it well, must know how to use it well, must have time to use it well, and must be able to afford to use it well." The opportunity to have knowledgeable people living on the land who have a sense of ownership, empowerment, and independence is a primary requisite for a sustainable agriculture.

versity, Blacksburg); John Allen (University of Nebraska, Lincoln); Sonya Salamon (University of Illinois-Urbana); Jim McNelly (St. Cloud, MN); Fee Busby (Winrock International, Morrilton, AR); John Ikerd (University of Missouri-Columbia); Don van Dyne (University of Missouri-Columbia); and Patrick Madden (Glendale, CA).

10. Wendell Berry, *What Are People For?* (San Francisco: North Point Press, 1990), p. 147.

Sustainable economic development

Community economic development strategies are currently undergoing changes consistent with sustainable agriculture. The strategies of industrial recruitment are giving way to growth-from-within policies. This is in line with the business theories of Reich and others, which include investment in entrepreneurs within the community to build small business and strengthen the local economy.[11] Local buyer-supplier projects reduce risks associated with fiscal resources leaving local communities by replacing imports with locally produced goods and services. As major corporations and branch plants relocate for inexpensive labor, efforts to recruit these businesses are increasingly regarded as an expensive and ineffective strategy for economic development. Attracting large companies may provide a large number of jobs, but these jobs often pay poorly and may be unstable. Economic development professionals are beginning to concentrate on improving the quality of jobs rather than the quantity of them.

Sustainable agriculture is a growth-from-within approach to rural economic development. It is an asset-based strategy where human capital is highly valued and enhanced through cycles of education, increased innovation, increased investment, increased value, increased employment opportunities, and higher wages. It is an alternative to the industrial agribusiness farming

11. Alvin Toffler, *Power Shifts* (New York: Bantam Books, 1990).

model of low wages, declining emphasis on education, declining rural communities, and an overall decline in quality of life.[12]

New realities of management

As American business has faced the challenges of maintaining competitiveness in global markets, management strategies have changed. The model of centralized production, high volume, and standardized units with little flexibility worked well in the past; however, in the past ten years about two-thirds of new nonfarm jobs were associated with small businesses. A recent National Science Foundation study found that small businesses produce 24 times as many innovations per research dollar invested as large businesses do.[13]

Reich reported that worldwide competition compresses profits on products that are uniform, routine, or standard.[14] Higher earnings are concentrated in businesses that are knowledge intensive and solve problems for customers or meet social needs. Large enterprises must downsize and decentralize into smaller and more flexible units. Toffler indicates that a technology not directly based on human activities will have the greatest impact in our lifetime on economic development and will create a new system of wealth.[15] As business is moving away

from many of the principles that evolved with the industrial agribusiness model of farming, conventional agriculture must also change. It must aggressively invest in people, management skills, and education. Sustainable agriculture places emphasis on equity, empowerment, and high levels of management skills and is consistent with trends in the business world. The increased knowledge needed to manage resources by sustainable means suggests a trend toward smaller farms that allows the manager to remain personally connected to diversified ecosystems and enterprises. Sustainable agriculture strategies provide opportunities for local ownership, hands-on management, and long-term commitment to the local community. A high level of farming skill increases returns to management and leads to greater profitability for sustainable agriculture farms. Farming becomes profitable for farmers and for rural communities as more dollars remain in the community.

Implications

The well-being of rural communities is essential to the future well-being of the United States. A viable rural economy can use existing resources of land and experienced farmers to provide a strong agricultural component to the rural community, supplying raw produce and opportunities for local value-added enterprises and jobs. Urban citizens benefit as well from a healthy, sustainable, rural economy. They benefit not only through the improved quality of natural resources and a high-

12. Robert B. Reich, "The Real Economy," *Atlantic Monthly*, pp. 35-52 (Feb. 1991).

13. Charles Stein, "Corporate Giants Try to Cut Themselves Down to Size," *News and Observer*, 14 Dec. 1991.

14. Reich, "Real Economy."

15. Toffler, *Power Shifts*.

quality food supply but also through the support of strong rural partners to relieve urban pressures on in-migration of unemployed or underemployed workers.

It is known that different farming systems have different implications for communities and the associated quality of life. Sustainable agriculture relies on a knowledge of the land and the ecology that supports the production of food and fiber. The strength of this approach lies in the human intellectual capacity to work with nature and maintain productivity. It empowers farmers and communities to strengthen local economies through dependence on people rather than on fiscal resources. The management of resources to enhance the dignity of work and improve the quality of life is powerfully connected to the resulting knowledge and productivity that is the best strategy to keep agriculture productive and to preserve the natural resource base for intergenerational equity.

A RESEARCH, EDUCATION, AND POLICY PHILOSOPHY FOR THE TWENTY-FIRST CENTURY

The current concept of sustainable agriculture mandates the viability of a twenty-first-century family farm model for U.S. agriculture. The structural attributes of this model are that

— the farm is owner operated;
— hired-worker days do not exceed farm-family-worker days;
— the farm is a partnership of, usually, no more than three families;
— the farm is structured as a joint management-labor relationship;

— the farm is diversified;
— there is emphasis on use of on-farm resources;
— there is common use of site-specific and real-time decision making; and
— there is a diverse set of enterprise statements.[16]

The enterprise statements associated with this model address the type of production system, economic goals, environmental quality goals, natural resource conservation goals, and quality-of-life goals.

The structural attributes of the twenty-first-century family farm are very different from those of large-scale commercial farms and part-time farms, both of which are common today. If these three distinct types of farms are identified as viable options for U.S. agriculture in the twenty-first century, they will require separate research, education, and policy initiatives that are targeted specifically to each model system. This contrasts with the past fifty years, when U.S. agricultural research, education, and policy have resulted primarily in a single system of agriculture: the large-scale conventional or industrial agribusiness model. To have an agriculture in which alternative types of farming systems prosper, separate policy initiatives and targeted research and education programs must be implemented for each type.[17]

16. After Strange, *Family Farming*.
17. National Research Council, Board on Agriculture, *Alternative Agriculture* (Washington, DC: National Academy Press, 1989); idem, *Sustainable Agriculture Research and Education in the Field* (Washington, DC: National Academy Press, 1991); Clive S. Edwards et al.

CONCLUSION

The new coalitions between farmers, ranchers, nonprofit private organizations, agribusiness, government, and academia have placed a new emphasis on quality of life as a focal point for sustainable agriculture. These efforts are beginning to catalyze interactions between the social and biophysical components of the professional sciences. In 1993, SARE held the first of a series of regional workshops designed to assist in integrating quality-of-life issues into systems-oriented policy, research, and education initiatives. For this to have a significant impact on U.S. agriculture, however, SARE will have to continue to foster the philosophy of

meaningful involvement of progressive farmers and ranchers in all agricultural policymaking, research, and education activities. The role of progressive farmers and ranchers in these areas must include policy development, decision making in relation to how resources are allocated, active participation in research and education programs, and development of appropriate oversight protocols. These roles will not only assure the inclusion of quality-of-life issues within the boundaries of sustainable agriculture but will restructure U.S. agriculture and return the role of the twenty-first-century farmer to that of producer of food, feed, and fiber, steward of our natural resources, and primary citizen-leader for our nation.[18]

Sustainable Agricultural Systems (Ankeny, IA: Soil and Water Conservation Society, 1990); Charles A. Francis, Cornelia B. Flora, and Larry D. King, Sustainable Agriculture in Temperate Zones (New York: John Wiley, 1990); National Science Board, Science Indicators - 1976 (Washington, DC: National Science Foundation, 1977), pp. 91-128.

18. Paul B. Thompson, "Constitutional Values and the Costs of American Food," in Proceedings of the 8th Annual Scientific Symposium (Chevy Chase, MD: Institute for Alternative Agriculture, 1991), pp. 64-74.

ANNALS, *AAPSS*, **529**, September 1993

Agriculture's Role
in a New Rural Coalition

By DENNIS U. FISHER

ABSTRACT: Many rural areas in the United States are in serious trouble as they experience decline over an extended period of time. Rural communities are increasingly being affected by changes in the national and world economies with little capacity to react. Selective out-migration has seriously reduced the size of the leadership pool. The remaining community and business leaders find themselves in a policy environment that is hostile or, at best, not helpful as they attempt to adjust to or take advantage of changing conditions. A key reason for this policy environment is the lack of any voice, other than production agriculture, speaking for rural communities. Although it is waning, the strength of the agricultural voice has repressed formation of any broad-based coalition that could speak to the wide variety of issues facing rural areas. To develop a supportive policy, however, a broad-based coalition must be formed. The very groups that have unwittingly preempted the voice of rural communities—agribusiness firms and farm organizations—may be in the strongest position to develop this coalition. This endeavor could be in the best interest of the agricultural establishment. Not all rural communities will survive, but they all should have a policy environment that will help them try.

Dennis U. Fisher is professor of agricultural economics and extension economist for development and policy at Texas A&M University. He also directs the Rural Policy program within the Economic Development Program Unit of the Texas Agricultural Extension Service. In this role, he has conducted and participated in rural policy workshops at the national, regional, and state levels. He has experience in industry consulting with retail, service, and manufacturing firms throughout the United States, providing advice on economic development, market analysis, and other business and economic areas.

103

WHO speaks for rural America? Where is the voice of our rural communities? It would seem that the stress of economic restructuring, selective out-migration, loss of rural hospitals, and closure of rural schools would generate a desperate call for help, but no such cry has been forthcoming. Other than requests from agriculture, no clear and distinct voices are being heard. This lack of an effective voice for rural areas is clearly demonstrated by William Nagle's comments: "Rural development policy does indeed lack a broad constituency. The proof is in that thundering silence that greeted the 1985 abolishment of [the U.S. Department of Agriculture's] Office of Rural Development Policy and more importantly the curtailment or abolishment of Federal rural development programs."[1]

James Bonnen describes the process by which rural areas have effectively lost their voices during the agrarian transformation. He argues that the commodity interests, general farm organizations, and agribusiness firms in partnership with Congress and the executive branch contributed to this demise and continue to block the formation of effective rural coalitions.

What happened in the agrarian transformation was a deinstitutionalization of rural America, an erosion of the base of the human and institutional resources of communities. It did not just undermine the population base for small town businesses and for schools. It first focused power in farm organizations and interest groups and then, with the decline of the agrarian sector, left behind rural communities whose basic institutions were underdeveloped and weak. No empowered rural community political institutions or interest groups developed in the agrarian transformation. . . . Commodity interest groups and their contentious partners in agribusiness and the general farm organizations have dominated what passes for rural policy since the Great Depression. . . . Agricultural interest groups have preempted the rural political domain and continue to dominate it. The executive branch and the Congress have joined in close partnership with these agricultural interests to manage the agrarian policies since the 1930s. This has institutionalized an agrarian voice for rural America that effectively excludes rural community interests.[2]

While these conclusions are unsettling, agricultural interests appear to have contributed unwittingly to the decline of the rural voice, and their strength continues to inhibit formation of a broad-based rural coalition. Is it possible that these same agricultural interests could orchestrate formation of a rural coalition? In this article, I will argue that the agricultural establishment is in the strongest position to create this coalition, that pursuing this endeavor would be in its best interest, and that a broad-based coalition may be the only option—or at least the best option—for

1. William J. Nagle, "Federal Organization for Rural Policy," in *Towards Rural Development Policy for the 1990s: Enhancing Income and Employment Opportunities*, Congressional Research Service and the Joint Economic Committee of the Congress, 101st Cong., 1st sess., Joint Committee Print 101-50, Sept. 1989, p. 236.

2. James T. Bonnen, "The Political Economy of U.S. Rural Policy: An Exploration of the Past with Strategies for the Future" (Staff Paper no. 90-54, Department of Agriculture Economics, Michigan State University, July 1990), pp. 4-5, 7.

preserving and possibly enhancing agriculture's political influence.

I will be addressing three questions. Is a rural coalition essential? Why should the agricultural establishment attempt to create a rural coalition? Will a rural coalition hold together and get the job done?

IS A RURAL COALITION ESSENTIAL?

Without policy changes, rural areas will probably continue to decline or at least be severely hampered in their ability to adjust to changing conditions. A rural coalition is essential to stimulating the needed policy changes.

Rural economic decline

The economic stresses on America's rural areas are well documented.[3] The migration of rural people to urban areas is but one indication of the lack of economic opportunities in rural areas. This migration has continued over the past fifty years, with a short reversal in the 1970s. The rate of net migration between 1986 and 1987 was greater than occurred during the decades of the 1950s or 1960s.[4] During the first part of the 1990s, the net migration out of rural areas fell to just over 100,000 people annually. But this masks an actual migration of 1.7 to 1.8 million people into some rural areas and 1.8 to 1.9 million people out of other areas. Therefore, some rural areas, particularly in the Great Plains and Midwest, continue to experience large out-migration.[5] This is not to say that all rural communities are in a state of decline. Urban-fringe communities, areas dependent on tourism and retirement destination, and communities that have diversified their economies have fared better than the remainder of rural America. Of those rural areas experiencing stress, not all will survive, but all should be given the chance to try. The challenges are certainly great enough to warrant formation of a rural coalition.

Hostile policy environment

The current policy environment is hostile toward rural areas. For example, many challenges yield themselves to single-community solutions in urban areas but require multicommunity approaches when faced by rural areas. Solid-waste disposal, health care, and education are critical examples. Unfortunately, government programs are normally designed to be delivered through single government units, and the solutions usually involve consolidation. Little attention is given to alternative solutions that will preserve community identity.[6]

3. U.S., Department of Agriculture, Economic Research Service, Agriculture and Rural Economy Division, *Rural Economic Development in the 1980s: Preparing for the Future*, ERS Staff Report no. AGES870724, July 1987.

4. David Freshwater, "A Synopsis of the Proceedings of the Rural Development Symposium," in *Towards Rural Development Policy for the 1990s*, p. 15.

5. *Rural Conditions and Trends*, 3(1) (Spring 1992).

6. Dennis U. Fisher, Ronald D. Knutson, and Howard Ladewig, "Policy and Multicommunity Development," in *Multicommunity Collaboration: An Evolving Rural Revitalization Strategy*, RRD 161, ed. Peter F. Korsching,

To add to this dilemma, rural interests rarely receive attention when policy changes are being considered. Robert Greenstein, director of the Center on Budget and Policy Priorities, indicated that he was not aware of any consideration of the impact on rural areas during congressional or administrative discussions of welfare reform.[7] With the exception of farm policies, policies affecting rural areas are generally discussed in terms of their impact on metropolitan areas, and little or no attention is given to their effect on rural residents.

Not only are rural interests not considered by government policymakers, but the institutional capacity for such an examination also is a rare commodity, particularly at the state level. According to Kenneth Fern of the Council of State Governments, "Only five full standing committees now exist in our ninety-nine state legislative chambers that bear the name 'Rural Resources' or 'Rural Development' as a part of their officially assigned policy making purview, and two of these five committees are in a single state."[8] At both the state and federal levels, government is organized to ignore rural interests.

Timothy O. Borich, and Julie Stewart (Ames: Iowa State University, 1992).

7. Robert Greenstein, "Welfare Reform in Rural Areas," in *Towards Rural Development Policy for the 1990s*, pp. 35-40.

8. Kenneth Fern, Jr., "Coalition/Consensus Building for Rural Development Policy," in *Understanding of Public Problems and Policies —1989*, ed. Walter J. Armbruster and Teddee E. Grace (Oak Brook, IL: Farm Foundation, 1989), p. 77.

Are the trends reversible?

Are the negative trends affecting rural America reversible, or are the forces fueling rural decline deeply seated within the structural changes occurring in the national and world economies? If the answer to the second question is yes, then a rural coalition, even if effective in changing policy, would have minimal impact. Many of the forces affecting rural America are national and international in origin and certainly beyond local control. Adapting to and working with those forces, however, is essential for survival of many rural areas.

There is no definitive research on the number and location of rural areas—or urban areas, for that matter—that will fare well in the face of the changing world economy. However, some changes in technology make participation in the world economy possible for areas previously excluded. For example, the information age has made locational considerations for some businesses, such as computer-based collection companies and mail-order firms, less important than in the past. Rural communities will need the necessary infrastructure to take advantage of this emerging technology.

In general, rural areas need a policy environment that will enhance rather than frustrate their efforts to work with their changing world. The ability to make the necessary adjustments will depend upon the ingenuity of rural people and their leaders, working within a policy environment that is supportive. Some will be able to make the necessary adjustments.

*Will the costs of
the policy changes
be prohibitive?*

During this time of federal budget deficits and very tight state and local budgets, expensive policy changes would not be considered even if a coalition were formed. In some cases, the expense of a policy change would be prohibitive, but many changes can be achieved at little expense. An example of a high-cost change involves equalizing federal reimbursement between rural and urban hospitals and doctors for the delivery of comparable services. According to the Office of Technology Assessment, community and migrant health centers receive 15 percent less federal funding per patient served than their urban counterparts even though the rural centers are more dependent upon patients who are backed by federal funds.[9] In a 1988 presentation, Marsha Kilgore, who was then president of the Board of Directors of the National Rural Health Association, stated, "Our federal government under the Medicare program reimburses rural hospitals at about 40 percent less than urban hospitals for the same level of service."[10] While one could argue about the comparability of service levels, changing this disparity would obviously be costly.

Creating a positive environment for multicommunity cooperation is an example of a policy change that would involve little cost. As indicated previously, many rural issues lend themselves better to multicommunity solutions than to single-community approaches. Because most programs are designed to be delivered through single government entities, leaders attempting multicommunity approaches face substantial red tape as well as the normal resistance to working cooperatively with other communities. Changing the policy environment to remove the red tape or to provide incentives for or give preference to multicommunity approaches would add little cost to existing programs and should improve program effectiveness.[11] Some changes would be expensive, possibly prohibitively so, but others would have little or no cost and could provide substantial assistance to rural America.

Is a rural coalition essential? Yes, if interests in addition to farm commodity programs are to receive much consideration. Are the trends affecting rural areas irreversible? Some are, but rural leaders will be able to capture opportunities and make necessary adjustments better in a positive policy environment.

WHY AGRIBUSINESS FIRMS
AND FARM ORGANIZATIONS?

Declining rural communities directly and negatively affect agribusiness firms and the membership of

9. U.S., Congress, Office of Technology Assessment, *Health Care in Rural America*, OTA-H-434 (Washington, DC: Government Printing Office, 1990), p. 12.

10. Marsha Kilgore, "Response to Health Paper: Western Region," in *Focus on the Future: Options in Developing a National Rural Policy*, ed. Sue H. Jones (College Station: Texas A&M University System, Texas Agricultural Extension Service, 1989), p. 173.

11. Fisher, Knutson, and Ladewig, "Policy and Multicommunity Development," in *Multicommunity Collaboration*, ed. Korsching, Borich, and Stewart, pp. 323-32.

farm organizations. For example, deteriorating rural economies result in decreasing asset values for agribusiness firms and their employees, as well as for the members of farm organizations living in rural America. As sales of goods and services decline, agribusiness firms face declining markets for their end products and less competitive markets for purchasing inputs. This will ultimately require developing alternative markets, possibly international markets, as the conditions for buying and selling in rural America deteriorate. The reasons fall into four categories.

Return a portion

Agribusiness firms and the members of farm organizations have made their profits and income from trade in rural areas and therefore should put something back. This reason may or may not be strong enough to motivate participation in the rural policy process, but it will no doubt be used extensively once the decision to participate has been made.

*Membership and
    employees need help*

The membership of farm organizations and the employees of agribusiness firms located in rural areas are suffering directly from declining rural communities and economies. The loss of jobs, income, and public and private goods and services is affecting the quality of life experienced by rural residents. The values of assets, both business and personal, are deteriorating. The impacts are direct, personal, and immediate.

A significant proportion of the employment of agribusiness firms is located in nonmetropolitan counties: 48 percent for input industries, 36 percent for processing and marketing industries, and 18 percent for wholesale and retail trade of agricultural products.[12]

Farm households are heavily dependent upon off-farm income, according to Petrulis, Carlin, and Francis. "Farm households increasingly depend on off-farm employment to improve the level and stability of total household income. Income from off-farm jobs, investments, and transfers accounted for over half of all U.S. farm household income over the 1984-88 period. Low farm business income no longer necessarily correlates with low total farm household income."[13]

Fisher and Knutson argue that farmers have a great stake in rural development. "Farmers have the greatest stake in rural development, but farm organizations have not recognized the importance of rural development policy to their constituency. Farm organizations have every reason to step into a leadership position on rural development policy. These organizations could join forces with the agribusiness sector since both have an important stake in rural issues."[14]

12. Mindy Petrulis, Thomas A. Carlin, and Wyn Francis, "Agriculture-Related Employment," *Agriculture Information Bulletin* (United States Department of Agriculture, Economic Research Service), no. 613, p. 2 (Sept. 1990).
   13. Ibid., p. 1.
   14. Dennis U. Fisher and Ronald D. Knutson, "Politics of Rural Development," in *Understanding of Public Problems and Policies—1989*, ed. Armbruster and Grace, p. 71.

Swanson argues that rural development is the key to survival of the family farm. "Indeed, strengthening the rural community appears to be the best strategy for preserving the family-type farm." The connection is off-farm employment.[15]

Markets deteriorate

As rural communities decline, the labor force deteriorates through selective out-migration. Those with the best opportunities elsewhere leave. That is, a higher proportion of those individuals of prime working age and the best-educated leave the area for better employment opportunities. This out-migration damages not only the labor force but also the pool of individuals available for public leadership positions and for ownership and management of private enterprises. Maintaining a competitive agriculture becomes increasingly difficult. Firms that become less competitive are a more expensive source of raw materials and a poorer market for farm inputs. Consequently, agribusiness firms are forced to develop new markets, possibly international markets, to replace those being lost.

This argument, while very powerful, suffers from being long-run in impact. The changes previously indicated will indeed happen and they have been occurring, but they may not catch business leaders' attention. Barring a drastic change in the rate of these trends, many rural markets may be lost before corrective action is taken.

Enhance political clout

The loss of political clout for the agricultural sector has been occurring over a long period of time as America has become urbanized. The process of losing congressional committee chairmanships and representation has been extensively discussed. This decline is not surprising. The number of people living on farms continued to drop during the 1980s and included less than 2 percent of the U.S. population in 1990.[16] However, about 27 percent of the U.S. population resides in rural areas. A coalition representing over one-fourth of the American population should generate significantly more influence than one representing less than 2 percent.

Forces other than population loss are eroding farm political clout. Other groups are beginning to reach into areas that farmers previously considered to be their exclusive domain. The following statement was signed by the presidents of the American Society for the Prevention of Cruelty to Animals, the Humane Society of the United States, and the Massachusetts Society for the Prevention of Cruelty to Animals and was endorsed by 104 of several thousand animal protection groups. "We shall work together to secure legislation that requires the basic behavioral and physical needs of farm ani-

15. Louis E. Swanson, "Rethinking Assumptions about Farm and Community," in *American Rural Communities*, ed. A. E. Luloff and Louis E. Swanson (Boulder, CO: Westview Press, 1990), p. 33.

16. U.S., Department of Commerce, Bureau of the Census, *Residents of Farms and Rural Areas: 1990*, Current Population Reports, ser. P-20, no. 457 (Washington, DC: Government Printing Office, 1992).

mals to assure the following minimum standards: the freedom to be able to stand up, lie down, extend their limbs or spread their wings and make other normal posture adjustments; an adequate supply of nutritious food; adequate veterinary care, and an environment that suits their physical and behavioral requirements."[17]

Farm organizations and agribusiness firms may want to begin forming a broad rural coalition that examines broad interests to forestall erosion of their own influence due to population loss and/or encroachment by other special interest groups. A broad-based rural coalition could result in increased political influence for the agricultural establishment. Of course, political objectives would have to be modified to accommodate the interests of other members.

When should such an effort start? It should start as soon as possible in order to be the most helpful to the leadership of rural areas. The agricultural establishment might have an even more compelling reason for starting soon if it considers the benefits of forming a coalition while agricultural influence is still strong enough to contribute to the effort. What agribusiness firms and farm organizations bring to this process is an organized but limited-focus coalition that has access to the rural part of the policy process. As that influence diminishes, the agricultural establishment will have less to contribute to the process.

17. Harold D. Guither and Michelle Van Buer, "The Evolution, Ethics, and Politics of Animal Protection" (Experiment station bulletin AE 4675, University of Illinois, Aug. 1991), pp. 8-9.

WILL A BROAD-BASED RURAL COALITION WORK?

What are the necessary and sufficient conditions in order for coalitions to form? Specific and direct benefits to an identifiable group are a strong incentive.

A lesson from agriculture

A lesson from the formation of the farm organizations is instructive. Prior to the 1930s, agricultural organizations were loosely knit organizations formed for social and professional purposes, but they had no strong political influence. This changed quickly with specific commodity legislation. James Bonnen credits the Agricultural Adjustment Acts of 1933 and 1938 with providing sufficient motivation for forming permanent commodity interest groups. "When you create legislation that provides specific benefits to limited groups, such as farmers or only wheat farmers, and when those selective goods substantially affect the welfare of that group, you also have created a sufficient incentive for organizing permanent (i.e., stable) interest groups."[18]

Other rural interest groups have not enjoyed such incentives. The rural health care delivery people are an exception. They have experienced a major negative incentive that seems to have spurred their organizational efforts and political influence. The lower reimbursement rates under the Medicare and Medicaid programs have provided a stick rather than a carrot,

18. Bonnen, "Political Economy of U.S. Rural Policy," p. 6.

but the result seems to be similar. The rural education people are not as well organized, but no legislation or government program has affected them as directly or as negatively as those recently affecting rural health care professionals.

Single-issue or multiple-issue coalition?

Without legislation that precipitates organization, should a rural coalition be organized to address all issues or to focus on specific single issues? Single-issue areas like rural health care are the most likely to produce specific legislation that will affect an identifiable group with specific benefits. Consequently, a coalition could be organized much more easily around a single-issue area. Unfortunately, a coalition formed around a single issue would not be equipped to deal with the problems facing rural communities. Fixing part of a community's problem may do little to improve conditions. Organizing around the variety of issues facing rural America is more likely to generate effective legislative solutions. However, those solutions would affect segments of the coalition differently, possibly having divisive rather than cohesive effects. If history is a valid predictor, the single-issue approach would probably be the easiest to organize. Without a broad coalition, however, the issues critical to rural America probably will not be addressed and single-issue groups will continue to address congressional committees predominated by urban interests.

THE STRATEGIC POSITION
OF AGRIBUSINESS FIRMS
AND FARM ORGANIZATIONS

Is there a third approach with a high probability of success in terms of both forming a coalition and addressing the spread of issues facing rural America? Agribusiness firms and farm organizations are in a position to take a better approach. Fisher and Knutson argue that agribusiness firms and farm organizations own the rural part of the policy process in the United States.[19] Most of the policy process is rightfully and understandably urban because most of the U.S. population is urban. The only part that is rural comprises those policies considered by the agriculture committees of Congress. This is not to say that only those pieces of legislation passing through the agriculture committees affect rural areas but that the agriculture committees are the only ones with predominantly rural constituencies. The farm organizations and agribusiness firms are the two groups that influence these committees. Any timely impact on rural policy will require the participation of groups already franchised. Keeping rural issues on the policy agenda will require relatively prompt action.

Have agribusiness firms and farm organizations not done enough by locating in rural areas and putting their purchasing dollars and payrolls in those areas? While these firms and organizations have undoubtedly made a major contribution to rural America, the present article identifies some

19. Fisher and Knutson, "Politics of Rural Development," pp. 62-72.

compelling reasons why they might want to expend additional effort to ensure that the problems of the nation's rural areas are addressed. These groups appear to be the only ones positioned to respond in a timely manner to the need for a rural voice that can be heard by policymakers.

WILL SUCH A COALITION BE SUCCESSFUL?

Will a broad-based rural coalition be successful? The challenges will be fragmentation of focus and conflicting goals. Congressional staffs focus attention on those issues that relate directly to their areas of responsibility. Consequently, those attempting to influence policy may not be heard when their topics are not directly related to the staff person's area. The congressional staff member may view the issue as being under the purview of another committee. Not surprisingly, William Browne's research findings indicate that lobbyists were best able to influence the process "where their concerns fit the decisions being deliberated."[20] Unfor-

tunately, rural issues often do not fit well into any single committee or single piece of legislation. The collection of messages coming from the coalition could be tailored to ameliorate this problem.

A broad coalition, by its very nature, will encompass groups with conflicting goals. This could be the most serious challenge of all. Whether or not such a coalition will hold together depends on whether members perceive their efforts as more effective with the coalition than without it. Will the political influence of members be enhanced sufficiently by the coalition to compensate for the cost of compromise? That is a good question. If a rural coalition is formed, the nation may get an answer.

What happens if a broad-based rural coalition is not formed? One can only speculate. Such a coalition offers some hope of reversing the present trend and strengthening agricultural influence. Rural areas will probably continue to experience a generally hostile policy environment with the exception of selected issues. Forming a coalition would be preferable to finding out what happens without one.

20. William P. Browne, "Access and Influence in Agriculture and Rural Affairs: Congressional Staff and Lobbyist Perception of Orga-

nized Interests," *Rural Sociology*, 54(3):375 (Fall 1989).

ANNALS, *AAPSS*, **529**, September 1993

Rebuilding Rural America:
The Southern Development Bancorporation

By BRIAN KELLEY

ABSTRACT: The Southern Development Bancorporation is a development bank based in rural Arkansas. The term "bank" is in some sense a misnomer; Southern is actually a collection of five development companies, for-profit and nonprofit, only one of which is a regulated bank. The other four groups are a venture capital fund, a real estate development corporation, a self-employment microenterprise program, and a manufacturing services program. Founded in 1988, Southern delivers a range of financial and nonfinancial assistance to rural companies with the intent of expanding local firms and thus creating jobs and an improved economic base for the region. Since 1988, Southern has lent or invested $19 million in 150 firms in a 32-county region of rural Arkansas. This article examines Southern's present activity, how it is working to achieve its goals, and what insights it has gained to date in the challenging task of developing the rural economy.

Brian Kelley is vice president of Southern Development Bancorporation and the Arkansas Enterprise Group, Southern's nonprofit affiliate. He brings to his efforts in southern Arkansas 18 years of experience in development banking, manufacturing, and nonprofit organizations. He earned a bachelor's degree from the University of California, Santa Barbara, and holds a master of arts and a master of business administration from Stanford University.

FOUR years ago, Marsha Denning started a quilt manufacturing business in Desha County, Arkansas. She employs women living in this economically depressed region. For some employees, even though they are in their sixties, this is the first paying job they have ever held.

In four years, Denning has been able to garner over $100,000 in loans from three public sources of business financing and one bank. With those funds, she built a building, bought equipment and inventory, and hired employees. Her market has been regional craft and trade shows. She employs five women and five women who contract work at home. The plan was to market the quilts in Arkansas and other states to bring new money and new jobs into the region.

With all of these monies and organizational allies, one would expect the River Country Quilts story to be a success story. Unfortunately, that is not the case.

At this point, she owes $14,000 in back taxes for which she is personally liable, is operating at a loss, has not paid herself in a year, is possibly facing bankruptcy, and has used all her available capital. Probably every quilt that she sold since the beginning has been sold at a loss, and as a result she has been eating into her capital reserves for four years. What went wrong?

What went wrong is easy to state but difficult to remedy. Growing a successful business, even a small one, takes much more than money. Many established, first-generation businesses now operating were started during the 1950s or 1960s, when starting a business was simple by comparison with now.

Business administrative and management issues in the 1960s were less complicated. Marketing in the 1960s was less competitive. In Marsha Denning's case, the minute she walks outside her door in Desha County, Arkansas, she competes not only with New York and California, but also with Taiwan, Mexico, and China. This level of immediate, efficient, and sometimes fierce competition for even the simplest products did not exist forty years ago, but it most assuredly does now.

The agencies that lent Denning money did not provide any significant nonfinancial assistance with their investment. She had no solid accounting system, and she did not understand pricing, the limits of her market, or the need to find higher-margin markets. She did not track inventory or cash flow and did not pay sufficient taxes.

None of this resulted from dishonesty or lack of hard work: she is exceedingly honest, works very long hours for little pay, and has superior quilting skill. Her problems came from the fact that she was a good shop-floor person but an unskilled businessperson.

From her organizational sponsors' perspectives, it was much more difficult to provide management, accounting, and marketing help than to provide money. The absence of nonfinancial support for the business produced the unfortunate result.

Were a complex, multipart rural enterprise development program to be reduced to a single example, the story of Marsha Denning would be that example. Multiplied many times over in very different market sectors, her story demonstrates one of the primary rationales behind the creation of the Southern Development Bancorporation and its nonprofit affiliate, the Arkansas Enterprise Group.

The Southern Development Bancorporation is an innovative rural economic development group based in the city of Arkadelphia in southern Arkansas. Founded in 1988 by 26 private, public, and nonprofit investors, Southern is a rural analogue to South Shore Bank in Chicago, an urban development bank.[1] Southern's role is to be a catalyst for economic development in Arkansas and to benefit low- and moderate-income Arkansans while at the same time operating a profitable and sound financial institution. We think it thus embodies an innovative combination of public sector goals within a private sector structure. Our primary goal is to create additional regional income by helping people establish and then expand small, locally owned businesses that produce goods or services for export from Arkansas or that replace those goods and services consumed in Arkansas but presently produced out of state. The premise is that over time these small, locally owned firms will create more wealth-generating jobs than currently exist in the region, will remain in rural Arkansas, and will be better employers.

This article is composed of four sections: the organization and opera-

1. Much has been written on South Shore Bank, most notably Richard Taub, *Community Capitalism* (Cambridge, MA: Harvard Business School Press, 1988).

tions of the Southern Development Bancorporation; initial lessons from and insights into the process of rural economic development; some suggestions about the interdependent nature of community and economic development; and, finally, thoughts about Southern's overall performance and some difficult questions that remain.

STRUCTURE AND
OPERATIONS OF SOUTHERN

Southern is composed of five operating companies, organized in a holding company format. Within this structure, there are two paths: for-profit and nonprofit. The for-profit side includes Southern Development Bancorporation as a regulated bank holding company; Elk Horn Bank, a $95 million rural community bank; and Opportunity Lands Corporation, a real estate development company. The nonprofit side, Arkansas Enterprise Group (AEG), includes the Good Faith Fund, a self-employment finance and training program; AEG Manufacturing Services, a capital and management support program for small manufacturing firms; and Southern Ventures, Inc., a small-business equity investment corporation. Because it is impossible for any entity to actually own a nonprofit organization, in that a nonprofit does not have shares and has specific Internal Revenue Service restrictions, there is no formal legal relationship between AEG and Southern except for some shared board membership. In the organizational chart (see Figure 1), this relationship is represented by a dotted line.

FIGURE 1
THE STRUCTURE OF THE SOUTHERN DEVELOPMENT BANCORPORATION

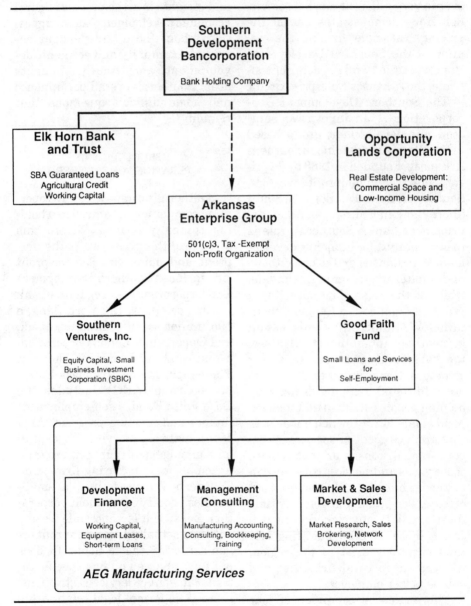

One concept of Southern is as a merchant bank that provides an extraordinary amount of nonfinancial support to its portfolio companies. Another view is that Southern is a nonprofit economic development group with a strong for-profit banking partner. Whatever the perspective, Southern was created to meet a variety of needs for a wide range of small enterprises. Southern's customers vary in size and sophistication from individual entrepreneurs going into business for the first time to established manufacturers in the process of expanding or exporting abroad. The smallest micro firms employ solely the owner and then only on a part-time basis. The largest company to receive assistance from Southern had sales of $6.8 million in 1991 and employs 165 people.

Southern's financial services range from long-term fixed-rate Small Business Administration (SBA) guaranteed loans to innovative joint ventures with small manufacturing firms. Nonfinancial assistance ranges from seminars for welfare participants about self-employment to customer-designed, national product marketing and brokering campaigns. A brief description of each of Southern's main programs follows.

AEG Manufacturing Services

AEG Manufacturing Services (AMS) delivers financial services to companies that cannot qualify for bank financing. AMS provides short- and long-term, fixed-rate loans, operating leases on production equipment, and Working Capital Investments. The Working Capital Investments program will provide a manufacturer with financing to fill a purchase order; AMS will provide the capital, while the manufacturer contributes the production capacity. AMS's return is fixed at the outset of the joint venture, as a percentage of sales. If the purchase is completed, delivered, and paid on time, then AMS makes a relatively high rate of return on the investment. If not, AMS stands to lose its entire investment.

The nonfinancial services that AMS provides are financial consulting, market assistance, and accounting services for small manufacturers. As an initial effort, to provide marketing assistance, AMS has created national marketing campaigns for local firms and engaged in marketing research. Additionally, AMS has helped to create and invest in a for-profit sales and marketing company, targeted at the wood products industry. These services are loosely modeled on development programs successfully operated in northern Italy and rural Finland. Through its investment and services program, AMS internally generates approximately 30 percent of its operating budget.

Good Faith Fund

The Good Faith Fund (GFF) was inspired by the Grameen Bank of Bangladesh. It targets low-income residents in southeast Arkansas who are interested in self-employment. GFF lends small amounts of money; the average loan disbursed since January 1991 has been $1,084. To borrow from the fund, an entrepreneur must participate in a series of eight training sessions and join a borrowing group. GFF relies not only on a security interest in the goods purchased but also on the peer-group pressure of the borrowing group to ensure repayment of its loans. Borrowing groups meet every other week to discuss their projects, receive training, collect loan payments, and make contributions to group savings accounts. About half of GFF's borrowing customers are women and over 80 percent are African American. Because GFF's microloan and technical assistance program are very staff intensive and the loans are quite small, the GFF loan portfolio has been able to only generate about 5 percent of its annual operating budget.

Southern Ventures, Inc.

Southern Ventures, Inc. (SVI) is a small-business investment company (SBIC) licensed by the SBA, wholly owned by the nonprofit AEG. Most of SVI's financial investments have been equity investments in small manufacturing and technical services companies. SVI is the only active venture capital company in Arkansas for transactions in the range of $50,000 to $250,000. It has invested in the manufacturing of waste water treatment facilities, aluminum casting, biochemical assay, and petroleum refining. When SVI makes an equity investment, it takes one or two positions on the company's board of directors and is very involved in the company's strategic planning and daily operations.

SVI is following the normal path of a venture capital group, albeit an unusual one, focused on rural development investments. By law, an SBIC investment term must be at least five years. SVI has yet to be profitable, but in 1992 it will earn 60 percent of its operating budget. Typically, a venture capital group spends its early years investing money and expects to

receive its return later, when its investments begin to turn over.

Opportunity Lands Corporation

The Opportunity Lands Corporation (OLC) develops commercial and residential real estate. In July of 1992, OLC completed renovation of vacant retail space, transforming it into two Enterprise Centers in Arkadelphia and Pine Bluff. Enterprise Centers are small—10,000 square feet—buildings located in downtown areas; they provide small, high-quality office space and a limited number of shared services. OLC has also managed rehabilitation and construction of low-income housing.

Elk Horn Bank and Trust Company

The Elk Horn Bank and Trust Company, a regulated commercial bank, contributes to Southern's development efforts through development loans. The bank originates, extends, or renews between 150 and 200 consumer, agricultural, small business, or residential real estate loans each month. Most of these loans would be made by local competitors on similar rates and terms. Southern considers an Elk Horn Bank loan to be a development loan only if other banks would not make the loan in the normal course of business on similar rates and terms. Development credits generally require additional underwriting and monitoring by loan officers and bank management. They often have relatively complex structures and require credit enhancement in the form of SBA guarantees to limit the exposure of the bank.

Between May 1988 and the end of June 1992, the Southern companies extended over $19 million in development investments, creating or sustaining employment for more than 700 people. Slightly more than half of the 145 enterprises that have received development loans or investment from Southern are minority owned.

Elk Horn and Southern are both profitable. With the exception of 1988, Elk Horn Bank has consistently earned at or in excess of the industry benchmark 1.00 percent return on average on assets. Losses and delinquency rates vary for each program, from high losses for the equity program (as is the norm in the venture capital business) and 8 percent delinquent or nonperforming for AEG to a 1 percent loss rate for Elk Horn Bank.

LESSONS LEARNED:
SMALL BUSINESS DEVELOPMENT

With experience, Southern has gained insights into successful strategies and techniques. Some of the clearer lessons will be discussed now.

*Multiple development
partners*

A successful long-term development process requires consistent and strong contributions from the private, public, and nonprofit sectors. Each sector has a specific, necessary, and unique role. This development tripod cannot stand unless all three legs are strong contributors.

Only the public sector can fund activities such as community leadership training, basic employee training, basic public investments in education and housing, and innovative public investments such as business incubators or investment funds targeted at specific market sectors. The public sector's role in economic development is demonstrated in European situations in which the public sector took the lead in the unavoidable risk of new investments, new market directions, and seed planting of new enterprise development. Only 3 percent of the initial funds that created Southern were public funds, but without the existence of the SBA's SBIC, microloan, and loan guarantee program, and various assistance programs of the Farmers Home Administration and the Department of Health and Human Services, Southern would be far behind its accomplishments to date. Recently, the state of Arkansas has made direct investments in SVI and has joined SVI and AEG in investing funds in several development companies.

The private sector creates the ultimate product of this effort, competitive jobs and enterprises. It is the private sector that has access to the greatest reservoir of finance, marketing, and management resources. All of the public funding available is only a drop in the bucket compared to the total funds needed to revitalize a rural economy. The private sector's access to abundant funds is demonstrated by Southern's activity so far; the great majority of its financial activity is through the for-profit Elk Horn Bank and through Southern Ventures, Inc., the for-profit SBIC. Finally, the private sector has the flexibility, market responsiveness, and discipline to supply venture and debt funds to individual firms, provide access to distribution networks and markets, and make the profit-driven—not political-influence-driven—investment choices that are difficult for the public sector.

Finally, the third leg of the tripod is in the nonprofit sector. Somewhat particular to the United States, the nonprofit sector can combine some of the best characteristics of the private and public sectors and is thus uniquely equipped to act as a bridge between the two. AEG has external goals that are public sector in nature: the creation of jobs and increased income for Arkansas's rural communities. Internally, however, AEG employs private sector strategies and goals: a program focused on bottom-line impact; private sector finance tools; fee-based management services and market support; and hard-nosed choices based on where AEG's resources can have the greatest impact on the region. A nonprofit such as AEG can be nimble and innovative enough to respond to changing community, business, and marketing connections.

Multiple types
of assistance

Just as it is necessary to have multiple sectors involved in rural development, it is necessary to make available to rural enterprises a range of development resources. Capital alone is insufficient. Without growing and profitable markets, all the financing in the world is useless. Similarly, without adequate management skills, the best product and most profitable market niche are insufficient.

For most businesses, the provision of these resources follows a sequence: first money, then management, and then marketing. Often the businessperson believes that he or she has three problems: money, money, and money. Sometimes this is true; sometimes it is not. Nonetheless, money is very often the squeaky wheel that brings the entrepreneur to the table. With this commitment and entrance to the business, it is then possible to work on the less urgent—though possibly more fundamentally important—business issues such as management skill, cost accounting, financing, product design, balance sheet structuring, product margins, market positions, market depth, product distribution, and employee management.

Reflecting this entrepreneurial need, Southern has been slowly expanding its resources and services. Southern now provides financing ranging from a $500 loan to a woman on public assistance who is beginning her own business to $350,000 in equity capital to $750,000 in long-term debt. Figure 2 suggests the progression of financial services offered by Southern. The equivalent offering of nonfinancial services at this point ranges from biweekly training sessions for Good Faith Fund participants to an ongoing fee-for-service accounting service for small manufacturers to very active and daily participation in SVI equity investment portfolio companies by staff members.

FIGURE 2

**GRADUATING TO CONVENTIONAL FINANCING IN THREE STEPS:
SOUTHERN DEVELOPMENT BANCORPORATION PROGRAMS**

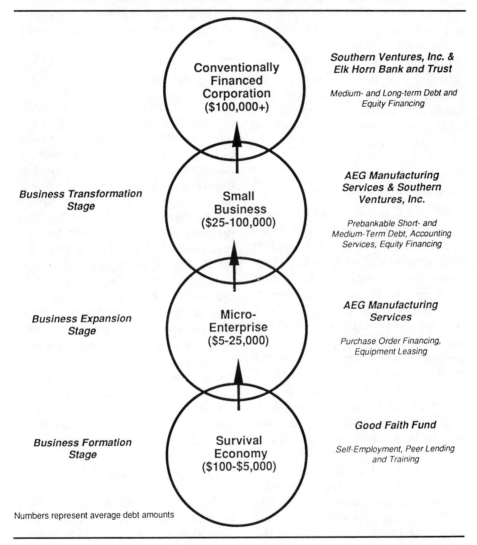

Numbers represent average debt amounts

Technical assistance

Inexperienced entrepreneurs cannot succeed with credit alone. They generally do not possess information adequate for developing a prudent plan and locating a profitable market niche. Individual technical assistance is generally too expensive for either the entrepreneur or funders to rationalize paying its full cost. When subsidized, however, technical assistance programs often lose market relevance and are generally mediocre in quality. To make technical assistance available to this level of entrepreneur in a cost-effective way, it has to be highly systematized, delivered to groups of entrepreneurs, and affordable for the users. This can be achieved through group entrepreneurial training programs, group lending, business incubators, and trade associations.

Firm growth versus individual development

Small businesses can be plotted on a pyramid, with many new, small businesses at the base that sell into local markets. The first tier comprises the self-employed. At the next level are businesses that operate from business locations, have employees, and provide local goods and services. Larger goods and services businesses serve regional markets; many are franchises. Larger businesses such as manufacturers, distributors, and wholesalers sell to large outside markets. For an economy to be healthy and growing, it must include the latter businesses.

Programs that operate in depressed communities encounter many businesses that are new and small and that serve very local markets. Small-business support at this level serves the individual development goals of entrepreneurs and their need for personal income. This is quite different from small-business support for existing firms, which serves the goal of firm growth. Firm growth has more immediate economic impact through the number of jobs and the amount of value added created. If

one has the goal of expanding the entrepreneurial community in depressed communities, however, both firm development and individual entrepreneurial development are necessary.

The role of information

In Southern's experience, information and market access rank as the most important ingredients behind business success in the traded or value-added sector. They are, unfortunately, the least developed arms of most economic or enterprise development efforts around the country. In a previous era, the key factors for success were often cited as location, location, and location; for some, cost structure was key. As we approach the twenty-first century, the need increasingly is for information, information, and information, especially in terms of product design, production technology, employee skills, and market savvy. Information makes the difference between success and failure or between significant margins—good wages—and barely survivable margins—minimum wage jobs.

Value-added businesses

Southern's experience argues against focusing scarce development resources on dying market sectors or on retail businesses. If a community has little or declining income from the outside economy or if its economy is based in a declining margin industry, then working with a local retail firm is futile. Local businesses do not increase the total amount of income available to community residents. The consumer sector is fundamentally based on the income or wealth generated by other, more primary industries. For that reason, it is necessary to clearly focus on firms that will affect the total income statement of the local community.

The role of the nonprofit intermediary

AEG's role, as what is commonly called an economic development intermediary, is being found in increasing numbers in rural and urban communities—for example, Arkansas, Vermont, Maine, Ohio, Michigan, Mississippi, Kentucky, and many places in Europe. Blending resources and strategies from the private and public sectors, these groups are successfully implementing multifaceted and coordinated responses to broadly based community and economic problems.

A high level of creativity and flexibility is one of the primary and critical assets that a nonprofit development group can bring to this effort. Neither governmental nor private sector entities have demonstrated significant amounts of flexibility, the ability to experiment and take risk, or nimbleness in the area of economic development.

RURAL COMMUNITY AND ECONOMIC DEVELOPMENT: TWO SIDES OF THE SAME COIN

Creating individual businesses and helping them grow is Southern's focus, not what is called community development. Therefore, the following comments on the relationship between these two activities are more exploratory and tentative than previous comments on the enterprise de-velopment process. The reason to explore this interaction, in spite of the uncertain ground that it represents, is that this may be an especially important subject for rural communities and rural economic development initiatives.

Rural versus urban development strategies

Underlying Southern's economic development strategy is a belief that rural economic development differs in critical ways from urban economic development. Experience across the country indicates that simply transplanting urban economic development strategies to rural areas is insufficient for success. The demographic, physical infrastructure, labor force, market access, public sector, and financial environments are significantly different and require a different response for economic development to be successful. While there are similarities between rural and urban economic development, the differences are critical and must be factored into the basic strategies and tactics of any program that hopes to be successful in reversing the decline of rural communities (see Table 1).

A rural community is more limited in community resources and leadership capacity because of low population levels. Unlike its more populous urban peers, a rural community has a much higher dependence on volunteers. To compound this difficulty, most government-funded economic development programs are administered from a regional or a statewide perspective, which makes it even more difficult for the rural commu-

TABLE 1
URBAN VERSUS RURAL DEVELOPMENT

Urban Economic Development	Rural Economic Development
Diversified economic base	Narrow, often single-sector economic base
Relatively easy access to market and sales	Difficult access to market and distribution channels
Many and different sources of capital	Few and narrow range of sources of financial capital
Wide range of employee and management skills	Limited employee and managerial skill range
Strong and diversified public investments	Limited, highly focused public sector investments
Broad public sector business resources	Very limited local government resources
Longer-term assistance less necessary	Deep and long-term assistance required
Substantial existing industrial capacity	Very limited existing industrial capacity
Many suppliers and peer businesses	Few suppliers and peer businesses
Many entrepreneurs to network with	Few entrepreneurs to network with

nity to gain access to public resources. The implication of this leadership shortage is that many programs that require local government participation—federal community development block grant funds, local business development activities, and so on—are often not utilized. By not participating in or having access to these development programs, the local community has more difficulty in moving beyond the limits of traditional private sector resources.

The rural economic development process

Figure 3 attempts to portray the development process and the interaction between community and economic development activities. The key points are that (1) economic development and community development are especially interdependent in rural communities; (2) community development occurs in stages, just as business development does; (3) community fundamentals such as education or quality of life, often absent in rural areas, attract competitive firms;

and (4) community development and economic development are processes that are constantly in motion.

The development process in any community can be described as an upward spiral that involves many elements. A successful process combines both economic and community development activities in a single cycle or flow composed of stages. It is not a finite project but an ongoing process. Success in rural communities requires the coordinated efforts of government, community leaders, nonprofit groups, entrepreneurs, and the private sector.

While the development process is essentially the same across communities, the emphasis and substance of each stage depends on the endowments and circumstances in each community. The creation of an active public-private partnership and the enterprises that result from the synergy between community and economic development are two of Southern's contributions to the development process.

The relevance of community development to economic development is

FIGURE 3
THE COMMUNITY AND ECONOMIC DEVELOPMENT PROCESS

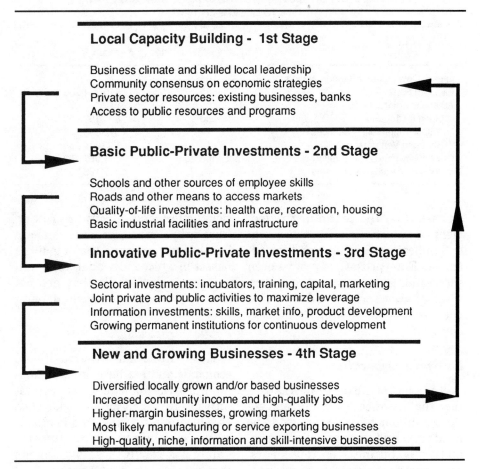

Local Capacity Building - 1st Stage

Business climate and skilled local leadership
Community consensus on economic strategies
Private sector resources: existing businesses, banks
Access to public resources and programs

Basic Public-Private Investments - 2nd Stage

Schools and other sources of employee skills
Roads and other means to access markets
Quality-of-life investments: health care, recreation, housing
Basic industrial facilities and infrastructure

Innovative Public-Private Investments - 3rd Stage

Sectoral investments: incubators, training, capital, marketing
Joint private and public activities to maximize leverage
Information investments: skills, market info, product development
Growing permanent institutions for continuous development

New and Growing Businesses - 4th Stage

Diversified locally grown and/or based businesses
Increased community income and high-quality jobs
Higher-margin businesses, growing markets
Most likely manufacturing or service exporting businesses
High-quality, niche, information and skill-intensive businesses

that the health of the overall community environment is crucial for a rural business attempting to compete on a national or international basis. Without sufficiently educated employees, a business cannot flourish. If there is no access to adequate infrastructure, then ever increasing environmental and safety regulations will hamper business success. If the quality of roads and other transportation facilities is poor, then having access to larger markets becomes increasingly difficult. While all of these factors and others are important for business growth in any setting, they seem to be especially powerful in a rural setting.

CONCLUSION

In its four years of operation, Southern has completed the basic design of its programs, invested over $19 million in 150 enterprises (see Table 2), hired and trained staff, and

TABLE 2

**PERFORMANCE OF SOUTHERN DEVELOPMENT BANCORPORATION,
1988 TO DECEMBER 1992**

	Number of Businesses Invested In	$ Amount Invested
Southern Development Bancorporation		
Elk Horn Bank	35	$10,701,252
Arkansas Enterprise Group		
Good Faith Fund	80	$ 192,000
AEG Manufacturing Services	24	$ 2,393,769
Southern Ventures, Inc.	14	$ 3,874,259
Opportunity Lands Corporation	not applicable	$ 1,967,452
Total loan and equity investments	153	$19,128,732

embarked on the continuing refinement of its activities. By these general indicators, Southern and the Arkansas Enterprise Group have been successful. There remains, however, a set of very serious and troubling questions, some of which are noted here.

Entrepreneurial culture

It is a fact of life in rural Arkansas that the historical economic and social conditions have not proved to be fertile ground for the growth of a population of business entrepreneurs. The business structure in rural America has tended to be large, monolithic, and commodity focused: agriculture, forestry, mining, and a whole range of branch plants focused on production only. The consequence of this has been to orient much of the population toward a paycheck rather than the self-determination of locating successful market niches. This is in contrast to many urban areas that enjoy cultural and economic histories rich with small business and entrepreneurial activities. This issue may place increased emphasis on educa-

tional efforts, on selective recruiting from urban areas, or on the role of incubators and incubating businesses in which individuals can learn entrepreneurial skills that are not heavily present in the environment.

Public infrastructure

Given the decline of the traditional economic and tax base of rural communities, the ability of these communities to invest in public goods such as education, housing, and health is being seriously eroded. Unfortunately, it is exactly these investments that provide a key part of the social context in which firms can grow to be nationally and internationally competitive. In light of the increased importance that successful firms place on employee education and skills, the quality of education is especially important. Health and housing are close behind. If they are in poor condition, many firms will not locate in the area or will be forced to move from it. That is a catch-22. The local tax base needs the strength of growing firms to help it improve its public infrastructure, but those firms will not locate or grow in rural America due to the existing poor quality of its infrastructure. A creative organization such as Southern can play a vital role, but it cannot replace the role of the public sector in creating a healthy context for business growth.

Scale and impact

Compared to many of its development peers in rural America, Southern has been quite successful, given its brief history. However comforting this is, it is misleading. The more relevant issue is, How well is Southern doing in achieving its goal of fundamentally affecting the rural Arkansas economy? The answer to this is more troubling. Of the 1300 small manufacturing firms in southern Arkansas, Southern has been able to affect only about 40 of those firms, or 3 percent. The question that remains is, At what level can Southern feel that it has actually affected the low- and middle-income residents of this region, the goal for which it was created?

Money versus information

Southern has been successful in supporting a wide range of businesses and enterprises. It is increasingly clear, however, that information and skill, not money, will make the company of the twenty-first century successful. Financial support is necessary, but very far from being the solution. The challenge that lies ahead of us is to find systemic and large-scale methods to distribute information and improve skills. Some work is being done by Southern and others in exploring strategies such as networks, incubators, and associations, but these efforts are young and their scale is still small.

I raise these concluding questions not to be negative about this effort or Southern's progress but rather to keep our sights high and to keep from ignoring the remaining and very fundamental unsolved questions of rural America. I am looking forward to reading in the 2003 issue of *The Annals* how these issues have been resolved!

ANNALS, *AAPSS*, **529**, September 1993

The Forest Service's Investment in Rural Communities

By RUTH McWILLIAMS, RONALD SARANICH,
and JENNIFER PRATT

ABSTRACT: This article presents a brief synopsis of the United States Department of Agriculture Forest Service's current rural community assistance efforts. The Forest Service, in close cooperation with rural America, has refocused its efforts from strict natural resource community production to sustainable investment in the future of rural communities. By working as a partner with rural America in identifying community needs and solutions, the Forest Service wants to help rural residents pursue and realize opportunities based upon available natural resources. The Forest Service mission explicitly recognizes the agency's commitment to help rural America address rural development concerns and remain a vital contributor to the nation's competitiveness.

Ruth McWilliams is Assistant Director for Planning, Development, and Marketing of the Cooperative Forestry Staff of the U.S. Department of Agriculture's Forestry Service. She received her master's degree from the University of Maryland and her bachelor's degree from Cornell University. During the last 15 years, she has held various positions in the Agriculture Department related to rural and economic development, dealing with rural electrification, transportation, and natural resources.

Ronald Saranich is a President Management Intern. He is doing a rotation assignment with Cooperative Forestry related to rural development.

Jennifer Pratt is a President Management Intern on a rotation assignment with Cooperative Forestry related to rural development.

SINCE 1897, when Gifford Pinchot became its first leader, the Forest Service has been guided by conservation precepts. Through the years, as new technologies have been developed and new insights have been gained, the application of these conservation principles has varied. The agency has not strayed from the basic concept embodied in its forest management approach, however, namely, that of "protecting environmental quality while also make available resources which people need."[1]

In line with its conservation leadership responsibilities, the Forest Service has broadened its focus to recognize an agencywide responsibility for a more coordinated, comprehensive approach to rural development in line with its mission of "caring for the land and serving people." The agency's approach to rural community assistance is not only community driven but also accomplished through public and private partnerships.

Today, the Forest Service no longer regards rural development as just a by-product of land management efforts but as a goal of the agency. This commitment to rural America is conveyed by the words of the agency's Chief, Dale Robertson: "Rural development has a high priority in the Forest Service and is a highly relevant part of our mission."[2]

BACKGROUND

Although rural development is not altogether a new responsibility of the Forest Service, its efforts in this area needed to be more focused on community needs and coordinated to a greater extent with other federal government efforts. In the 1980s, the Forest Service began to examine more expansive approaches to helping rural communities. The broader focus now stresses helping rural communities diversify their local economies through the wise use of all forest resources, not just timber.

In 1987, at the national conference "Community Stability in Forest-Based Economies," the concept of ensuring the economic well-being of communities through a continuous supply of timber was discussed, and other strategies were identified for assisting communities in economic transition. The Forest Service took an agencywide position that multiple-use management could legitimately support local efforts toward economic diversification and thereby assist the larger community while supporting its traditional industry partners.[3] It was an important initial step in redefining the agency's role and responsibilities to rural Americans.

In 1989, the Forest Service received Economic Diversification Studies money from Congress, the agency's first funds targeted directly at economic development in rural commu-

1. Lisa Cohn, "Searching for Harmony," *Forest Perspectives*, 2(3):7 (Autumn 1992).

2. Dale Robertson to Regional Foresters, Station Directors, Area Director, and Washington Office Staff, letter titled "Rural Development Strategic Plan," 28 June 1990.

3. George Leonard, "The Role of the Forest Service in Promoting Community Stability," in *Community Stability in Forest-Based Economies*, ed. Dennis C. LeMaster and John H. Beuter (Portland, OR: Timber Press, 1980), pp. 79-81.

nities. In the same year, the agency participated in a review of the rural development efforts of the U.S. Department of Agriculture (USDA) that was released by Secretary Yeutter in a report titled *A Hard Look at USDA's Rural Development Programs*. The report recommended that the department clarify its commitment to rural development, strengthen coordination of rural programs, improve its ability to implement those programs, and enhance the department's capacity for strategic action. Shortly thereafter, the Forest Service formed its own National Rural Development Task Force and Steering Committee to assess the agency's capability and develop a plan for guiding the agency with a unified approach to rural development.

In January of 1990, President Bush announced his Initiative for Rural Development, and in June, the Forest Service completed its national strategy for the 1990s, titled "Working Together for Rural America." A cornerstone of the President's initiative was the creation of State Rural Development Councils. The President's initiative offered guidelines and a focus for rural development efforts across the federal system. The Forest Service responded to the challenges set forth through the initiative and positioned itself to more effectively assist rural communities.

Also late in 1990, a new farm bill was passed. In this bill, the Rural Development Title of the Food, Agriculture, Conservation, and Trade Act of 1990, the Forest Service is authorized in Subtitle G to assist economically disadvantaged rural communities located in or near national for-

ests to diversify their local economic base. This was a particularly significant step in the Forest Service's evolving position and helped to further legitimize the agency's role in rural development, which was recognized by the USDA in its annual rural development report titled *Putting the Pieces Together*.[4]

Most recently, the President's Council on Rural America released its report, *Revitalizing Rural America Through Collaboration*. By emphasizing locally driven development and the need for flexibility in federal programs, this report further supports the direction being taken by the Forest Service in its refocusing efforts.

THE FOREST SERVICE'S NATIONAL STRATEGY

Chief Dale Robertson established the Forest Service's National Rural Development Task Force in 1989 with two main objectives in mind. The first, to review the agency's rural development efforts, was to be achieved through the second, the development of a national strategy. Completion of the strategy[5] confirmed the agency's position as an active rural development participant with significant resources—human, technical, financial, and natural—to help communities. Representing all levels of the Forest Service and all its deputy areas—namely, the National

4. Edward Madigan and Roland Vautour, *Putting the Pieces Together: Annual Rural Development Strategy Report*, Department of Agriculture, Aug. 1991.

5. U.S., Department of Agriculture, Forest Service, *A Strategic Plan for the 90's: Working Together for Rural America*, June 1990.

Forest System, State and Private Forestry, Research, International Forestry, Administration, and Programs and Legislation—the task force developed the strategy to help in clarifying the agency's commitment and positioning itself for the future. The strategy contains a revised rural development policy for the Forest Service and six implementation goals. The policy states:

The Forest Service will provide leadership in working with rural people and communities on developing natural resource-based opportunities and enterprises that contribute to the economic and social vitality of rural communities. The Forest Service can make lasting improvements in rural America by helping people solve their local problems in ways that enhance the quality of the environment in accordance with our existing authorities.[6]

Through its six goals, the task force refined the agency's position on rural development and offered guidance on using its available resources. The goals are as follows:

— to communicate to both Forest Service employees and the public that rural development is a key part of the Forest Service's mission;
— to include rural development in agency resource decisions to achieve long-term economic development and improved quality of life;
— to participate actively in community rural development efforts;
— to understand and integrate the needs of diverse communities;

— to strengthen participation in cooperative USDA efforts at the local level; and
— to provide timely and current research and resource information.

Together, the policy and goals constitute a unified plan for the Forest Service to help rural America. Development of the strategy demonstrates that the Forest Service has listened to rural America's concerns and has accepted the responsibility to work cooperatively and proactively with it in addressing broad rural needs and concerns. Working in partnership with other public and private organizations is central to the agency's strategy. Through such relationships, the Forest Service expects to more effectively help communities to help themselves.

The Forest Service has consistently emphasized working closely with rural people and communities as an integral component of its national rural development strategy. Rural development accomplishments are achieved through both internal and external partnerships. As stated by Chief Robertson, the Forest Service is "so interwoven with local communities and economies that we need to share part of the responsibility for the well-being of those communities."[7]

Today, the emphasis is on helping the whole community, not merely the private sector or a subset of it. Recognizing that assistance to any one aspect of rural life is insufficient, the Forest Service is taking the approach

6. Ibid., p. 5.

7. Dale Robertson, keynote speech delivered at the Annual Western Regional Meeting of the National Association of Counties, Placer County, CA, 7 May 1992, p. 2.

that neither individual programs nor short-run solutions will help rural communities realize sustainable, balanced development. The agency strongly believes that unless communities themselves are intimately involved, in control, and in it for the long-run, rural development efforts will be neither successful nor sustainable. Therefore, locally driven development has become a guiding principle of the Forest Service's approach to rural development.

The national rural development strategy is a significant step in helping the Forest Service become a full partner in rural development efforts, challenging the agency's traditional way of doing business. The Forest Service has risen to the challenge and is moving ahead on its implementation in view of its mission and the many opportunities that exist to help rural America.

The Forest and Rangeland Renewable Resources Planning Act (RPA) of 1974 also provides the agency with an opportunity to "integrate social needs and resource management programs with an eye to the future."[8] As stated in the agency's *Forest Service Program for Forest and Rangeland Resources: A Long-Term Strategic Plan*, the RPA Program "is built on three components: roles for Forest Service programs (that is, the agency's philosophical stance based on its legal mandates and experience), consideration of contemporary resource issues, and a long-term program strategy."[9]

8. U.S., Department of Agriculture, Forest Service, *The Forest Service Program for Forest and Rangeland Resources: A Long-Term Strategic Plan: Summary, Recommended 1990 RPA Program*, May 1990, p. S-1.

9. Ibid., p. S-7.

The RPA requires the Forest Service to prepare a recommended program for agency activities every five years. The 1990 RPA Program enumerated nine critical roles for the Forest Service. One of the roles was titled "Contributions to Rural Development." For 1995, the Forest Service is pursuing a broader perspective regarding agency mission. For instance, rural development issues are an integral part of community assistance and shared responsibilities.

OPPORTUNITIES

The Forest Service anticipates continued commitment to rural community assistance over the years. As a result of the departmental and agency efforts, the Forest Service is poised to respond to the challenge of increasing its assistance to rural America. The agency, using research done by Margaret Thomas for the U.S. Department of Commerce's Economic Development Administration titled "Recouple—Natural Resource Strategies for Rural Economic Development," recognizes that many opportunities exist to assist rural America. The following community-based opportunities identified by Thomas help the Forest Service address the diverse, pressing needs facing rural America and link agency resources to community needs:

— organizing diverse community interests for resource-based economic development and conservation by diverse community interests—for example, land owners, government officials, business leaders, and others— to develop common visions and cooperative ventures; catalyzing the private sector to satisfy rural needs on their own volition; and creating institutions to fill existing gaps;

— fostering value-added processing in order to produce good incomes through, for instance, the conversion of existing primary processing plants into secondary manufacturers while developing new facilities;

— emphasizing alternative goods and services from the forest by, for instance, inventorying, planning, and managing for special forest products as well as services related to cultural, historical, and amenity resources;

— enhancing productivity of existing services and manufacturing firms through, for instance, use of waste products and increases in the efficiency of extant operations;

— strengthening the marketing of commodity and amenity resources by, for instance, working with communities to promote and collectively market products and areas of interest, and stimulating new market sectors, both domestic and international;

— promoting technology transfer while improving and increasing information by, for instance, conducting research and applying existing and new technologies to solve specific problems; and

— improving local human capital through, for instance, employee training and vocational efforts.[10]

Thomas observes,

The selection of forest resource strategies for rural economic development will depend on many factors. Consideration must be given to (a) the type, quantity, quality, and ownership of the forest resource, (b) the market potential for more or improved productivity in primary or secondary processing in the area, and (c) the market potential for alternative goods and services from the forest resource. But equally important, consideration must be given to the history of regional cooperation for economic development in the area. New and creative ways to link the natural resource-based entrepreneurs to more traditional economic development efforts should be near or at the top of any action plan for forest resource specialists.[11]

In the national strategy in *Working Together for Rural America*, the Forest Service identified four resources —human, natural, technical, and financial—available to help rural communities achieve their development goals. Even though the Forest Service manages a natural resource base, it is interested in broad development strategies that encompass amenity as well as commodity-based resource uses. Human resources are people from all areas and levels of the organization who collectively provide a wide range of skills and knowledge. Forest Service employees can provide an interpersonal link between communities and rural development programs. Natural resources such as rivers, wildlife, timber, scenery, and range are marketable, and associated sites and facilities managed by the Forest Service and others may be

10. Margaret G. Thomas, *Forest Resource Strategies for Rural Development* (Washington, DC: Department of Agriculture, Oct. 1990), pp. 2-6.

11. Ibid., p. 7.

available for community use. Technical resources include diverse areas of expertise, computer capabilities, feasibility studies, and planning processes. Though limited, the financial resources of the agency consist of grants, cooperative agreements, and cost-sharing partnerships.

Currently, the agency's rural community assistance efforts emphasize opportunities for both targeting goods and services from forest resources and strengthening marketing. A real need exists for the Forest Service to invest its resources in helping to organize community actions, improve local capital, and target value-added processing through an expanded agencywide effort.

OVERVIEW OF RURAL COMMUNITY ASSISTANCE EFFORTS

The Forest Service's response to the events that have been discussed included bringing already existing programs together with new ones under the umbrella of the Rural Community Assistance program. These efforts now consist of the following core funding programs: Economic Recovery, Rural Development, and Economic Diversification Studies. Leadership for coordinating the overall Forest Service effort and administering core programs is the responsibility of the agency's State and Private Forestry branch.

The agency's rural community assistance programs are an integral part of the comprehensive federal effort in terms of both their orientation and the means by which they are delivered. Because of the Forest

Service's decentralized organizational structure, funding decisions are made as close to the local level as possible. Regional Foresters and the Area Director are given the flexibility to make funding decisions based on their own understanding of community and regional priorities and in consultation with others, such as state and local agencies and organizations.

Although the Forest Service's Washington Office does not make decisions on how to disburse rural development program monies to states or communities, it does initially allocate program funds to each Forest Service region. In preparation for fiscal year 1993, fund allocation processes were developed that included need-based factors.

Economic Recovery Program

The Economic Recovery Program is mandated by the Food, Agriculture, Conservation, and Trade Act under the Rural Development Title (Title XXIII). The Forest Service's principal authority is enumerated in Subtitle G (Rural Revitalization Through Forestry), chapter 2 (National Forest-Dependent Rural Communities Economic Diversification Act of 1990). The purposes of this law are

(1) to provide assistance to rural communities that are located in or near national forests and that are economically dependent upon forest resources or are likely to be economically disadvantaged by Federal or private sector land management practices;

(2) to aid in diversifying such communities' economic bases; and

(3) to improve the economic, social, and environmental well-being of rural America.[12]

Assistance is provided to help communities organize local action teams, develop local action plans, and implement projects contained in them.

For fiscal year 1993, Economic Recovery funds were allocated based upon measures of timber dependency and community need per congressional language and Forest Service responsibilities. These funds are intended to assist communities dependent on national forests where the timber supply is declining and the communities are "likely to be economically disadvantaged by Federal or private sector land management practices."[13] By law, eligible communities are located in counties with total earnings of 15 percent or greater of the total primary and secondary labor and proprietary income resulting from natural resource industries and within 100 miles of a national forest. Economic Recovery funds in fiscal year 1993 amounted to $5 million.

Fiscal year 1992 was the first year that the Forest Service received and distributed Economic Recovery funds. With these funds, the Forest Service field units organized or certified 171 local action teams, resulting in the certifying of 127 local action plans. A total of 185 counties or communities obtained financial assistance for 102 individual activities or projects. Examples of funded projects included restoration of an abandoned, environmentally damaging

22-acre landfill site along the Bitterroot River in Latah County, northern Idaho; inventory of the community assets of Fremont County, Wyoming, which led to the establishment of the Bighorn Sheep Center in DuBois; and identification of community leaders in southern Mississippi to provide them with leadership training.

Rural Development Program

The Cooperative Forestry Assistance Act of 1978 (Public Law 95-313) grants authority to the Forest Service for a variety of activities related to rural development and associated with forest lands and resources. The agency's Rural Development Program, which originally was an initiative funded by Congress, is now an ongoing effort of the Forest Service to help strengthen rural communities and diversify and expand local economies, especially in communities where the economy is tied directly to natural resources. The program works with rural communities that have more persistent or long-term problems by helping them develop local, regional, or statewide strategies based on available natural resources and carry out activities to strengthen local economies. Communities need not be dependent on federal lands or natural resources to be eligible for this assistance.

Rural Development funds for fiscal year 1993 were allocated based on two criteria. The first addressed those areas where the Forest Service maintains a vested interest. The agency has a bona fide interest in those lands it manages—the national

---

12. Food, Agriculture, Conservation, and Trade Act, Subtitle G, chap. 2, § 2373.b (1990).
13. Ibid., § 2373.b.1.

forests and grasslands—but also has an interest in other forest lands owned and managed by private individuals and companies, states, and Native Americans. The second criterion used to allocate Rural Development funds involved a long-term measure of need. Rural Development funding for fiscal year 1993 totaled $4 million and was allocated nationwide.

In fiscal year 1992, all Rural Development funds were designated by Congress for the Northeast and Midwest and were administered by the Forest Service's Northeastern Area State and Private Forestry staff. With these funds, over 100 projects were conducted by participating state forestry organizations through partnerships with a variety of cooperators. Projects included state demonstration programs, special-emphasis projects, training, business development, and marketing assistance.

Economic Diversification Studies

The Economic Diversification Studies program accomplishes a specific purpose: to have feasibility studies conducted in order to help rural communities dependent upon a single forest resource find ways to diversify their local economies through any means. The studies are funded through cost sharing. The criteria developed and used by the Forest Service to select studies for funding are economic dependency and diversity; economic need; practicality and feasibility; costs and benefits; and ability to share funds.

In fiscal year 1992, 137 proposals were submitted. Of these, 13 were chosen for funding, which totaled $543,000. Examples of the funded projects include a study of the potential impacts of a hardwood sawmill and other value-added hardwood manufacturing on the Hoopa Valley Indian Reservation in Humboldt County, California; a study to identify alternatives—the establishment of new enterprises while sustaining the current forest-related business and industry—that could diversify the economy of Liberty County, Florida, and thereby improve the quality of life for the residents; and development of a comprehensive strategy for the commercial utilization of timber in the beetle-infested forests of the Kenai Peninsula in Alaska. Fiscal year 1993 funds disbursed also totaled about $500,000, and, as in previous years, final decisions regarding funding were made by the Forest Service's Washington Office.

RELATED RESOURCE PROGRAMS

The full extent of the agency's rural development efforts are found not only in the core rural community assistance programs but also in other Forest Service programs administered by other branches of the service, such as the National Forest System and Administration. Additional endeavors, such as those related to recreation, cultural and historical resources, wildlife, fisheries, range, minerals, geology, and human resources, provide both direct and indirect support for sustainable rural development efforts. These efforts provide and improve opportunities for people to use natural resources. Although sustainable rural development is not a primary goal of these programs, they contribute significantly to agency efforts through specific resource activities carried out in conjunction with a variety of partners at the national, state, and local levels.

Examples of National Forest System programs that assist in rural development include the National Recreation Strategy; Eyes on Wildlife; Windows on the Past; and the Job Corps. These and other initiatives and programs are in effect at 156 national forests in 43 states. The agency's employees and their technical expertise also contribute to rural America in a variety of ways.

Examples of contributions resulting from the National Forest System include a fish habitat in the Chugach National Forest, Alaska, that is being developed near Begich, Boggs Visitor Center at Portage Glacier. Streams and ponds are being created, and soil and vegetation are being established to add nutrients for habitat enhancement. The project combines improvement of a high-use recreation area with a major tourist attraction, Portage Glacier.

Another example involves the national forests as a source of building stone. The national forests are touting their building stone as a commodity to improve rural economies, as evidenced by the partnership between the Minnesota Department of Natural Resources (Mineral Division) and the Superior National Forest. Three quarries on the Superior are

currently undergoing development, and the potential for a granite fabrication plant as a value-added economic activity is being explored. The project is an example of Forest Service mineral activities providing a new source of manufacturing for rural communities.

Through Human Resource Programs, the Forest Service has a special opportunity to help rural communities. The agency's Human Resource Programs are being refocused to strengthen rural economies by providing human and natural resource benefits while administering programs in work, training, and education for the young, the unemployed, the underemployed, the elderly, and others with special needs living in rural areas. In Idaho, for instance, the Forest Service is working with several state and local agencies, a state college, and community organizations in the Clearwater Valley to attract retirees for tourism development and relocation purposes. A workshop has been held, and a workbook is available for use by interested parties.

The agency's Human Resource Programs operate from 18 Job Corps Civilian Conservation Centers in 12 states under an interagency agreement with the U.S. Department of Labor. The centers provide not only education and vocational skills training for young people but also accomplish natural resource and local community work valued at $20 million annually. The centers tend to be located in rural areas and therefore provide an opportunity to better align agency investment in human capital with the development needs of rural communities.

The agency's Forest Products Conservation and Recycling program is administered by State and Private Forestry. The program supports the network of technical partners needed to deliver assistance concerning high-value-added processing; innovation through special, nontimber forest products; enhancement of productivity related to existing manufacturing and waste utilization; marketing forest products; and transfer of technology. These programs are coordinated through state forestry organizations and involve a range of activities including pilot projects, business plan development, capital investment, information assessment, and direct technical and marketing assistance.

Overall, Forest Products Conservation and Recycling encourages and facilitates the wise, more complete use of the forest resource to enhance economic development and stimulate better stewardship of the forest. Assistance is provided to increase economic opportunities through market and community development; to reduce the environmental impact of harvesting and processing forest products; to improve the use of wood wastes and residues; and to extend the useful life of forest products.

RESEARCH PROGRAMS

The Forest Service's national research strategy, Enhancing Rural America, complements the national rural development strategy by providing the scientific and technological support for the Forest Service to carry out [its] policy. The focus of this effort is rural communities, and as such the research will be conducted with community and social vitality in mind and within the context of the value system of rural communities.[14]

As a result, the Forest Service is addressing economic, quality-of-life, and resource management issues central to strengthening rural America. *Enhancing Rural America* states:

Among land-managing agencies, the Forest Service is in a unique position to conduct and lead this type of research. The geographic breadth of the organization, the ability to conduct research across the entire spectrum of natural resources, relationships with National Forest System and State and Private Forestry, long-term program continuity, and existing partnerships all contribute to the capabilities of Forest Service Research in this area.[15]

Key research opportunities include the following:

— understanding rural communities and the intrinsic value that people place on a rural way of life to help ensure that the overall Forest Service effort is on target and meets the needs of rural communities; an example is the identification of culturally diverse life-styles and values in rural America in order to better understand how quality of life is defined and enhanced;
— diversifying and enhancing the economies of natural-resource-dependent communities by providing scientific technological

14. U.S., Department of Agriculture, Forest Service, *Enhancing Rural America National Research Program*, 19 June 1991, p. 3.
15. Ibid., p. 4.

support, such as developing value-added structural products from underutilized tree species, examining economic impacts of tourism, and developing recycled products from waste materials;

— understanding the dynamics of resource, economic, social, and technological change in rural America by, for example, improving planning and evaluation methods related to change; and

— identifying institutional barriers affecting rural communities and limiting rural development efforts; an example is the improvement in methods for incorporating greater public participation into natural resource decision making.

A SOLID COMMITMENT

The Forest Service is dedicating itself to successfully addressing the needs of rural communities through the development of new approaches and programs. Its commitment extends throughout the organization. Rural community assistance programs, in conjunction with agency programs concerning areas such as recreation, wildlife, range, minerals, research, and human resources, provide both direct and indirect support for sustainable rural development efforts.

The opportunities for continued, active involvement in rural community assistance are endless. The Forest Service has taken significant steps to organize its efforts and is implementing a variety of rural development activities in partnership with others. In the past two years, with minimal funding, the Forest Service has made great strides toward meeting its rural community assistance goals. It has fostered greater understanding, both within its ranks and among rural communities, of the role the agency can play.

The Forest Service fully expects to continue as an active partner in the rural development process and sees an enhancement of its role in the future. To this end, the agency is currently undertaking a mid-course evaluation of its efforts and intends to conduct a more formal evaluation at the end of the decade. The rural development process is a complex, dynamic, challenging one, and the Forest Service is committed to it for the long run. Most important, the Forest Service is committed to the rural communities it serves.

ANNALS, *AAPSS*, **529**, September 1993

Rural Development Systems:
Lessons from Europe and Northern Michigan

By H. RICHARD ANDERSON

ABSTRACT: Fragmented economic development efforts that are not coordinated either strategically or operationally have limited impact. Across rural America, individual economic development agencies have lacked the capacity to use their complementary strengths to shape a vision of how to develop a region. Often, these efforts do not relate to the real customers of rural development, the existing firms that create most new jobs. The projects that are implemented are of short term and limited scale, and the real systems that influence the direction of an economy are ignored. Many European countries seek to improve the competitiveness of a region through accelerating the modernization of firms. It takes a systems approach to enhance the private initiative of firms by improving the relationship between firms and the supporting relationships of institutions involved in training, technology, and finance. Lessons can be drawn from this approach, and a new rural model for taking a systems approach to improving the competitiveness of firms in northern Michigan is discussed.

H. Richard Anderson, AICP, is a practitioner of rural economic development and president of Northern Economic Initiatives Corporation (NEICorp), located in Marquette, Michigan. In 1985, he was selected to direct the Northern Economic Initiatives Center, NEICorp's predecessor. Graduating from Michigan State University with a bachelor of science degree in urban planning, he earned a master's degree in administrative services/public administration from Northern Michigan University. In 1992, he was part of a Michigan delegation organized to evaluate European vocational education and economic development programs.

R URAL policy planners and the practitioners of rural development have taken different paths when confronted with the challenge of relieving the traditional credit, capital, training, and development obstacles encountered by firms in remote disadvantaged areas. Policymakers have the luxury of looking at the whole, and practitioners tackle single themes. The challenge to both worlds is the balance between the complex systems and forces at work shaping economic conditions and the lack of resources to alter these forces. Policymakers and practitioners are confronted with these questions: How does one go about transforming a region that historically supplied commodity-based resources—agricultural products, wood, copper, gold, and iron ore—to outside markets exporting the value-added jobs that typically accompany processing and manufacturing? How can employment be sustained past the cycles that characterize a boom-and-bust economy? How is confidence inspired in enterprises wishing to reach distant markets, compete in trade, secure adequate financing, and create employment for the benefit of the community? Can rural firms adjust to international competition through product differentiation and quality, rather than competing by means of a low-wage strategy? In what ways can the behavior of public and private institutions having enormous capacity be influenced to contribute to this transformation? Finally, can this economic transformation respect the rural character of a region and the quality of its natural environment?

Many of the leading practitioners of rural economic development and the industrial modernization movement have looked to Europe for the answers to these questions.[1] While lessons can be drawn from Europe, the solutions are at home. Rural communities must unleash their own talents if they want to sustain economic growth and the vitality of rural life. Business owners and educators must work together to invest in the creative capacity of the citizenry in order for a community to assert its identity and direction in the face of external economic forces. This is particularly true for rural areas formerly dominated by commodity and natural resource extraction industries and dependent on their boom-and-bust business cycles. In rural areas, this historical pattern has been further exacerbated by the retrenchment of resource extraction industries, the restructuring of agricultural economies, and the pressure to move low-wage manufacturing to lower-cost regions. Communities have been buffeted by external forces over which they have had little control. By contrast, an indigenous economic strategy that relies on the innovative abilities of citizens is a superior means of achieving economic stability and an improved quality of life.

Domestic regional and local development programs organized in geographic districts and separated from

1. See Stuart A. Rosenfeld, "Technology Innovation and Rural Development: Lessons from Italy and Denmark," *A Report of the Rural Economic Policy Program Aspen Institute for Humanistic Studies* (Washington, DC: Aspen Institute for Humanistic Studies, 1991).

industry associations, educational units, and financial institutions have distinct drawbacks in inspiring indigenous economic growth when compared to the European system of governmental partnership between the public and private sectors. This article provides one practitioner's view of the American and European approaches and offers a model for taking a long-term comprehensive and systems approach to local economic development in northern Michigan.

DEMONSTRATIONS AND PILOT PROJECTS: THE DOMESTIC DILEMMA

In the past twenty years, this country has relied on limited pilot projects contributing much-needed experience but wholly inadequate in confronting what amounts to a systems problem. Rural programs have been inadequate because they, by and large, work outside the economic fabric and are disenfranchised from mainstream institutions that influence an economy. Additionally, rural development programs are topical in nature and are organized within economically artificial boundaries.

Economic development in rural areas has been championed by county economic development corporations, community development corporations, private industry councils, community action agencies, and regional planning districts. With some notable exceptions, these nonprofit intermediaries intervene with programs tending to concentrate in one or two areas from a menu of traditional approaches including direct financing, technical assistance, training, and housing. These services are provided directly because they are not offered by the mainstream institutions of banks, consulting firms, educational institutions, industry associations, and developers.

The transactions of an intermediary relative to the size of the economy it is attempting to influence are minimal. This leaves program accomplishments to be defended as demonstrations. The hope seems to be centered on finding successful models demonstrating impact and success to federal and state governments that may formalize the program approach through grant support. Scale is dependent upon the scope of direct services and the grants to support the activity.

What is worse, the remedy for what ails a rural economy has been topical in nature. Interventions from industrial park development and recruitment to micro-enterprise support and peer-group circle lending programs tend to happen in isolation, never penetrating the underlying influences of a dysfunctional economy. Even the latest fad of industrial collaboration—networks of small and medium-sized firms encouraged to mimic the economies of scale of large firms—in some instances has become the principal intervention rather than part of a multistrategy triage.

While industrial collaboration and networking are features of highly flexible and innovative economies, they have been seized upon by some American policymakers and economic development professionals as the physical embodiment of a vibrant economy rather than as part of an integrated system incorporating other factors such as skill development, finance, and technology. American industry made the same error in the 1970s by adopting quality circles as the way to become a total quality organization. It was convenient to do so, as quality circles could be seen and rather easily duplicated. But establishing a quality circle in an otherwise hierarchical organization where the other elements reinforcing quality are missing is no more able to transform an organization than industrial networks can transform a region. Program efforts in the United States seem to miss this point.

Programs to promote local economic development are organized within political boundaries, essentially economically meaningless borders. Additionally, rural programs funded and organized around political boundaries at the county or regional level encourage turf battles. Bordering economic development agencies have literally fought over poverty as they try to position themselves as the single agency responsible for development.

Organizing rural economic development around local units of government results in faulty feedback to program staff. The customer becomes the local government rather than the private enterprises the programs were established to serve. Importance is placed on new business when rural jobs are created from existing enterprise. Change has to be physically perceptible and happen in the right area. Local firms lose interest in contributing money to these efforts over time because they are not the direct beneficiaries. Finally, budgets are small—and they fluctuate—leaving small-scale single-issue programs to work on short-term priorities.

Enthusiasm for declaring a boundary is tempered by the short time horizon of expectations held by the stakeholders of local programs. Political jurisdictions that fund local programs expect quick results. Staff view their alternatives in this political and time-sensitive context; priorities become confused. While practitioners compare the process of local economic development to watching a tree grow, their boards and directors want transplants, regardless of the season, location, and the ability of the ecology to support that type of growth.

The result is that rural development typically turns to recruitment by offering incentives to new employers. New policies have been proposed that lower the business burden in enterprise zones by packaging tax breaks, fewer environmental regulations, subsidized infrastructure, and real estate. These approaches may change the rural landscape by attracting investment that is motivated by a low cost advantage, but they do not address the arguably more important influences that shape the business environment, including work force skills, finance, technical assistance, and trading and supplying relationships.

A public policy environment puts the focus on competing for firms rather than making firms more competitive.[2] A shift in domestic policy has begun, but comprehensive models have yet to emerge.

2. Ibid., p. 34.

BEYOND DEMONSTRATION:
THE EUROPEAN SYSTEMS
APPROACH TO DEVELOPMENT

In visiting peer programs in Europe, one gets the sense that the playing field is entirely different from that in the United States. The historical context of these programs is deeply seated in the early stages of the Industrial Age. How many American practitioners of economic development start their program descriptions with Napoleon's view of commerce, industry, and government? Yet the precursors of present-day industrial modernization programs in Europe have their roots in French *chambres de commerce*, established during the French occupation of the Rhineland in the Napoleonic era to advise governmental bodies on promoting trades and crafts. Napoleon sought to enhance the competitiveness of industry by "causing the sciences to cooperate in its improvement. . . . Indeed, under his reign, chemistry and mechanics were applied to the improvement of all branches of industry."[3] The focus shifted from providing service to firms by government-led programs to firm-governed, market-motivated programs. After Napoleon's defeat, chambers of commerce were created through Prussian law as self-administering organizations. They were responsible for their own elections and finances; the chambers also protected and educated their members and advised the government.

Today's European-style chambers of commerce bear little resemblance

3. Prince Napoleon-Louis Bonaparte, *Napoleonic Ideas* (New York: Harper & Row, 1967), p. 62.

to their American counterparts. In Europe, quasi-governmental associations of self-managed industrial and trade groups seek to enhance competitiveness among members through direct services on such matters as work force training, access to finance, and new technology. Sector organizations consisting of specific kinds of industry collaborate with government in a way that has been criticized as a conflict of interest in the United States. Indeed, the word "lobbying" seems a foreign notion to European sector leaders seeking to advance the common interest with government in accelerating competitiveness. The emphasis is not so much on the reduction of the tax and regulatory burden of government but on how government resources can accelerate modernization through intervention and partnerships.

Industrial associations and chambers in the United States seem more interested in providing help to their members indirectly by lobbying state and federal government to lower governmental regulations and costs and directly through cost-saving self-insurance funds and other joint-risk management activities.

Moreover, accelerating economic development in Europe almost always takes a holistic approach. The notion of subsidiarity—the articulation of program approaches at the European Community, member nation, or subnational levels—asserts a kind of federalism across Europe by assuming that coordination of roles and program intervention are offered by the lowest and most appropriate level of government. For example, at the European Community level, the

Commission of the European Community bases its whole structural adjustment plan on the necessity of having environment, quality-of-life, education, and economic development policies in place. The European Community then utilizes the catalysts of internal market and commercial policies to focus on developing their key accelerators of technology innovation, research and development, education, and training to focus on developing small to medium-sized businesses by providing required business services.[4]

The member nations of the European Community have distinct public-private partnerships to promote economic competitiveness. These partnerships typically find legitimacy through legislation and are governed in part by their customers.

For example, at the national level, the Netherlands Re-Structuring Company (NEHEM) is a systemswide intermediary seeking to "strengthen the competitiveness of corporate life in the Netherlands." NEHEM does this by involving the ministries of government in the selection of a board of directors that oversees staff, consultants, and European Community resources who prioritize industrial-sector projects. Customers of NEHEM include financial institutions, trade unions, individual firms, sector employer organizations, and special ministries. These sector projects involve customers in continuous improvement of quality, physical dis-

4. Letter to the author from James Malnight of the Malnight Company, Grand Haven, MI, 20 July 1992. See Commission of the European Communities, *Industrial Policy in an Open and Competitive Environment: Guidelines for a Community Approach*, 16 Nov. 1990.

tribution and logistics, infrastructure, environment, management attitude, strategic alliances, human resources management, and education. (See Figure 1).

From a policy standpoint, the programs of the European Community —along with national programs like NEHEM—improve firms' chances to succeed by increasing product quality, market position, and firm efficiency, as well as investing in human capital. When institutions like NEHEM work responsibly with large numbers of firms, private initiative is stimulated; also, entrepreneurs take risks to pursue business ideas or expand their business operations. If there is one lesson from Europe, it is that the competitiveness of firms can be accelerated within institutional frameworks that have permanence and scale and that work in the economic fabric.

A SYSTEMS APPROACH
FOR THE DEVELOPMENT
OF NORTHERN MICHIGAN

In today's global economy, natural resources are no longer the major source of rural competitive advantage. Regions such as Michigan's Upper Peninsula, blessed with an abundance of raw materials, can no longer rely on these commodities as their primary sources of wealth creation.

Supplementing natural resource production with human resource development may be the only way to sustain rural economies. To do this is far more complicated than mining ore or harvesting crops and trees. Approaches must be synchronized at the macro and micro levels of the economy.

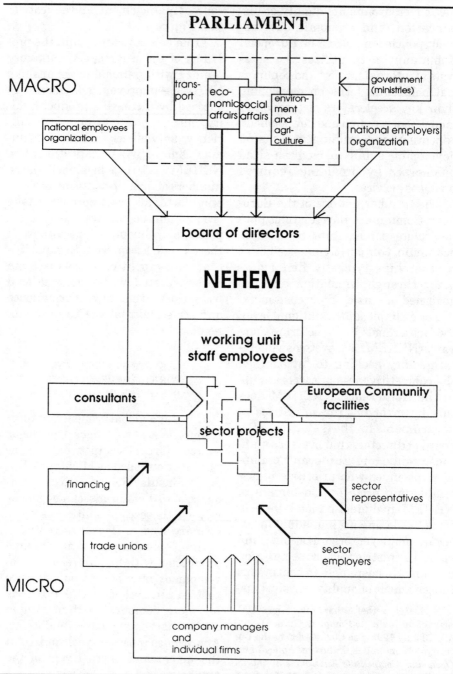

FIGURE 1
PUBLIC-PRIVATE PARTNERSHIP FOR
DEVELOPMENT IN THE NETHERLANDS: THE CASE OF NEHEM

A new initiative in northern Michigan borrows concepts pioneered in Europe by building the existing business support infrastructure. It stimulates new forms of enabling behavior among firms and supporting institutions that dominate education and finance.

Michigan's Upper Peninsula is defined by Lake Superior to the north and Lake Michigan to the south. It shares a border with Canada and is connected to Michigan's Lower Peninsula by the Mackinac Bridge. The Upper Peninsula has a population of just over 300,000 people, or 19 people per square mile.

Geographic isolation and a boom-and-bust economy have helped create a region with uneven growth, a labor force participation rate 15 percent lower than the state rate, and unemployment rates averaging 20 percent higher than the state average over the past two decades. Between 1979 and 1989, personal income in the Upper Peninsula counties lagged rural, metro, and overall income levels as measured against both state and federal figures. According to 1988 data, the Upper Peninsula derived a higher percentage of personal income through transfer payments than any other region of Michigan or the state as a whole.[5]

Through each boom-and-bust cycle, the wage and salary employment of mining and government expanded and contracted. This led the region into good times—and also took it into near depression. These cycles have tempered entrepreneurial diversification and may have shaped and influenced the behavior of institutions having a great impact on the economy: government, lenders, and educational institutions.

State and local government looked to major projects and industrial recruitment to provide employment for the region. At best, these provided mixed results and required massive subsidy. Lenders were seen as cautious, bypassing opportunities in countercyclical industries. Educational institutions were seen as training residents who would find jobs elsewhere.

Could the reactive behavior of these mainstream institutions unwittingly aggravate cyclical trends? This question focused attention on how an intermediary could support private initiative and realign mainstream institutions to stimulate diversity and sustain employment.

The catalyst for the project to study this question became two unlikely partners—Northern Michigan University, a rural university, and Shorebank Corporation, a development bank based on the South Side of Chicago.[6] Yet each partner offers unique strengths. Northern Michigan University's mission of education and programs in business assistance combine with Shorebank's experience in development, finance, and entrepreneurial support.

---

5. Roger J. Vaughan, "Framework for Economic Development in Michigan's Upper Peninsula" (Report prepared for Michigan Department of Commerce, 1989), pp. 1-13.

6. For a description of another rural development program affiliated with Shorebank, see Brian Kelley, "Rebuilding Rural America: The Southern Development Bancorporation," this issue of *The Annals* of the American Academy of Political and Social Science.

The project's programs include the North Coast Business and Industrial Development Corporation (BIDCO), a for-profit subsidiary of Shorebank Corporation that offers subordinated and long-term seed debt and equity; a Loan Production Office (LPO) of the South Shore Bank (a bank of the Shorebank Corporation) offering conventional bank debt and Small Business Administration-guaranteed loans; and Northern Economic Initiatives Corporation (NEICorp), a nonprofit company that offers business development assistance, manufacturing networking, micro-enterprise loans, and an innovative design institute.

The model that emerged is founded on two simple principles. The first is that the performance of a firm is tied to the individual performance of management and management's ability to rationalize and access capital, technology, market opportunities, and work force skills. Second, the performance of a region is tied to the collective performance of firms and their ability to accelerate innovation, competitiveness, and exporting ability. It seems that the latter three characteristics happen more often when firms cooperate with each other and find institutions that support their financial, work force, and technical needs.

Figure 2 depicts the relationships between the various parts of the northern Michigan model.

The objectives of the model are to

— create an integrated credit and technical-assistance institution to create jobs that would not otherwise exist;
— reorient the focus and behavior of the Upper Peninsula econ-

omy toward diversification and value-adding manufacturing;
— shift capital allocation within the private sector, leveraging needed private resources and changing long-term lending behavior;
— improve firm net worth, capacity to innovate, cost-effectiveness, and competitiveness;
— feature a customer-focused evaluation component that monitors activities, retargets programs, improves program delivery, and generates data on development outputs;
— generate a measurable and positive impact on the Upper Peninsula economy; and
— develop a model that, if successful, can be replicated substantially in other rural areas.

To reach these objectives, the challenge for the partners rests on converging institutional commitment of technical assistance, capital, and work force skills development.

Technical assistance

NEICorp has set out to diversify the Upper Peninsula economy by encouraging the formation and growth of value-adding small and medium-sized enterprises that compose its customer base. NEICorp does this in two ways. First, with direct service to customers, NEICorp

— provides expertise and guidance on business direction and expansion by focusing product line and market development efforts; helping identify and making operational improvements in financial, human re-

FIGURE 2

NORTHERN MICHIGAN UNIVERSITY AND SHOREBANK CORPORATION'S DEVELOPMENT MODEL FOR NORTHERN MICHIGAN

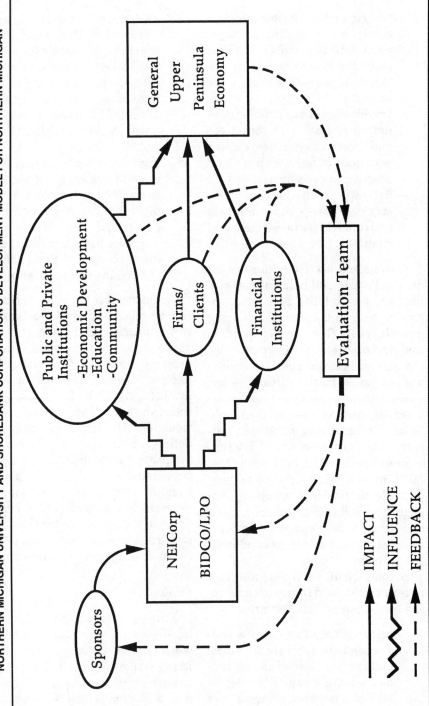

SOURCE: Stephen DeGoosh, assistant professor, Department of Geography, Northern Michigan University, Marquette, MI. Reprinted by permission.

source, and work flow management; and providing management with new tools to address everyday problems and an interested "partner" to help solve them;

— provides direct assistance in evaluating technology alternatives and integrating those choices with marketing, work force, and production capabilities; and

— delivers financial packaging services to help improve access and compete for investment and credit.

Customized service addresses individual needs and helps a customer improve profitability and make informed judgments about managing growth, cash flow, credit, production, and markets. NEICorp provides the service because similar services are not found in the private sector. The customary providers of small-business counseling—certified public accountant firms, bank loan officers, insurance agents, and lawyers —do not participate in this market. NEICorp is looking for ways to demonstrate profitable markets by engaging consultants to deliver one-on-one services and encouraging local associations of businesses to address the problem.

Second, NEICorp builds industry networks intended to create reinforcing relationships between firms by

— bringing together firms within a sector to collaborate on issues, making the individual participants more competitive. Members of a network compare and contrast common interests, problems, production issues, and marketing constraints; focus on how these issues, when confronted jointly, will enhance the individual competitiveness of the participants; and identify individual strengths that can be allocated by the network to minimize weakness within the network;

— organizing firms to participate in joint training activity as a cost-effective means to accelerate modernization within the group; and

— grouping firms by market niche to collectively underwrite the costs of reaching distant markets.

Collaboration between firms is a characteristic of flexible and innovative economies. Yet the competitive advantage for most businesses means keeping secret all of the things that differentiate one from another: ideas, production methods, market contacts, and so on. These attitudes stem from how the firm and its owners define advantage. NEICorp is attempting to redefine advantage by demonstrating bottom-line benefits from networks. As networking becomes a characteristic of competitive firms in the region, natural business patterns will emerge and will become self-initiating and self-sustaining.

Capital

Financing and capital access for businesses in the Upper Peninsula were viewed as barriers to growth. Many Upper Peninsula firms appear to have limited access to venture capital, and commercial and industrial credit seems constrained. Virtually no moderate- or high-risk venture capital flows into the region. Many commercial banks do not utilize government-guaranteed programs intended to promote small-business development. Many lenders also have conservative collateral requirements that restrict the ability to borrow, and they do not offer short- or medium-term commercial credit.

To address this problem, the BIDCO seeks credit opportunities for businesses that will create jobs, generate sales growth, and increase profits. Although not limited to a particular industry, the BIDCO seeks opportunities with a high value-added component to the product or service.

The BIDCO loan products may be used in combination with bank loans, Small Business Administration loans or guarantees, private financing, or other sources of financing. BIDCO financing usually ranges from $50,000 to $250,000. The BIDCO also provides assistance in business management, including product development, financial and cash management, and work force training.

The LPO is designed to fill the gaps in the financial marketplace by providing government-guaranteed term credit to small businesses that require financing for fixed assets or working capital but that cannot qualify for conventional term credit. The LPO will, in effect, serve as an extension of the bank's Commercial Lending Department and will provide the South Shore Bank with a physical presence in the Upper Peninsula for commercial credit purposes. The LPO will not, however, operate as a deposit-taking branch office for the South Shore Bank.

The approach is intended to supplement and leverage existing sources of credit and capital available to the Upper Peninsula business community. It will not replace existing lenders as a credit source but rather provide loans in the appropriate size and structure, working in tandem with primary financing offered by local lenders. It will, in essence, be a private source of gap financing to fuel economic development in the region. As progress is made in demonstrating profitable markets to local lenders, other financial institutions may enter the business, releasing additional capital.

The Shorebank Corporation was organized in 1973 to demonstrate that declining urban neighborhoods in Chicago could be revitalized by a nontraditional but profit-oriented approach to business credit and housing rehabilitation. Shorebank has, by careful design, supplemented its traditional banking products and services with human and real estate development affiliates able to attack problems that are beyond the business and regulatory reach of a commercial bank alone.

The Shorebank Corporation has, over the past 18 years, earned a reputation for its "development banking" initiatives in rural as well as in urban settings. It now operates in five minority communities in Chicago with a total population of about 300,000. Shorebank also designed, organized, and provides management advisory services to the Southern Development Bancorporation, a bank holding company that has been implementing a rural economic development initiative in Arkansas since 1986.

Work force skills development

With technical assistance and industrial networks under way and the development bank operational, NEI-Corp is exploring the work force development needs of value-adding small and medium-sized enterprises.

This project is in the planning stages and is inspired by both European and domestic models. The Upper Peninsula is fortunate to have a comprehensive educational infrastructure. Educational institutions in the Upper Peninsula include two public community colleges, two private two-year colleges, and three public four-year universities that have two-year associate programs. Additionally, secondary education is adopting the tech-prep curriculum approaches encouraged through federal legislation. These schools have opportunities to coordinate with one another and improve their relationship with nearby small and medium-sized enterprises.

Recently, a consortium of Upper Peninsula secondary and postsecondary schools was organized by Northern Michigan University. With the staff assistance of NEICorp, the consortium is studying ways in which technical and vocational work force development can improve the performance and innovation of industry. Programs of interest include

— models that integrate design and technology concepts into math, science, and language curricula from the early grades

on and build an awareness of innovation;

— training programs articulated through a strict system involving private employers and public and private vocational education centers; and

— European training systems displaying a fierce dedication to value-adding small and medium-sized enterprises and defining their core competency around the evolving training needs of nearby industry.

The Upper Peninsula Consortium is modeling its activities after the Consortium for Manufacturing Competitiveness, a network comprising colleges with outstanding industrial technology resources and vocational education programs from each of the 14 southern states. The original design called for the colleges to work cooperatively to develop innovative approaches and share ideas and experiences with other colleges in the state. Although each college has its own training niche based upon the customer or industry demand in its locality, the lessons learned are shared. Thus, as each individual institution takes a step forward, so does the entire region. Having its roots in industry networking with area firms, NEICorp quickly saw the advantages of this approach.

The potential of the Upper Peninsula Consortium may be as a catalyst to develop and modernize small and medium-sized enterprises. Its programs must be market motivated to provide talent and new skills to industry, ease the introduction of new technology, improve work force productivity, and lead product innovation.

REMAINING CHALLENGES
FOR THE UPPER PENINSULA

NEICorp, the BIDCO, and the LPO will choreograph technical assistance, capital, and human resource development resources through the industrial networks it has established, along with the customized delivery of services to individual firms. Together, they must enlist the mainstream institutions of finance, education, and business support services to participate in the development of the economy. These institutions have real power to reorient the economy through scale, permanence, and access to customers. The challenge for the northern Michigan program will be to provide useful services to customers and demonstrate their value to the supporting institutional infrastructure. Over time, perhaps a decade or more, such action could transform the underlying features of a resource-supplying region to an economy that produces employment in competitive value-adding industries.

The challenges for the Upper Peninsula, like most rural areas, will be formidable.

Rural areas tend to specialize in routine manufacturing. These are industries which rely more on production workers and have a relatively low proportion of managerial, professional, and technical jobs. ... Routine industries in rural areas have typically made standardized products for U.S. markets, using assembly-line production methods and employing less-skilled and less-educated workers. Competitiveness has generally depended on economies of scale and low-cost, rather than on product innovation.[7]

Economies that focus their energies on innovation lead markets; those focusing on lowest-cost production tend to follow. Innovation and productivity produce competitive advantages, higher-margin goods and services, and, in turn, a higher standard of living. Rural regions can compensate for two primary disadvantages—distance from the customer and access to markets—by differentiating their products through quality and design. Innovation is a competitive advantage for firms that are engaged in the production and export of goods from a local economy. Establishing this competitive advantage requires building a tradition of design excellence and a supportive environment fostering interaction between youths, tomorrow's innovators; their teachers and mentors; the region's employers and entrepreneurs; recognized designers and innovators; and professionals with knowledge of markets, technology, and management.

A long-term strategy designed to cultivate the creative talents of a community and develop an indigenous industry base must involve the systems of an economy that interact with youths, the work force, and firms tackling problems in a hands-on environment. As noted educator Larry Rosenstock states, "The entire community—its educational institutions, community support agencies, neighborhoods, families and local employers—must be involved in strategies affecting the prosperity of their community and the development of its children."[8]

7. Philip Shapira, "Strategies for Rural Manufacturing Modernization: Assessing Best Practices" (Paper delivered at the Modernization Forum, Detroit, MI, May 1991).

8. Larry Rosenstock, "The Walls Come Tumbling Down: The Overdue Reunification of

If this is not accomplished, rural regions risk a growing detachment between home, school, and work life, perceiving them as separate and unrelated rather than as equally important elements in a balanced, rewarding life. This fragmented view often leads youths to see few local opportunities and perhaps contributes to rural out-migration. Rural institutions and the business community need to bridge this fragmentation to provide young people with a practical vision of entrepreneurial possibilities and inspire confidence among existing enterprises to establish new and profitable opportunities. Sustaining rural development requires this vision.

Vocational and Academic Education," *Phi Delta Kappan* (Feb. 1991).

ANNALS, *AAPSS*, **529**, September 1993

Federal Aid for
Rural Economic Development

By ANNE BERBLINGER

ABSTRACT: Federal economic development programs for rural communities work. They do indeed help rural communities to create new jobs, raise income levels, diversify their economies, sustain local businesses and help them grow, and create new businesses. In this article, programs are described, and the author shares some thoughts on federal aid for rural economic development.

Anne Berblinger was 1992 chair of the Oregon Rural Development Council. She has been the Oregon representative for the U.S. Economic Development Administration (EDA) since July of 1983. As Economic Development Representative, she has organized three multicounty Economic Development Districts serving eight rural counties and developed six regional small-business revolving loan programs and over forty public works projects for EDA funding. She has a master's degree in regional planning from the University of North Carolina at Chapel Hill.

THE Economic Development Administration (EDA) is a very small agency in the Commerce Department. We have a program budget for fiscal year 1993 of just over $217 million.[1] We offer a handful of programs, including grants with a matching-share requirement for public works and development facilities, a tiny program of grants for technical assistance, planning grants to help defray the staff costs of multicounty Economic Development Districts (EDDs), Indian tribe economic development programs, grants to establish regional or inner-city small-business revolving loan funds, and grants to assist areas experiencing major plant closings or other economic dislocations.

Most of our grantees are local governments or EDDs, the regional partnerships of local government and local private sector representatives created through our planning grant program. Through the planning grant program, EDA has established a network of these regional rural economic development organizations, which serve most of the economically distressed counties in the nation.

We work with economically distressed areas, using one- or two-year unemployment rates for counties as our primary measure of distress but also considering factors such as per capita income and out-migration. We work with urban as well as rural areas.

To be eligible for financial assistance under our programs, a rural community needs to participate in an economic development planning process carried out at a countywide level either by a volunteer committee or by an EDD. This planning process involves a public-private collaboration to produce what we call an Overall Economic Development Program (OEDP). OEDPs range from perfunctory exercises to high-quality documents produced by effective and inclusive participatory processes. The trend at least in Oregon is toward the latter. It is the OEDP process that is largely responsible, in my opinion, for the success and popularity of our other programs. In Oregon, all but 5 of 33 economically distressed counties are served by EDDs. Each of the Oregon EDDs has an excellent planning process and produces a high-quality plan.

RURAL ECONOMIC DEVELOPMENT IS LOCAL

The programs that we deliver to rural communities are delivered for the most part through and by local government or through public-private partnerships in which local government participates. This is appropriate because businesses make decisions and jobs are created at the local level. If all politics is local, so is all economic development.

EDA's programs do work in the places for which they are designed to work—in distressed communities, at the local or regional level. What they do best is to help local government create the conditions that encourage the stability and expansion of local business by removing impediments to development. These impediments can be insufficient infrastructure, lack of capital for business expansion, and many others. Every outside

---

1. In 1980, our budget was over $600 million. Neither this figure nor the 1993 budget figure is corrected for inflation.

study of EDA programs shows that they do work—that they do contribute to job creation in both rural and urban communities.

With our minuscule budget, we cannot hope to counteract the overwhelming macroeconomic forces affecting rural America. What we can do is help keep hope alive in rural communities, help them to replace some of the jobs that have been lost, support and reward sound planning and realistic thinking about the future. In addition, we can test our tools and approaches to find out which are effective and in what circumstances.

The best way the federal government can provide tools for rural development is to make those tools accessible to and appropriate for local government and other local community leaders. The federal government should in turn maintain high expectations and rigorous standards for local governments and other entities that are recipients of federal assistance. Among these expectations should be realistic and inclusive planning; attention to the needs of minorities, women, youths, workers, and citizens with special needs; cooperation and collaboration with neighboring communities and with the private sector; and real commitments of time, energy, and local resources to the development objective over time. The standards should not include success with every project—the federal government will not serve rural areas if it does not encourage and share in risk taking.

Should the federal government continue to be in the business of direct delivery of resources for economic development to small communities? Is that not the state's job? I would pose the question a little differently: how can the federal government, as it creates or changes resources for rural communities, interfere least with and support most the existing programs and delivery systems that work, whether these programs and delivery systems have been created locally, by states, or by other branches of the federal government? The first answer to this question is for those in the position of creating or changing rural programs to know what does exist and what does work. The second answer is to design programs to be flexible and responsive so that they can be easily coordinated with existing programs and delivery systems.

Some federal programs may best be delivered to rural communities through block grants to states. Indeed, for those states that have programs designed to empower local government in the economic development arena, a block grant program may be the best delivery mechanism. Where block grants are used, program evaluation should ask the same questions about each state's performance that we feds should ask about our own: how do these programs perform at the local level where development happens, and how satisfied are the ultimate customers—local communities—with the delivery of the programs?

LOCAL AND REGIONAL:
THE APPROPRIATE SCALE

Having stressed that local governments—cities, counties, port districts, and so on—are the best partners for federal economic development assistance, I will now seem to contradict myself by saying that the most efficient and effective way to deliver many economic development programs in rural communities is through regional organizations serving a number of local areas. Almost every small town and county would like to have its own economic development practitioner on staff, its own industrial park, and its own local revolving loan fund (RLF) to finance small business. It is not instantly apparent to local elected officials that cooperation, not competition, with their immediate neighbors is the most effective approach to improving their own community's economy. Federal programs should be structured to encourage and reward the most effective behaviors on the part of local leadership, and thinking regionally is such a behavior.

EDDs provide professional economic development planning and other services on a scale that works well. In a good EDD, the staff usually has more demand for service than they can handle, a situation that hones the prioritizing skills.

The Small Cities Community Development Block Grant program in Oregon—a program of the federal Department of Housing and Urban Development—used to make grants to tiny cities—for example, Drain, with a population of 1100; Sublimity, with a population of 1600—which the cities in turn would loan to a business as part of an incentive deal to create jobs for low- and moderate-income people. As the loan was repaid, a revolving fund was created, but it was only available to businesses within the city limits. Most cities and counties that were recipients of such grants at first jealously held on to the prerogative and honor of operating these loan funds themselves. Over time, however, many, if not most, have delegated the job of running these programs to EDDs, which have in place the well-trained and experienced staff required to operate an RLF. But the distortion created by the availability of this resource in only one community in a region—in Drain but not in Sutherlin, Elkton, Oakland, Yoncalla, Rice Hill, or Roseburg, all within a 20-mile radius—remains intact.

EDA at one time made RLF grants to individual small counties—and to states—but our experience showed us that the best scale for such a program is a region of about 100,000 to 300,000 people.

COORDINATION—BY DEFAULT, A LOCAL RESPONSIBILITY

The 1992 Catalog of Federal Domestic Assistance lists 25 programs administered by nine different departments or agencies under the heading of economic development. At the end of the listing, it refers the user to eight more headings. I can think of at least one or two federal economic development programs that did not make it into the index under this heading.

Are federal economic development programs fragmented? Obviously! Who is responsible for coordinating these programs? Nobody in the federal government has been assigned the authority to coordinate federal economic development programs. Are they ever coordinated? Absolutely!

The most skilled and sophisticated state, local, and regional economic development organizations coordinate these federal programs on the ground. For example, in Oregon, EDDs, all of which operate EDA revolving business loan funds, also package Small Business Administration (SBA) 7(a) Loan Guarantees and SBA Section 504 Debentures. They contract with counties and cities to operate RLFs resulting from Community Development Block Grant projects and Urban Development Action Grant projects. Some have applied for the Farmers Home Administration (FmHA) Intermediary Relending Program, which is soon to be operated by the new Rural Development Administration. They also use several business finance programs sponsored by the state of Oregon. Each of these programs provides loans for small business expansions and start-ups. They have different rules and requirements, which make them more or less suitable for specific deals that the EDDs are trying to set up. The EDDs in Oregon provide a one-stop shop for public sector business finance programs. For every deal that needs public sector finance, the EDDs determine which source of funding is most appropriate.

Coordinating the small business finance programs is relatively easy. SBA, FmHA, and EDA each require a local representative loan board to approve loans. The requirements for loan boards are different, but not contradictory. If an EDD wants to, it can use the same loan board for all the programs.

There are plenty of programs with contradictory requirements. EDA's requirements for the boards of directors of EDDs clash with the Soil Conservation Service's requirements for the boards of Resource Conservation and Development Councils, another multicounty program with some areas of potentially fruitful coordination with EDD responsibilities. In some cases, local officials have maneuvered through the differences and created one board that serves both functions. In other cases, efforts to do so have been discouraged by one of the two agencies.

A prerequisite for EDA projects is the OEDP adopted at the county or regional level. A prerequisite for projects under the Forest Service's Economic Recovery Program is a local economic development plan prepared by a team led by a Forest Service official. These requirements are mandated by the authorizing legislation for the programs. In Oregon, EDA and Forest Service staff, state agencies, and EDDs have, with the encouragement of Forest Service officials in Washington, D.C., worked together to minimize the duplication of planning efforts and documents.

FRAGMENTATION OR HEALTHY COMPETITION?

If there are thirty kinds of toothpaste on the grocery store shelf to choose from, why should there not also be multiple economic development products offered by the federal government? Maybe it is duplication, but is it not also competition? These products differ from each other more than Crest and Tom's of Maine toothpaste do. One program is aimed at providing jobs for people of low and moderate income, another at providing family wage jobs. One will fix an existing pollution problem but not allow funds to be spent to provide capacity for growth. Another can be used to fix a pollution problem only when growth and jobs will result as well. Construction using EDA programs must comply with Davis-Bacon, meaning that union-scale wages must be paid, while construction using FmHA programs does not have this requirement.

The differences in programs start with differences in legislation; they originate, after all, in different congressional committees. As programs develop over time, policy decisions—some documented in published regulations and guidelines, and some passed down in a bureaucratic oral tradition—limit or expand the program's possibilities. The agency culture—risk averse or risk encouraging—influences the degree to which a community can fit a program to its needs.

Newcomers to local economic development efforts are often overwhelmed by the complications, but a little experience can allow a local economic development professional to mix and match the resources in innumerable ways to get the job done. Often, however, there are clear needs that cannot be met. Sometimes market forces do not work, or the potential project falls through the proverbial crack.

There is another, more serious point where the market competition analogy fails. In fact, the programs do not compete, because there are almost no consequences resulting

from performance. The ones that work best do not always get more money, and the ones that do not work very well usually do not get less money. What produces more money for a program or an agency is a real or perceived increase in the significance of the problem that the agency or program is supposed to be addressing. (For example, riots in Los Angeles produced Enterprise Zone legislation.) If the people who work in these programs were not dedicated to solving the problems, this process could lead to a perverse result: if the problem is made worse, the employee's job is ensured.

Agency leadership and management are usually committed to improving programs, and often programs are improved. Outside studies may make excellent recommendations that are conscientiously implemented. Congress or the administration may tweak program provisions. Employees may be trained to be more effective. But there are no serious, rigorous standards for evaluating the achievement of agency or program goals in local communities, the only place that counts. There is no mechanism for expanding successful programs or changing or discontinuing programs that are not addressing the needs effectively.

HUMAN INFRASTRUCTURE

Rural communities need experienced people who have substantial time to commit to work on rural development problems. In a few fortunate communities, volunteers with expertise, often retired people, can commit the time to see a project through from start to finish. But the majority of rural communities do not have this luxury. Small-town government staff is often limited to a handful of people with expertise in record keeping, running the utilities, law enforcement, and other traditional maintenance responsibilities. Elected officials are essentially volunteers, with no pay or only token pay. In a survey of Oregon cities and counties, 85 percent responded that the lack of paid, professional staff to work on economic development projects was a problem for their community.[2]

EDD staff, Resource Conservation and Development Council staff, Extension, Small Business Development Centers, and many other federally supported programs can and do help with this problem, but the need far outstrips the resources available.

The lack of paid professional staff leads directly to another problem raised over and over again by rural communities: they do not even know what resources are available to help them with their economic development needs. They rely on a hodgepodge of sources for such information, and no one entity has the responsibility or the resources to bring all the information together and keep it up to date.

PAPERWORK

A chronic and justified complaint about federal programs for rural development is the paperwork.

There is a good—or at least a plausible—explanation for every piece of paper required in an application.

2. Survey by the Oregon Rural Development Council, Leadership Committee, Jan. 1992.

Most of the explanations serve the purpose of reducing risk for the government and/or for those responsible for making decisions. Unfortunately, there is often no appropriate proportion of risk to paperwork burden. There are instances of draconian solutions to minuscule problems and threats, solutions that create an increased paperwork burden for local applicants.

No one seems to have the responsibility to ask, Is this piece of paper or documentation really needed to ensure compliance with whatever law or regulation applies here? Will the agency use this information for anything? Does it need this exhibit to carry out its real-world responsibilities? Is the risk this documentation seeks to avert proportional to the paperwork required, or is it so small or remote as to be acceptable?

This was not always the case. Around 1973, the federal Office of Management and Budget (OMB) standardized and simplified the applications for federal assistance. It made a big difference at the time. The main device was substituting assurances of compliance with requirements for documentation of compliance. While OMB still has the responsibility for reviewing and approving application forms, there does not seem to be any oversight that prevents the ongoing addition of more documentation to approved forms.

Another source of excess paperwork is using complete applications or complicated preapplications for competitions, where many more proposals are solicited than can possibly be funded. This simplifies life for the feds who review the projects and make decisions as to which should be funded, since it saves them from surprises. They can make the determination that a project can comply with all the requirements at the same time that they determine that it can win the most points or come closest to meeting the selection criteria. But from a local point of view, this is backward. Local people often feel that the feds should find out what projects are most competitive first and then help the applicant figure out how to meet the technical requirements. This, in fact, is the way OMB Circular A102 describes the function of the preapplication. But the typical federal preapplication calls for information far beyond what would be called for to merely familiarize the agency with the proposed project and establish its competitiveness. That means that for every successful application and happy applicant, there are several disgruntled losers who have spent perhaps hundreds of hours on useless paperwork.

Too often, feds take the position—most of them unconsciously—that if they really want the project to be funded, they should not complain, that they have nothing better to do. In fact, they have lots of better things to do! The paid professional staff or volunteer time that is consumed by unnecessary paperwork is the single most valuable development resource that rural areas have.

RURAL DEVELOPMENT
COUNCILS, A STEP IN
THE RIGHT DIRECTION

Oregon is one of eight pilot states in which State Rural Development Councils were organized as part of a presidential initiative on rural development. Our council includes representatives of federal agencies with rural development responsibilities, state agencies, local government, nonprofits, corporations, and small businesses. The mission of the council is "to promote rural development by focussing governmental, private, and non-profit resources to assist rural Oregon in building long-term livability."

Under the presidential initiative, federal agencies are asked to become more flexible, responsive, and proactive in helping rural areas undertake strategic planning, empower themselves, and address their problems and opportunities.

The Oregon Rural Development Council has a work plan that includes

— making information about resources for development more accessible to rural communities;
— identifying barriers to the effective use of resources and recommending changes to regulations, procedures, and legislation to remove those barriers;
— identifying opportunities for creative collaboration by federal, state, and other partners on rural development projects;
— supporting the efforts of rural communities to obtain the services of paid professional staff to implement their development plan; and
— providing appropriate information about rural issues to target audiences, such as the employees of council member agencies.

Our council has about seventy members. We meet monthly in rural communities around the state, and the heart of each meeting is a local presentation. Our meetings are open, and we invite participation by anyone who is interested. Our agenda and our work plan are determined by the expressed needs and concerns of rural communities.

Our council has been in operation for about a year and a half. It takes a long time for a group like ours to get organized and start functioning as a team, and the issues we are working on do not lend themselves to quick victories. Nonetheless, we have in the council a vehicle to address the issues and problems described in this article.

ANNALS, *AAPSS*, **529**, September 1993

Multicommunity Networks:
A Rural Transition

By TED K. BRADSHAW

ABSTRACT: Rural America is in a difficult transition due not just to the economy but to the changing relations between cities and towns in the rural-urban continuum. Small-scale places are no longer isolated and simple but are part of a global interdependence that redefines cities and suburbs and creates rural regions. In the new rural region, traditional rural problems of poverty and lagging social services persist, but in addition a whole new set of problems and opportunities that originate outside the community affect a whole rural region. Rural development efforts, in response to the new small-community interdependence, are harder and more complex. Instead of the trend toward narrower, single-purpose programs, the rural development paradigm for the 1990s should be one of multijurisdictional networks for the development of rural regions. Coalitions of small communities can solve many problems that individual communities working alone cannot tackle. Solutions come from leadership, strategic planning, and mobilizing local resources.

Ted Bradshaw is a research sociologist at the Institute of Urban and Regional Development at the University of California, Berkeley. Over the last two decades, he has written widely on rural development, economic development, California public policy, and technological change. He has just completed an analysis of comparative state economic development strategies, evaluated the impact of military base closures on rural regions, and participated in designing and evaluating rural development projects in both forest and agricultural regions of California.

W HY has rural development proven to be so difficult? Transitions in the rural economy—from agriculture and natural resource extraction to a manufacturing and service economy—are well documented. Labor savings from increased farm productivity have grown so rapidly that farm employment now produces only a few percentage points of rural income. This particular transition, however, has been ongoing and of major concern for over a half century now, and at the macro scale displaced farm labor has been reemployed within the national economy and in virtually all broad multistate economic regions with the possible exceptions of the South and northern Plains. The rural problem is that growth industries replacing agriculture are concentrated in cities, not rural towns. In the absence of effective rural initiative, there seems to be a universal truth that development tends toward the urban and that resource-rich areas become poor.[1]

But, from time to time and place to place, there are exceptions where rural development works. The brief turnaround of the 1970s and the continuing rural growth today in nearly half of nonmetropolitan counties illustrate that rurality is not doomed. Some communities see industry expanding and incomes growing. The hard problem is to figure out what to do about the places that are not making the transition to the rural advanced industrial society.[2] The an-

swer may lie not so much in the economy as in the changing structure of communities.

The purpose of this article is to explore how rural development programs could meet the needs of small communities that are finding the transition hard—where the key problem is interdependence rather than isolation. Most development assistance is organized around community competition rather than cooperation, resulting in ineffective and shortsighted development programs. A multijurisdictional development strategy is outlined to overcome these problems.

THE CHALLENGE OF
RURAL REGIONALISM

Rural isolation was the pressing issue at the turn of the century, and sociologists made news by discovering that urban culture reached even to the "small town in mass society."[3] More recently, the emphasis was on the urban-wildland interface and micropolitan areas. The major transition, however, appears to be a blurring of the entire continuum of community from central city to hinterland, with regional links becoming more essential.

As urban and rural culture have become increasingly intertwined, the question arises as to what constitutes

---

1. Ted K. Bradshaw, "The Elusiveness of Rural Development Theory and Policy: Domestic and Third World Perspectives Joined," *Sociological Practice*, 8:58-71 (1990).

2. The U.S. nonmetro population grew by 4 percent during the period 1980-90, down

from 14 percent in the previous decade. Growing nonmetro counties include those adjacent to metro areas, retirement and recreation counties, and nonmetro counties in the West, especially California, Nevada, Arizona, and Alaska. "Rural Population Growth Slows During 1980-90," *Rural Conditions and Trends*, p. 18 (Spring 1991).

3. Arthur J. Vidich and Joseph Bensman, *Small Town in Mass Society* (Princeton, NJ: Princeton University Press, 1958).

rurality anymore. Indeed, rurality can no longer be defined by industry, isolation, socioeconomic status, or values. It must be defined as those areas with low density of population, and this is associated with small scale.[4] Within rural low-density areas, there can be a great deal of specialization and connectivity within a larger region. The transition from the dominantly agricultural village to the global small town is not happening easily.

Three major changes in the character of community make the transition to the new rurality hard: decreasing rural dependence on central places; the regional linkage of specialized places; and the external origin of local problems and resources.

Rural areas are less
dependent on
central places

The role of the central city has changed considerably, and, along with it, the entire hierarchy of places has eroded. The central city used to be the center for all types of specialization. Located around ports, rail terminals, power sources, or natural resources, urban industries became the motor that drove culture and community. According to central place theory, small cities around the central city provided less specialized and increasingly local inputs, with small towns and farm communities supporting just the most basic services, such as general stores and gas stations. The hierarchy of specialization implied that people went to in-

creasingly larger places to get more specialized goods and services.[5]

This pattern is breaking down at both ends of the continuum. Cities are no longer exclusive suppliers of highly specialized functions, with these being dispersed throughout the urban region. Specialized manufacturing firms in new growing computer, aerospace, biotechnology, and other industries are rarely located near traditional city centers, but in subregions and what Garreau recently called "edge cities."[6] Headquarters for Fortune 500 companies are rapidly shifting outside downtown areas. More jobs are being created in suburbs than in the city center, creating new intersuburb commute patterns that now are double the number of trips to the central city. The function of the old central city is increasingly to serve as a place where regional, national, and global decisions are made.[7] This function is supported by specialized information, expertise, and hospitality.

At the rural end, isolation is breaking down and many functions that were constrained to the cities are dispersing because of the attractive uncongested rural environment. Better telecommunications and transportation have allowed many

4. See Ken Deavers, "What Is Rural?" *Policy Studies Journal*, 20(2):184-89 (1992).

5. For a review of central place theory and evidence of its breakdown, see Harley E. Jojansen and Glenn V. Fuguitt, *The Changing Rural Village in America: Demographic and Economic Trends since 1950* (Cambridge, MA: Ballinger, 1984).

6. Joel Garreau, *Edge City: Life on the New Frontier* (New York: Doubleday, 1991).

7. Peter Hall, "Managing Growth in the World's Cities," *Berkeley Planning Journal*, 6: 19-35 (1991); Robert Cervero, *Suburban Gridlock* (New Brunswick, NJ: Rutgers University, Center for Urban Policy Research, 1986).

types of businesses and firms to locate quite specialized functions in rural communities, ranging from back-office data processing or telephone customer service operations to specialized high-technology manufacturing plants. Computer software, publishing and printing, agricultural machinery, sporting goods equipment, and mail-order sales are examples of industries that have become especially prevalent in rural areas. In addition, some firms in virtually every industry can be found in small towns across the nation. Since close proximity is no longer necessary for most business functions, firms can disperse farther and farther from the center city.

Thus the options for small communities seem greater than ever before, but it is increasingly difficult for community leaders to participate in the negotiations about what role their community plays in the changing and rapidly evolving urban landscape. Because of their small size and limited understanding of what their options really are, small communities usually lack an integrated approach to their future.

*Specialized places
are linked in a
regional network*

Just as the central city has ceased to be the central node for more and more business functions, rural places are becoming more specialized and interdependent with each other. Even small rural communities are selecting functions that are distinctive, such as county seat and governmental services, educational institu-

tions and related knowledge services, retail sales, business equipment, recreation and culture, or even poverty and economic depression. These specialized small places are interlocked in a region in the same way that neighborhoods are interlocked in a city, with many specialized functions that all add up to a vibrant whole. The pattern of rural interdependence can be called a "ruralplex."[8]

The potential level of interdependence is often underestimated. One indicator of the multicommunity regional network of rural communities is the Wal-Mart strategy. Many of the rural Wal-Mart stores have been placed on the outskirts of a town or between several small towns. The idea is that the store has a regional draw and can compete for business in several or many small towns. What Wal-Mart knows is that the loyalty to and competition between small towns are eroding and that people cover wide distances in order to get what they want.[9] Community, as Melvin Webber showed, no longer implies a discrete place but can be viewed as "spatially extensive, processual systems in which urbanites interact with other urbanites wherever they may be. For it is interaction, not place, that is the essence of the city and of city life."[10] In rural areas, personal and business net-

8. This term was mentioned at the Small Town and Rural Development conference in Stevens Point, WI, Mar. 1982, but the source is unknown.

9. See, for example, Alan Ehrenhalt, "Up against the Wal-Mart," *Governing* (Sept. 1992).

10. Melvin M. Webber, "The Urban Place and the Nonplace Urban Realm," in *Explorations into Urban Structure*, ed. Melvin M. Web-

works link small specialized communities in the same way that small communities were once linked to central cities, and neighborhoods are linked within cities.

For rural communities, this is a hard transition. Communities have history, politics, high school football teams, and shared dreams. These are difficult to give up. Moreover, the functional geography linking these small towns has developed faster than the civil geography, and new political and organizational structures are largely unavailable and politically unacceptable.

Local problems and resources are external

In small towns across the country, the problems of lagging development and dependency increasingly originate outside the community, and solutions increasingly involve local mobilization of outside resources. This duality of increasing external dependency, on the one hand, and local initiative, on the other, is expressed nicely in the environmentalist motto, "Think globally, act locally."

Rural problems are often induced by changes in the regional, state, national, and international arenas. Today, employment in rural food packing firms is being affected by international corporate and political decisions. The North American Free Trade Agreement promises massive consequences for rural employment, with both short-term problems and the need for long-term restructuring. Already packing firms in California

are receiving Mexican broccoli, and some California crops are being sent to Mexican processing plants.[11] Southern textile and clothing firms that moved into small towns during the 1970s are now moving to lower-priced foreign operations. At the same time, some rural college communities have found rich opportunities in attracting foreign college students to enroll. Foreign tourism as well as export is a key growth sector for small communities.

Not all external change is foreign, however, with much of it coming from other parts of the nation and from nearby cities. Problems of ozone pollution, with its urban origins, is reported to be responsible for at least a 10 percent crop loss in the San Joaquin Valley;[12] trees die in forest areas, and acid rain ruins rural water and fish. Other problems include urban-related traffic through rural areas, theft and vandalism on farm and forest land, rapid increases in housing values as urban owners buy rural housing and land, consolidation of small downtown shopping areas into malls and discount stores, and the elimination of rural manufacturing plants and businesses due to environmental restrictions or technological change.

At the same time that the problems originate externally, the resources to deal with the problems are also externally controlled. Financial resources for communities used to be

ber et al. (Philadelphia: University of Pennsylvania Press, 1964), p. 147.

11. Raul Hinojosa-Ojeda, Sherman Robinson, and Kirby S. Moulton, "Free Trade with Mexico: Economic Impacts," *California Agriculture*, pp. 5-6 (Sept.-Oct. 1991).

12. Harold O. Carter and Carole Nuckton, *California's Central Valley: Confluence of Change* (Davis: University of California, Agricultural Issues Center, 1990).

negotiated at the local bank, but with the rise of branch banking and global money markets, even if the bank is locally operated, the financial resources for even the most isolated community are governed by state and national investment practices—funds are invested in short- and long-term notes, and loans are bought and sold on larger markets according to regulations and standard practices. Federal grants and loans used to be a major development resource, but program after program has been cut, leaving rural areas dependent on other resources for development. Utilities, churches, colleges, hospitals, and other public-serving institutions are similarly controlled outside local communities, and their ability to contribute to an integrated development plan remains external.

The conditions for development are likewise shaped by external influences. Local land-use regulations are used to govern rural planning, but these are increasingly shaped by state and national environmental, industrial, and fiscal policies. Setting land-use patterns in an attractive way involves agreements and assistance from the many interests external to the local community that can make local successes and failures.

With a feeling of growing dependency, many rural communities face a harsh reality. Their increasing ties to urban America seem to promise opportunity, but rural communities compete poorly and changes are coming very fast. Many options are poorly understood, and communities often act too late to shape their own destiny. In short, the options for rural communities are overdetermined by external forces, and gains quickly turn into a new level of dependency.

THE CHALLENGE OF DEVELOPMENT PROGRAMS

Development is a complex process, and debate has raged over what the necessary interventions are that will lead to improved well-being for disadvantaged people and communities. With the increasing regional interdependence of rural communities and their economies, the debate is the appropriate response to the rapidly changing regionally based community structure.

The federal role in rural development has long been recognized through specific area programs—for example, the Appalachian regional commission—or industrial assistance to agriculture, forestry, and fisheries. Rural areas have also benefited from the broad range of development programs that have not been area specific and from programs that are not intended as development programs. For instance, increased social security benefits paid since the 1970s have allowed retired people to move to rural areas. Another example is the interstate highway system, which was established to link cities. It opened up the vast rural areas in between cities to easy access, stimulated commuting for employment, and helped establish a new generation of rural industries.[13]

13. Ted K. Bradshaw and Edward J. Blakely, "Unanticipated Consequences of Governmental Programs on Rural Economic Development," in *Rural Economic Development in the 1980s: Prospects for the Future*, ed. David L. Brown et al. (Washington, DC: Economic Research Service, 1988), pp. 235-54.

Rural development challenges have increased over the years. Wayne Rasmussen has argued that, in the early days of rural development, people had clear needs that could be quickly solved and easily documented; these included programs that provided paved roads and highways, electricity, municipal water and sewage systems, postal delivery, and telephones. Federal investments in these programs improved rural living and enabled the growth of both modern agriculture and industry. In spite of the solution to these problems, however, rural economies failed to keep up with the pace of urban development. Rasmussen feels that recent efforts have had to deal with more intractable problems, such as unemployment, persistent poverty, and inadequate housing.[14]

The case must also be made that the pace of change has increased, with rural agendas expanding to include environmental protection and enhancement, equal rights, worker safety, global trade, and a broader array of federal entitlements than would ever have been imagined. Rural no longer necessarily means agricultural, isolated, and culturally deprived; rural areas now share many urban qualities, though in a less dense setting. In short, the rural development challenge today is to stimulate an intensely complex system in which rural areas are part of a global marketplace but are constrained by a historical small-town mentality. Rural development pro-

grams that fail to meet the challenge of global complexity are increasingly irrelevant to solving the real development needs.

Meeting the challenge of rural development requires a development paradigm that has two major pillars. First, in spite of the global implications, development must be focused on the local level. Without a doubt, the most important lesson of the last twenty years of community development is that the local community itself must take the lead in mobilizing outside resources for community benefit. Development must be done with rather than to a community. There is little that will happen locally without active mobilization of local interests to start to resolve local problems and to reduce local dependency. Local people need to set their priorities, and, if they do not, development is unlikely. In part, this is because many other small poor places are trying to get the attention of those who would assist. In part, it is because the assistance that is available involves the ability to contribute partial resources to a project rather than to start a project from scratch. While communities are increasingly tied to the outside world, these ties lead to bifurcation, with large and rich places becoming larger and richer while small and poor places become worse off.[15] This trend can be countered, however, by local leadership that persistently helps

14. Wayne D. Rasmussen, "90 Years of Rural Development Programs," *Economic Development Perspectives*, 2(1):2-9 (Oct. 1985).

15. Ted K. Bradshaw, "In the Shadow of Urban Growth: Bifurcation in Rural California Communities," in *Forgotten Places: Unequal Development in Rural America*, ed. Thomas A. Lyson and William W. Falk (Lawrence: University Press of Kansas, 1993).

make deals that bring external resources into the community. The objective of rural development must be to assist local leadership in reversing the flow of resources from small places.

The second pillar of rural development is the need for a multifaceted approach. While rural electrification or providing access to modern farming technology might have been a single, focused solution to many problems in the past, reversing the cycle of rural dependency today requires more than transfer-type programs where providers offer rural people some things that they need. Sewer systems, water systems, and industrial parks may be preconditions for development, but they are not adequate by themselves.

The best example of the failure of single-purpose programs is the large number of rural industrial parks built during the 1970s. Large numbers of these remain empty. In Wisconsin, the surplus could cover anticipated expansion through the year 2010;[16] in California, industrial parks in the forest regions were about 80 percent empty, years after they were built.[17] What is lacking is the social and organizational infrastructure for effective economic development that would generate an effective strategy for starting, expanding, and building firms that utilize a diversity of community resources, including available industrial park space. Generating new business opportunities in rural areas is thus one part of an overall economic development strategy that includes a wide array of social and infrastructure programs. By themselves, the components do not constitute development.

MULTIJURISDICTIONAL NETWORKS FOR RURAL DEVELOPMENT

A new model is needed. Several community-based organizations started during the War on Poverty era may provide an example. During a research visit to California's Mendocino County in the early1980s, I inquired about growing employment opportunities because it was apparent that the population and economy were both growing rapidly. Officials told about various small employment gains in traditional firms but knew of no major source of growth. Later that day, I met with the head of North Coast Opportunities, a nonprofit organization for social service and employment development. It turned out that, in its various activities, this organization had become the second-largest employer in the county, was working with small cities as well as rural communities, and was helping poor people to find their way into mainstream businesses and organizations. Over the years, it has spun off dozens of projects as profit and nonprofit companies—in, for example, weatherization, arts and crafts, light manufacturing, and health care—expanded its activities into small communities in nearby counties, and retained a

16. Ted K. Bradshaw et al., "New Challenges for Rural Economic Development" (Working Paper 400, Institute of Urban and Regional Development, Berkeley, 1983).
17. Dena Belzer and Cynthia Kroll, *New Jobs for the Timber Region: Economic Diversification for Northern California* (Berkeley, CA: Institute of Governmental Studies Press, 1986).

core entrepreneurial spirit. None of its activities could have succeeded on a single-community basis, and the experience gained in one reinforced the experience in others.

If the challenge is to provide diversified resources to locally initiated programs in a network of interconnected communities, rural development programs will necessarily be complex and their task will be difficult. While single-focus programs have a great deal of accountability and results can be easily identified, many of these programs fail to achieve the larger goals of rural development. On the other hand, many of the broad-based community organizations started during the 1970s have either lost sight of their mission or been embroiled in political turmoil and scandal. In spite of these mistakes, community organization remains a better model for rural development than do single-purpose programs such as industrial park construction.

Community leadership model

The model for community intervention that is most widely used in the development process provides a good starting point. At its simplest, intervention into rural communities involves a willing community and an expert or team of experts who will help it reach goals it selects. Usually the development process involves the following five steps:

1. Current or potential community leaders are identified and mobilized to participate in the process.

2. Training in leadership skills and economic development is provided to this group.

3. The leaders begin to work in their community, and they conduct an assessment of its strengths and weaknesses. From the assessment, a set of possible projects to meet community needs is developed and prioritized.

4. A community project or set of projects is identified that will help the community and develop local capacity, and outside technical assistance is provided to help the community accomplish its project goals.

5. The successful completion of the project reinforces the leadership and is institutionalized so that additional projects can be completed with less assistance.

In one form or another, this model has provided assistance to hundreds of communities and is at the core of much of the work done by foundations, extension, and nonprofit corporations. In this model, though, assistance is provided to one community at a time, and a project is fairly discrete. Typical projects include, for example, the formation of an economic development corporation, the establishment of an incubator, the upgrading of infrastructure, and securing better funding for businesses. These efforts are important to the local community, but there is a lack of widespread benefit beyond the community.

A number of efforts are under way to make this model more efficient. For example, clusters of 4-10 nearby communities are included in common training programs, and assistance is provided more economically to groups in the cluster. These efforts seem quite well suited to midwestern areas, where there are many similarly sized small towns near each other. Another way to make assistance more efficient is to utilize video and other media in the training process. With better-structured training modules, more people can be helped, and they will have a better learning experience as well. Finally, technical assistance can be streamlined by using practical modules that cover important information on relevant steps in making community assessments, carrying out projects, or utilizing outside resources. These detailed modules can provide assistance in the technical phases of all community projects. In short, some progress is being made in establishing a more efficient community development strategy that will help rural areas.

The emphasis, however, is still to take a focused look at the problems and resources of one community at a time and to do a project that will have local significance as though each community is in competition with and isolated from nearby communities. The growing interdependence of rural communities stands in sharp contrast to a single-community approach. It is clear that fostering, utilizing, and enriching multicommunity ruralplex coalitions that jointly work on mutual problems is both sensible and more efficient than having each community work independently on what are usually closely interrelated problems.

Regional problem-solving approaches are very attractive. Increasingly, the problems facing rural places are general problems for which small communities are poorly equipped to assume benefits. For example, a large resort or recreational facility in one community has significant implications for nearby communities that have increased traffic, seasonal employment, and potentially greater pressure on housing stock by people who work away from the community but use community services such as schools. Changes in the location or raw-material needs of packing plants can leave local suppliers without markets. Environmental changes or regulations—with respect to, for example, endangered species, air quality, or water—may alter the use of broad areas around many communities. Immigration changes can affect many agricultural workers. A large employer usually draws workers from many communities. Medical care needs are becoming so specialized that rural cooperative health programs are mandatory. In short, the relevant unit of analysis for understanding rural problems is increasingly regional, a fact well-known by those trying to solve problems.

Solutions to the problems are also larger than any one community. For example, regional employment diversification programs can mitigate the impact of any one industry. Farm worker housing is better provided regionally, as resources can be allocated more efficiently over the larger area. Marketing of both products and recreational activities is best done regionally. Communities can share provision of social services, with one specializing in educational services, another in business services, and yet another in human services. Community coalitions can be beneficial in a number of ways.

Multijurisdictional leadership

Depressed communities need assistance in identifying leaders who can develop a vision for the community and who have the personal contacts to mobilize participation from diverse segments of the community. In the same way, in a multijurisdictional setting, leaders need to be identified who can function across the region.

The challenge for regional leadership is greater than for local leadership precisely because regional boundaries are usually unofficial or weak and leadership is lacking or powerless. In many parts of the nation, councils of government have been established, but they have very limited powers and cannot impose taxes to obtain funds. In Vermont, this was a serious problem due to the township structure, which carried out virtually all local government functions, with counties limited to just courts. However, based on planning requirements, state subregions were established that became the basis for economic development organization. A new multijurisdictional structure was required for planning and for establishing economic development corporations and similar bodies.

In other cases, coalitions of communities can form based on shared interests or the effort to deal with a problem together. Watersheds, ecosystems, tourist regions, or highway corridors have all become regions based on the need to cooperate and respond to problems. The leadership problems for these multijurisdictional groups are significant because the groups span many types of formal jurisdictions—communities and counties, special districts, and overlapping planning areas. While boundaries of new interest coalitions may or may not be fixed or coincide with the boundaries of other organized groups, the key is that leadership must develop that distinguishes the shared interests of the coalition from the otherwise competing interests of the participants.

Strategic planning

A multijurisdictional rural development project has the advantage of a large enough scope to include some of the major ongoing and planned activities in the area. Planning has an important role in all development projects regardless of scale, but, in a multijurisdictional project, it becomes especially significant. With limited resources, inadequate information, and poor technical skills, small communities need more assistance in setting priorities and identifying resources than any other component of the development process. Once a development strategy is established, cooperation between communities can be profitable, and the costs and benefits will be clear to all.

Resource mobilization

Finally, regional coalitions in rural areas need to be able to mobilize resources from among themselves as well as from external organizations in order to solve rural problems successfully. The advantages of a rural coalition for overcoming some of the difficult disadvantages of small communities include sharing, economies of scale, specialization, and leveraging.

Sharing. Over the long term, communities can learn to draw on the expertise and experiences of other communities in their region rather than relying on central cities. This pattern of mutual assistance is best exemplified in the use of circuit riders to provide planning capacity in small rural towns. The benefit is not just that communities share expertise; the planner helps keep channels of communication open, too.

Economies of scale. One of the most important functions of the coalitions is that program implementation, purchases, and the like can benefit from programs simultaneously in several communities. For example, housing rehabilitation programs can take advantage of bulk purchases of materials or negotiating better contracts with specialized providers. In many community projects, the largest single real cost is the administrative one of setting up and managing the work that is being done. In joint projects, this cost is shared and the tasks often done better.

Specialization. Several communities joining together can provide a degree of expertise and even equipment that can benefit the whole region.

Leveraging. When several communities are involved, the potential increases to multiply the effort of a project to link it to other projects. To return to the housing example, when several communities are involved in a joint program, it may be feasible to develop efforts to train local contractors to do the work, avoiding large contractors from nearby cities. The training program might be funded from several sources including the Job Training Partnership Act, community colleges, and private sources. The trained contractors could then be an ongoing resource in their community.

CONCLUSION

Rural development requires innovative responses to match the changing character of rural communities. Development efforts must not look at the community in isolation but must be strategic about forging linkages between communities to respond to external problems that they share. Moreover, in this response, local leaders need to be able to access a network of urban and rural resource providers, as no one source is capable of providing adequate assistance.

Policies for rural development need to provide more mechanisms for this type of multifunctional and multijurisdictional response. The decline of broad-scope interventions that assist communities is particularly counter to the type of response that is needed. In meeting the challenge of the future with programs that meet the complexity of the communities they are serving, development programs will not only be more effective, but they will be more efficient in the use of state and federal funds as well.

Report of the Board of Directors to the Members of the American Academy of Political and Social Science for the Year 1992

MEMBERSHIPS AND SUBSCRIPTIONS
AS OF DECEMBER 31

Year	Number
1982	9,536
1983	8,904
1984	6,564
1985	5,704
1986	5,606
1987	5,151
1988	4,674
1989	4,903
1990	3,932
1991	4,378
1992	3,088

PUBLICATIONS
NUMBER OF VOLUMES OF *THE ANNALS* PRINTED (6 PER YEAR)

1982	74,211
1983	68,236
1984	52,154
1985	52,800
1986	53,201
1987	43,629
1988	53,497
1989	40,269
1990	39,000
1991	37,246
1992	34,900

FINANCES
SIZE OF SECURITIES PORTFOLIO
MARKET VALUE AS OF DECEMBER 31

1982	390,119
1983	485,809
1984	384,312
1985	369,389
1986	373,320
1987	387,997
1988	345,634
1989	284,732
1990	139,451
1991	164,537
1992	150,560

NUMBER OF VOLUMES OF *THE ANNALS* SOLD (IN ADDITION TO MEMBERSHIPS AND SUBSCRIPTIONS)

1982	7,562
1983	5,877
1984	5,230
1985	5,910
1986	5,119
1987	5,314
1988	13,283
1989	4,802
1990	5,005
1991	3,766
1992	3,681

STATEMENT OF INCOME AND RETAINED EARNINGS FOR THE YEAR ENDED DECEMBER 31, 1992

Income
Royalty—Sage Publications	$120,000
Sales of review books	1,095
Royalties and reprint permissions	4,660
Miscellaneous	11,257
Total Income	137,012

Operating Expenses
Salaries	74,317
Payroll taxes	8,214
Pension expense	7,932
Employee benefits	8,799
Depreciation	9,953
Insurance	7,349
Postage	3,093
Repairs and maintenance	5,369
Professional and contracted services	12,036
Book review costs	1,240

Office expense 1,599
Utilities 11,550
Miscellaneous 6,328
    Total Operating Expenses 157,779
    Loss from Operations . . . . (20,767)
Other Income (Expenses)
Investment income (net) 5,739
    Net Income (Loss) . . . . (15,028)
    Retained Earnings—January 1 99,870
    Retained Earnings—December 31 84,842

Report of the Board of Directors

During 1992, the six volumes of THE ANNALS dealt with the following subjects:

January   *China's Foreign Relations*, edited by Allen S. Whiting, Professor and Director, Center for East Asian Studies, University of Arizona, Tucson

March   *World Literacy in the Year 2000*, edited by Daniel A. Wagner, Professor and Director, National Center on Adult Literacy, University of Pennsylvania, and Laurel D. Puchner, Doctoral Candidate, University of Pennsylvania, Philadelphia

May   *Drug Abuse: Linking Policy and Research*, edited by Eric D. Wish, Acting Director, Center for Substance Abuse Research, University of Maryland, College Park

July   *The Future: Trends into the Twenty-First Century*, edited by Joseph F. Coates, President, and Jennifer Jarratt, Vice President, Coates & Jarratt, Inc., Washington, D.C.

September   *Affirmative Action Revisited*, edited by Harold Orlans, an independent scholar in Chevy Chase, Maryland, and June O'Neill, Professor and Director, Center for the Study of Business and Government, Baruch College, City University of New York

November   *Political Islam*, edited by I. William Zartman, Jacob Blaustein, Professor of International Organization and Conflict Resolution and Director of African Studies, School of Advanced International Studies, Johns Hopkins University, Washington, D.C., and Charles E. Butterworth, Professor, University of Maryland, College Park

The publication program for 1993 includes the following volumes:

January   *White-Collar Crime*, edited by Gilbert Geis, Professor Emeritus, and Paul Jesilow, Assistant Professor, University of California, Irvine

March   *Free Trade in the Western Hemisphere*, edited by Sidney Weintraub, Dean Rusk Professor, Lyndon B. Johnson School of Public Affairs, University of Texas at Austin, and Distinguished Visiting Scholar, Americas Program of the Center for Strategic and International Studies, Washington, D.C.

May   *Religion in the Nineties*, edited by Wade Clark Roof, J. F. Rowny Professor of Religion and Society, University of California at Santa Barbara

July   *Citizens, Protest, and Democracy*, edited by Russell J. Dalton, Professor of Political Science and Chair of the Department of Politics and Society, University of California, Irvine

September   *Rural America: Blueprint for Tomorrow*, edited by William E. Gahr, Associate Director, Food and Agriculture Issues, U.S. General Accounting Office, Washington, D.C.

November   *Interminority Affairs in the U.S.: Pluralism at the Crossroads*, edited by Peter I. Rose, Sophia Smith Professor and Director of the American Studies Diploma Program, Smith College, Northampton, MA

During 1992, the Book Department published over 160 reviews. The majority of these were written by professors, but reviewers also included university presidents, members of private and university-sponsored organizations, government and public officials, and business professionals. Over 500 books were listed in the Other Books section.

Forty requests were granted to reprint material from THE ANNALS. These went to professors and other authors for use in books in preparation and to nonprofit organizations for educational purposes.

OFFICERS AND STAFF

The Board reelected the following officers: Marvin E. Wolfgang, President; Richard D. Lambert, Vice President; Anthony J. Scirica, Secretary; Elmer B. Staats, Treasurer; Henry W. Sawyer, III, Counsel. Re-

appointed were: Richard D. Lambert, Editor, and Alan W. Heston, Associate Editor.

Respectfully submitted,
THE BOARD OF DIRECTORS

Elmer B. Staats
Marvin E. Wolfgang
Richard D. Lambert
Lloyd N. Cutler
Henry W. Sawyer, III
Anthony J. Scirica
Frederick Heldring
Lynn Curtis
Mary Ann Meyers
Milton L. Rock

Philadelphia, Pennsylvania
20 November 1992

Book Department

INTERNATIONAL RELATIONS AND POLITICS

KAMINSKI, ANTONI Z. *An Institutional Theory of Communist Regimes: Design, Function and Breakdown.* Pp. xi, 414. San Francisco: Institute for Contemporary Studies Press, 1992. $29.95. Paperbound, $15.95.

This is one of the few books about the breakdown of Communist systems to reach American audiences written by a social scientist who lived under one of them. Antoni Kaminski is a sociologist by training and a high-ranking official in the Polish Ministry of Foreign Affairs. In this excellent study, he seeks to explain the disintegration of Communist systems, and the USSR in particular, by reference to their institutional design and ideological foundations. Lenin's practical and theoretical contributions receive much well-deserved emphasis. While Kaminski highlights Marx's notions of human nature, he reminds us that these ideas also played a paradoxical role in the foundation and evolution of these systems. Given Marx's optimistic view of human nature, it is not surprising that he and his followers paid little attention to the need for autonomous political and cultural institutions that would have fostered political democracy and pluralism. Correspondingly, "the presumption of the rulers' wisdom" became axiomatic in each Communist system and deprived these governments of mechanisms for detecting error in devising and implementing their policies.

This massive and comprehensive study also examines Western theories of Communist systems. While not disputing that Communist states represented a form of modernization, Kaminski emphasizes that, whereas Western-style modernization led, through the weakening of traditional institutions, to the liberation of the individual, exactly the opposite happened in Communist societies, where the weakening of traditional institutions "left lonely individuals facing an anonymous, all-powerful state." In short, Communist modernization was an enterprise

179

quite different from the earlier Western variety with profoundly different results.

This book will help to settle the contentious issue of the link between Marxist ideas and ideals and the institutional practices of the now-defunct Communist states. Were the latter mere parodies of Marxist ideals or heirs to these doctrines? In Kaminski's view, they possessed "some of the key institutional features postulated by the main currents of socialist thought," which helps to explain "why Marxist intellectuals in the West are sometimes so painfully ambivalent in their attitudes to the abuses committed by Soviet regimes." The author has little doubt that "without understanding the Marxist-Leninist foundations of Communist regimes, we cannot understand their institutional design. . . . Acting upon an erroneous theory . . . has consequences."

Perhaps the central proposition of this rich and thoughtful volume is that the demise of these systems has been taking place because their institutions and guiding ideas have proved incapable of dealing with the industrial, technological, and social developments of our times. While this is not an entirely new idea, Western analysts tended to believe, before the dramatic events of the last year or two, that modernization and a reformed variety of Communist systems were compatible, that modernization would humanize and pluralize these systems rather than fatally undermine them and highlight their lack of legitimacy. These systems cannot reform themselves because as soon as they try to allow more public expression and autonomy, their lack of legitimacy reveals itself.

Written before the dissolution of the Soviet Union and hence dated in some of its conjectures and concerns—for example, the policies of Gorbachev—this book will greatly help the reader to grasp the essential features of all Communist systems and what have been the seeds of the destruction that these systems harbored from their inception.

PAUL HOLLANDER

University of Massachusetts
Amherst

RUESCHEMEYER, DIETRICH, EVELYNE HUBER STEPHENS, and JOHN D. STEPHENS. *Capitalist Development and Democracy*. Pp. ix, 387. Chicago: University of Chicago Press, 1992. $45.00. Paperbound, $19.95.

This book focuses on the development of democracy in capitalist systems. The authors use a comparative historical model in which European democratic development is used to discover the prerequisites for democracy in developing nations. They examine the transformation of European states from autocracies to democracies during the nineteenth century, and they find that both economic crises and warfare during the latter decades of that century created new class alignments. Where the agrarian landlord elite class was reduced as the dominant force in society, other groups, particularly working- and middle-class elements (but not the bourgeoisie), forced a transformation to democratic rule. They argue that working-class mobilization in particular was crucial in most cases of democratization, a finding that differs from most other studies, including those of Barrington Moore.

Extending their model to South America, the authors identify several necessary preconditions for the establishment of democracy, including consolidation of state power, export expansion, industrialization, and an alliance between the working class and middle class. When only several of these conditions held, the establishment of democracy was difficult, as in Brazil and Uruguay. But in Bolivia,

Peru, Venezuela, and Chile, a mineral-export economy and an active working class combined to help form the foundations of democracy. Also key was the involvement of the military, which, when divided, gave more impetus to democracy than when it was unified, as in the case of Chile.

In Central America, the authors find that a combination of landlord power, U.S. political intervention, and Spanish traditions made the establishment of democracy difficult. But in the Caribbean, British traditions both weakened the landlord class and provided the philosophical underpinnings of participatory government.

The comparison across regions and time about class structure and democracy produce compelling findings. In both nineteenth- century Europe and in developing areas in the Western Hemisphere in the twentieth century, similar class alignments worked either to retard or to advance democracy. Strong landlord classes aligned with autocratic states hindered democracy while working-class and middle-class coalitions encouraged it.

Some readers, including this one, may wish that the authors had supported their findings with more data. Moreover, their findings on Europe are based exclusively on secondary sources. Otherwise, this is a carefully crafted book that will be essential reading for those interested in the nexus between capitalism and democracy. Unfortunately, it will be less helpful in explaining the potential for democracy in former Communist nations where transformations of both the political and economic systems are now in gestation.

DAVID S. SORENSON

Air War College
Maxwell Air Force Base
Alabama

AFRICA, ASIA, AND
LATIN AMERICA

KRYZANEK, MICHAEL J. *Leaders, Leadership, and U.S. Policy in Latin America.* Pp. xii, 249. Boulder, CO: Westview Press, 1992. $45.00.

Michael J. Kryzanek has written a book on a topic neglected in the recent study of Latin American politics. The contribution is noteworthy because of the connection it establishes between national leaders and U.S. policy toward Latin America. After an initial discussion on leadership types and U.S. interests in the region, Kryzanek focuses on three classes of leaders—military, civilian, and revolutionary—and examines Washington's response to them in different periods. (In this section, Kryzanek's profile on Daniel Ortega and the insights into television and public relations packaging are of particular value.) Thereafter, Kryzanek presents three issues or areas that leaders must contend with in the 1990s: drug traffic, foreign debt, and U.S. intervention. Two concluding chapters evaluate the success and failure of, as well as the prospects for, the region's leaders in the domestic and international arenas.

Although the book provides a general panorama of leadership types and specific case studies of how U.S.-Latin American relations have been influenced by particular brands of leadership styles, Kryzanek's work is not satisfying on a deeper level. The dissatisfaction is a result of two problems: one concerns the book's scope and the other, the ideological undercurrent. First, the work falls into broad generalizations that specialists will find disconcerting. Dichotomies, such as "authoritarian" and "democratic," do not do justice to the complexity and nuances of leadership in a region where it is not uncommon for some military to act more democratically than democratically elected civilian presidents—remember Fujimori in Peru. In short, knowledgeable readers will find the discussion on models of leadership, in chapter 1, lackluster. For example, seldom does Kryzanek connect leaders to followers, and he fails to elaborate on continuity and change in the region's political culture, which seems to be part of his explanatory variable.

Second, throughout the book Kryzanek uncritically espouses ideas and an ideology that are sources of scholarly and policy debates. He assumes that modernization and democracy go, or should go, hand in hand in a progressive continuum. His perspective on authoritarianism is not only surprising but contradictory as well: "authoritarianism with its penchant for stability and revolution and with its emphasis on mass mobilization and income distribution. . . ." The problem is, again, related to generalization. Not all authoritarian, or democratic, regimes behave exactly the same way. Moreover, the ideological undertow is evidenced in statements such as "A revolution spread throughout the hemisphere and Soviet influence increased [since 1959]." The author's endorsement of privatization, free trade, and the entire neoliberal reform package, on the other hand, and his penchant to raise the specter of Marxism, on the other, undermine an otherwise competent work.

Kryzanek's comments on the prospect for improved U.S.-Latin American relations in the 1990s—based largely on the possibility that "pragmatic" leaders will emerge in the region—dismiss the obstacles imposed by power asymmetry, divergent interests, and the record of U.S. interventions in the region regardless of individual leadership type.

As an admirer of Kryzanek's coauthored *Politics of External Influence in the Dominican Republic* (1988), I ex-

pected a uniformly high caliber of scholarship from his latest work as well.

DAMIAN J. FERNANDEZ

Florida International University
Miami

SHEPARD, ROBERT B. *Nigeria, Africa and the United States: From Kennedy to Reagan.* Pp. xi, 193. Bloomington: Indiana University Press, 1991. $24.95.

JEAN, CLINTON M. *Behind the Eurocentric Veils: The Search for African Realities.* Pp. xxi, 113. Amherst: University of Massachusetts Press, 1992. $19.95.

Postcolonial Africa's importance to the United States is the subject of a longstanding debate on the fringes of American foreign policy. To some, the African subcontinent has been little more than an irritating distraction from the important struggles taking place in more geostrategic locations across the globe. To others, Africa's economic potential gave it sufficient geopolitical weight to warrant American attention. To yet others, finally, an assortment of moral and historical considerations mandates a voluntaristic foreign policy toward the subcontinent. Far from ending the debate, the end of the Cold War forces the United States to soberly reassess its interests in a continent of some fifty countries and several hundred million people that has the combined gross domestic product of an average midwestern state such as Michigan and accounts for less than 2 percent of the world's trade.

The two books under review both shed some light on these issues, albeit in very different ways and not necessarily intentionally. In *Nigeria, Africa and the United States,* Robert Shepard traces the evolution of American policy toward the African subcontinent through the prism of

Nigerian-American relations, from the Kennedy administration to Reagan's second term. The material covered is hardly new and will be well-known already to the specialist, but Shepard demonstrates some skill in showing how American policies toward Africa have usually been motivated by factors external to Africa and informed by a meager knowledge of African realities. Although his study devotes inadequate attention to the domestic motivations for American policies, Shepard does point to the recurring sense among decision makers and in public opinion of a link between domestic race relations and policies toward Africa. With a large population of African origin and a legacy of slavery and institutionalized racism, the United States has felt a special responsibility toward Africa, one that outweighs the economic and geostrategic considerations that usually inform foreign policy.

Behind the Eurocentric Veils describes a very different kind of relationship between the United States and Africa, but it does provide evidence for Shepard's argument that Americans have a tendency to see in Africa only what they want to see. In a polemical essay that attacks both "mainstream" and "radical" Western intellectual traditions as "eurocentric" and argues for an "Afrocentric" reinterpretation of world history, Clinton Jean goes so far as to suggest that the world would be a more peaceful and less oppressive place if African cultural norms dominated, rather than the Western intellectual tradition. Jean's unwillingness to define his conceptual apparatus with any consistency or precision and his fairly relaxed attitudes about evidence make for tough reading to all but the already converted. The student of Africa will be struck by the highly romanticized, almost mythical view of the continent offered in these pages. For all its progressive rhetoric, the Africa that the author conjures

to contest Western cultural hegemony is a preindustrial Garden of Eden populated by noble savages. Such myths perhaps fulfill some needs within the academy, but they are no more helpful for Africa as it approaches the twenty-first century than the fictitious descriptions in the old Tarzan movies.

NICOLAS VAN DE WALLE

Michigan State University
East Lansing

SIKKINK, KATHRYN. *Ideas and Institutions: Developmentalism in Brazil and Argentina.* Pp. xviii, 263. Ithaca, NY: Cornell University Press, 1991. $35.00.

This is an outstanding study of a topic central to Latin America's development after 1945. It will give both experts and students a clear understanding of the state-directed developmentalism in Latin America that attained hegemonic status among progressive regimes by the end of the 1950s and that still garners powerful support in political circles.

Ideas and Institutions is a well-crafted examination of the policies adopted in the second half of the 1950s by "two intense men who shared the same dream: to usher their countries into the future as modern industrial powers." Juscelino Kubitschek and Arturo Frondizi, presidents of Brazil and Argentina, respectively, attempted to use the powers of the state to mobilize the resources of their nations, to plan and so control economic activity, and to direct investment into the designated fields. Interesting as is Sikkink's analysis of Kubitschek's success in serving out his term and implementing many of his famous *metas* (targets), the work is more innovative in its discussion of Frondizi's presidency. Sikkink makes a strong case for Frondizi's having achieved far more success in promoting economic development than is generally granted him. His failure is essentially political. In this respect, Sikkink could have given more consideration as to whether any individual elected president of Argentina in 1958, given the deep polarization produced by Juan Perón's long years of rule, could have mobilized and retained broad support for an ambitious set of policies.

Good as the delineation of the Kubitschek and Frondizi presidencies is, the book excels in its handling of larger theoretical issues, particularly its discussion of the factors—ideas, institutions, and interest groups—that, in the author's opinion, make planned economic development possible. Sikkink has an enviable capacity for clear presentation of argument and analysis that makes her work a joy to read. Ideas she sees as indispensable do not just allow for the formulation of effective policies but form an ideological program attracting broad support. Autonomous, well-organized state institutions are required for the enactment of policies, while the marshaling of a broad coalition of committed interest groups, which support a program for national development because it promotes the groups' own interests, is essential. Without repudiating dependency theory, bogged down in determinism and normativism, Sikkink's work presents a fruitful approach to the vexed question of Latin America's stymied development in the years after 1945.

RODERICK J. BARMAN

University of British Columbia
Vancouver
Canada

EUROPE

FARMER, KENNETH C. *The Soviet Administrative Elite*. Pp. xii, 296. New York: Praeger, 1992. $49.95.

The world has not been kind to Communist ruling elites since the revolutions of 1989. Once regarded as virtually indestructible leviathans, Leninist single-party states are now in danger of becoming extinct. The rapid disintegration of the Soviet Union after the abortive conservative coup of August 1991 stands as one of the seminal events of our era. Today a handful of demoralized Communist elites still lord over isolated garrison-states in places like China, Vietnam, North Korea, and Cuba. But, far from being in the vanguard of progress, their days appear numbered.

Kenneth Farmer's monograph, *The Soviet Administrative Elite*, was conceived and executed before the deluge. In the concluding chapter, he manages to say a few words about the August 1991 coup and expresses some cautious optimism about the prospects of democracy in Russia and the other new republics. Nonetheless, the work as a whole reflects the latter stages of Gorbachev's tortuous efforts to reshape the Communist Party and Soviet society.

Still, this is a valuable and interesting study. Farmer examines the Soviet political elite as a corporate entity, providing a detailed description of its institutional structure, its historical development since 1917, and its relationship to the more enduring "deep structure" of Russian society. His anthropological approach borrows liberally from classical elite theorists such as Max Weber, Vilfredo Pareto, Gaetano Mosca, and Alexis de Tocqueville, while incorporating some of the insights of more contemporary elite theorists such as Suzanne Keller—particularly her concept of strategic elites—and John Armstrong. We are reminded of some of the eternal verities of elite theory—"the few govern the many"; "to know who is educated is to know who will rule"; and so forth—a literally noble body of knowledge that can be traced back to Plato and Aristotle.

Farmer's concept of the "deep structure" of Soviet society is central to his understanding of the Soviet political elite. Contrary to the tenets of orthodox Marxism, the Bolsheviks seized power in a society whose "deep structure" was "peasant-feudal" rather than modern, urbanized, and industrialized. The party-state apparatus that Lenin superimposed on this society absorbed, not surprisingly, many "peasant-feudal" characteristics: highly personalized relations between patrons and clients, distrust of outsiders, and an authoritarian style of command, among others. Although modern Russia and some of the other republics have well-educated, predominantly urban populations, Farmer's insistence that the "peasant-feudal" structure has not yet been completely uprooted appears accurate. This no doubt accounts for some of the difficulties in building market economic as well as democratic political institutions.

The Soviet administrative elite enjoyed a brief but turbulent reign. Lenin's Old Bolsheviks were decapitated during Stalin's Great Terror—undoubtedly the bloodiest "elite transformation" in history. Beginning in the late 1980s, Gorbachev engineered a more peaceable transformation of the elite, but it was not enough. The elite's considerable institutional flaws, convincingly portrayed by Kenneth Farmer, suddenly and shockingly proved to be the cause of its demise in the summer of 1991.

SCOTT NICHOLS

Southern Illinois University
Carbondale

McCLELLAN, JAMES E., III. *Colonialism and Science: Saint Domingue in the Old Regime*. Pp. xviii, 393. Baltimore: Johns Hopkins University Press, 1992. $52.00.

In *Colonialism and Science*, James E. McClellan III, professor at Stevens Institute of Technology, presents a three-part work dealing with the roles of science and scientific institutions in the French slave colony of Saint Domingue in the eighteenth century, ending with the beginning of the successful slave uprising in the last decade of the century. Based upon extensive reading in contemporary and later writings, as well as numerous primary archival sources, it is a history of slavery as well as a history of science in France and in the New World.

Part 1 is basically a history of Saint Domingue as a slave society and represents a solid contribution to the analysis of the development of what was once the world's richest island. Part 2, "Science in a New World Setting," is a thorough examination of various applied sciences, including medicine, botany, and meteorology, describing both the contribution of these sciences to the colonization process and the impact of the discoveries and the colonies upon scientific thought.

Part 3 provides an interesting discussion of the rise and fall of the one major scientific organization of Saint Domingue, the Cercle des Philadelphes, founded in Cap François in 1784, trailing behind only those of Philadelphia (1768) and Boston (1780) in North America. In addition to the institutional details of its official recognition by the French government, McClellan presents a quite useful description of its various papers and publications. Its end came, of course, with the onset of the Haitian Revolution.

McClellan argues that a "major moral of this tale is that science and organized knowledge did not come to Saint Domingue as something separate from the rest of the colonizing process but, rather, formed an inherent part of French colonization from the beginning," leading him to conclude that "French colonial science and medicine did not serve to advance the cause of human freedom as much as to reinforce the chains of human bondage." Perhaps so, but little is said about the role of science on the European continent, where slavery no longer existed, in the French New World colonies where slavery was less important, or in the slave colonies of the other European powers, and about why it might have been expected that such a central part of society and social thought would have, in the relatively short run, played any other role. Nevertheless, because of the information presented, the questions asked, and the description of the role played by seemingly modern developments within a slave society, *Colonialism and Science* will be of interest to historians of science and to historians of the settlement of the American colonies.

STANLEY L. ENGERMAN

University of Rochester
New York

PRYOR, FREDERIC L. *The Red and the Green: The Rise and Fall of Collectivized Agriculture in Marxist Regimes.* Pp. x, 550. Princeton, NJ: Princeton University Press, 1992. $59.50.

SCALAPINO, ROBERT A. *The Last Leninists: The Uncertain Future of Asia's Communist States.* Pp. xvii, 104. Washington, DC: Center for Strategic and International Studies, 1992. Paperbound, $14.95.

The stunning and almost completely unanticipated collapse of Soviet-bloc communism between 1989 and 1991 poses both theoretical and practical questions for students of Communist societies. Do systemic differences between Warsaw Pact communism and other models of Leninism, such as those found in China or Vietnam, help to explain why the former states have perished while the latter endure?

What, moreover, are the prospects for those Communist states that have, so far, survived the so-called end of the Cold War? These two fine studies, though very different in scope and execution, commonly contribute to our understanding of a landscape that is suddenly so very different.

The Red and the Green is an ambitious and sweeping analysis of the problem of agricultural development under Marxist rule. Drawing upon a formidable command of a diverse economic and political literature, and proceeding with a caution that befits such an effort at synthesis, Frederic Pryor highlights the differences as well as the similarities in the approaches of various Marxist regimes to this critical economic sector. He argues that "the reorganization of agricultural production units into large-scale state and collective farms has been the most radical change of economic institutions implemented by Marxist governments" and that, "although the organization of agriculture may not be the ultimate cause of bad agricultural policies, it is often the proximate cause since it increases the probability for certain inappropriate policies." In the Warsaw Pact in the late 1980s, Pryor believes, agriculture came to absorb more resources from the socialist economy than it was releasing, a circumstance at odds with the broad sweep of Western economic development, to say nothing of the particulars of Stalinist industrialization doctrine. Even with the collapse of communism, however, Pryor sees decollectivization as a slow and contentious process: "Some major institutional changes may occur in the short run only with difficulty, if at all, even if the institutions to be changed are dysfunctional."

However dysfunctional the remaining Communist regimes in Asia may be deemed, they nevertheless continue to cling to power. But what of their future? In his brief essay pondering the question,

Robert Scalapino concludes that "an era featuring the centralized, command economic strategy is ending, and despite nostalgia in certain quarters and temporary retreats, it cannot be restored." *The Last Leninists* sketches out four possible "scenarios" for Communist regimes in Asia—including a "muddling through," a sudden collapse, and a rapid transition to an open society—but regards as most probable a shift toward "authoritarian pluralism," by which is meant polities of the Chiang Kai-shek or Park Chung Hee variety. Readers will doubtless have their own opinions about the likelihood of the various outcomes Scalapino describes, but they are sure to find his masterful analysis of the current circumstances facing Beijing, Hanoi, and Pyongyang both rewarding and thought provoking.

NICHOLAS EBERSTADT

Harvard University
Cambridge
Massachusetts

American Enterprise Institute
Washington, D.C.

REID, DONALD. *Paris Sewers and Sewermen: Realities and Representations.* Pp. x, 235. Cambridge, MA: Harvard University Press, 1991. $39.95.

Sewage is an almost irresistible topic for a scholar seeking to explore a topic from both the inside and the outside and to reconcile linguistic representations and social realities. Donald Reid shows persuasively that the discourse of sanitary reformers moved uninterruptedly between the pragmatic consideration of sanitary needs and the metaphorical framework of social pollution. At one level, the outbreak of social revolution was viewed as equivalent to a backed-up cesspool and thus, conversely, more efficient sewers might obviate the class men-

ace. Upon their discovery that sewer workers were not the degraded figures of bourgeois humor, early nineteenth-century reformers such as Parent-Duchâtelet built a larger social vision. They hoped that cultivation might enable them to rejuvenate a corrupted working class.

While Reid is quick to identify reformist rhetoric, he is less keen to acknowledge reality or to explain how it relates to its representation. Reid seems to deal with middle-class reform mainly in rhetorical terms, but his treatment of working-class trade unionists largely dwells on their social practices. Although he surely does not intend this, the dichotomy between the middle class and the working class sometimes seems confused with the dichotomy between representation and reality. His attempt to analyze both middle-class social reformers and sewer laborers through a single representation-reality lens focused on the middle-class rhetoric of sanitary reform neglects the very different concerns of social reformers and trade unionists.

Ultimately, for both reformers and workers, the need to solve perceived problems provides the indispensable matrix for reconciling representations and realities. Although Reid neglects the topic, the outbreak of cholera and typhoid in a rapidly growing Paris forced sanitary reformers to recognize that sewage treatment was somehow related to the outbreak of epidemic disease. In the end, the need for improvements in public health stimulated the growth of sanitary reform and provided a public and political means for evaluating its success.

Preeminent among sanitation reformers, concern with epidemic disease was subordinated by sewer workers to the need to secure and defend the strong bargaining position they had secured through collective action and group solidarity. The privileged position of the sewermen as municipal employees and the support they received from allies among the professional engineers may have originated in concern with sanitation, but, as Reid acknowledges in a perfunctory fashion, these depended most heavily on political alliances and trade union support within the larger world of syndicalism and republicanism. The link between sanitary reform rhetoric and trade union rhetoric may have been real, but it seems too weak to unify the diverse issues treated in this book.

Reid's discussion of the sewermen's unionism is fascinating and important, but his failure to locate it within the larger context of unionism and popular politics probably leads him to exaggerate its significance. While its mutual-benefit social-insurance functions, particularly its collective farm for the aged and orphans, are highly interesting, the union's dependence on an increasingly conservative Parisian municipal council probably accounts for its sustained inattention to national or municipal politics. It is hard to buy Reid's celebration of its "innovative praxis" and his assertion that such political neutrality joined with mutual-benefit services represented an "exemplary . . . blend of antibureaucratic socialism, syndicalism and cooperatism."

MICHAEL HANAGAN

New School for Social Research
New York City

SCHUMANN, WILLY. *Being Present: Growing Up in Hitler's Germany.* Pp. xi, 212. Kent, OH: Kent State University Press, 1992. $29.00.

Cultural historians will probably be able to find reasons for the current popularity of everyday history. This is history as witnessed in the daily lives of ordinary people who do not normally appear in history books. Perhaps one reason for the large numbers of studies of this kind is the breakdown of grand theories of historical explanation, such as Marxism, socialism, and structuralism. The refuge of giving attention to little people and their day-to-day existence has its charms for those disillusioned with larger theories.

Willy Schumann's memoirs of growing up in Hitler's Germany are a good example of the strengths and weaknesses of this genre of history. Born in 1927 in northern Germany near the Elbe River estuary, Schumann experienced Nazism as a rather bemused young adolescent, both taken by and skeptical of all the Nazi transformations of traditional German life. His family was unambiguously middle class, respectable, hardworking, basically non-Nazi. In many ways, his reports about his life are strikingly unexceptional. He has some interesting early memories about the day Hitler came to power and drawing a swastika in the sand. He goes to elementary school and the local *Gymnasium*, joins the party's Hitler Youth, and finally serves in military units at the end of the war.

Along the way he comments cogently on a variety of subjects: the ways in which his schoolteachers resisted the nazification of German classrooms; his dislike of *All Quiet on the Western Front* because it was not heroic enough; the growing militarization of German life in the late 1930s; the deep effect of the war on homefront morale; his desire to be a soldier like his older brothers; and his gradual realization after 1945 that Hitler's regime was a fraud worthy of "collective German shame."

A drawback of Schumann's book is the very routinism of his experience and his inability to reflect more than superficially on what he once lived through. True, this is the story of the way he saw his life, but he did not see very far, and his life in Nazi Germany passed as if in a sheltered cove. His family lost no sons or daughters; there were no great conflicts of conscience during the war; and, as he reports, life after the war continued for all of them as if the Nazi episode had been a parenthesis of turbulence in the calm flow of German history. Incidentally, the author immigrated to America and became a professor at Smith College.

More illuminating examples of everyday history in Germany are Bernt Engelmann's *Hitler's Germany: Everyday Life in the Third Reich*, Richard Bessel's *Life in the Third Reich*, Detlev Peukert's *Inside Nazi Germany*, and Alfons Heck's *Child of Hitler*.

RICHARD M. HUNT

Harvard University
Cambridge
Massachusetts

UNITED STATES

BIRD, KAI. *The Chairman: John J. Mc-Cloy—The Making of an American Establishment*. Pp. 800. New York: Simon & Schuster, 1992. $30.00.

For several decades, from World War II until the mid-1970s, a group of uncommon men, many of whom were Eastern businessmen or Wall Street lawyers and bankers and members of the Council on Foreign Relations, were extraordinarily influential in the shaping of America's foreign and security policies, mostly by acting behind the scenes. No member of this so-called Establishment was more involved in high-level domestic and international affairs than was John J. McCloy. John Kenneth Galbraith described him as "without doubt the most important member of the Establishment." *Harper's* magazine called him "the most influential private citizen in America." The author of the book under review refers to McCloy as "the country's first national-security manager, a sort of political commissar" and as "the quintessential chairman of the American century."

During his long and varied career, John J. McCloy, born in Philadelphia "on the wrong side of the tracks," educated at Amherst and Harvard Law School, served as Assistant Secretary of War and Henry Stimson's right-hand man at the War Department; as an intimate adviser to eight presidents; as "the most sought-after lawyer on Wall Street"; as chairman of the World Bank, the Chase Manhattan Bank, the Ford Foundation, and the Council on Foreign Relations; as U.S. High Commissioner in Germany; as "arms control czar" in the Kennedy administration; as a member of the loyalty review board appointed to investigate the charges against Robert Oppenheimer, the Warren Commission, and other major investigatory bodies; as a behind-the-scenes negotiator in the Cuban missile crisis, the Iran hostage crisis, and other crisis situations. He wore many hats. On him, as Bird observes, "all the hats fit. . . . He seemed to be everywhere . . . and to know everything."

All of these and many other activities and services in the private and public sectors are described in considerable detail in this book. So, too, are McCloy's difficulties in the McCarthy era and during the Vietnam war. There are interesting accounts of his relations with presidents and other public figures in the United States and abroad—for example, Henry Stimson, Henry Kissinger, and Konrad Adenauer.

On the whole, McCloy escaped major public criticism. For his role in a few important matters, however, he was widely criticized. These included the internment of Japanese Americans during World War II, his muted views on the Holocaust, and his clemency decisions regarding Alfred Krupp and other leading Nazi collaborators.

On all of these issues, Bird reflects the critical views of McCloy's behavior. He seems to be particularly disturbed by the possible conflicts of interest arising from

McCloy's high-level operations in both the private and public sectors, McCloy's practice of "always" acting "in close collaboration with Washington," and McCloy's strong belief that it was America's destiny to lead the world.

This is the first full-fledged biography of "the Chairman," a remarkable man who was relatively unknown as far as the general public was concerned. It was a decade in the making. In preparing it, Kai Bird, a well-known journalist, consulted major archival sources, interviewed nearly 150 persons, and made an exhaustive examination of the relevant literature.

NORMAN D. PALMER

University of Pennsylvania
Philadelphia

BLUM, JOHN MORTON. *Years of Discord: American Politics and Society, 1961-1974.* Pp. x, 530. New York: W. W. Norton, 1991. $25.00.

In *Years of Discord*, John Morton Blum recounts the turbulent events of the Kennedy, Johnson, and Nixon presidencies from 1961 to 1974. In domestic politics, Blum emphasizes the powerful drive toward federal government reform in a wide variety of areas, including civil rights, public education, aiding the poor, welfare, and the economy. The New Frontier and the Great Society resulted in considerable expansion of government activity.

Blum correctly identifies the resistance to social reform, including the conservative coalition in Congress and the law-and-order appeals made by Nixon in the 1968 campaign. The quest for racial justice provoked reactions in the South that turned around Kennedy's views and helped Johnson to achieve passage of the 1964 Civil Rights Act and the 1965 Voting Rights Act.

Johnson's Great Society had some important successes, particularly the Head Start program, but Nixon sought to dismantle the antipoverty program and shift attention to welfare reform. By the mid-1970s, elected officials and voters were less interested in social reform as the economy soured due to the Arab oil boycott. More important, the lawlessness and corruption of Nixon's Watergate scandal resulted in voter cynicism and distrust with respect to government.

Blum also traces the concentration of power in the foreign policy imperial presidency. He is very critical of the Kennedy-Johnson-Nixon expansion of executive authority without consulting Congress or the American people. His conclusions are based upon the Bay of Pigs fiasco, the overreaction by Nixon to a Soviet threat during the 1973 Yom Kippur War, and, most important, the entire conduct of the Vietnam war, which dominated the Johnson and Nixon presidencies.

According to Blum and most other observers, the Vietnam war divided American society, ripped apart the Democratic Party at the 1968 Chicago convention, and prompted Nixon to begin covert activities against his "enemies" in the Watergate episode.

Years of Discord is an excellent source for historians, political scientists, students, and general readers interested in the dramatic and tragic events of the 1960s and early 1970s. A minor improvement—namely, differentiating the leadership styles of JFK, LBJ, and Nixon —would make Blum's epilogue more effective. While the three presidents dealt with similar problems, their approaches to persuading and educating the public were quite different. This might explain why LBJ and Nixon were two of our most flawed presidents.

ALAN SHANK

State University of New York
Geneseo

BODENHAMER, DAVID J. *Fair Trial: Rights of the Accused in American History*. Pp. x, 173. New York: Oxford University Press, 1991. $24.95. Paperbound, $9.95.

David Bodenhamer's book analyzes the development of the procedural rights that American society currently accords a criminal defendant. It explains how these rights have evolved over more than three centuries, beginning with colonial practices and concluding with the conservative jurisprudence of the Rehnquist Court.

The initial focus is on how the rights that are presently considered essential for a fair trial evolved out of English practices. Bodenhamer explains that early English criminal justice was based on an adversarial model in which litigants did battle—literally—and judges played the rather passive role of ensuring fairness in the process. He shows how innovations that the Normans introduced after conquering England modified this system of criminal justice and eventually produced the model that is still used in this country. The notable features of that model are an accusation by a grand jury and an adversarial trial of the charges before a trial, or petit, jury.

This system was brought to the American colonies and provided the basis for the system of criminal justice that evolved in the states. Bodenhamer explains that until the middle of this century, the administration of criminal justice remained a matter of state, not federal, law. Until the 1960s, the Supreme Court's position was that the Bill of Rights applied only to the federal government; states were not required to honor protections such as the Fifth Amendment right against self-incrimination.

For example, in 1914, federal law adopted the exclusionary rule—under which evidence improperly obtained cannot be used to establish guilt—as a remedy for Fourth Amendment violations, but the rule did not apply to the states. Consequently, state courts could—and did—entertain evidence obtained through conduct that violated the protection established by the Fourth Amendment.

During the 1960s, the Supreme Court, led by Chief Justice Earl Warren, fundamentally altered American criminal justice by holding that most of the rights granted by the federal Bill of Rights were binding on the states. As Bodenhamer explains, this was a highly controversial outcome because it greatly expanded the procedural protections for those accused of committing crimes. He concludes by noting the extent to which the Supreme Court—under Chief Justice Warren Burger and now under Chief Justice William Rehnquist—has retreated from the decisions of the Warren Court.

While not a comprehensive treatment, this book is an excellent survey of the evolution of procedural rights in American criminal justice.

SUSAN W. BRENNER

University of Dayton
Ohio

DAVIS, JAMES KIRKPATRICK. *Spying on America: The FBI's Domestic Counter-Intelligence Program*. Pp. x, 192. New York: Praeger, 1992. $21.95.

Only the most stable of personalities could take a balanced view of the dreadful excesses of the Federal Bureau of Investigation's Counterintelligence Program (COINTELPRO). Such equanimity distinguishes James Kirkpatrick Davis's *Spying on America*. Davis is no less offended by this sordid chapter in the bureau's domestic intelligence activities than have been previous authors on the subject, but his is more a tale of personal tragedies than a political call to action. Davis depoliticizes what was surely one of America's quintessentially political conflicts. Perhaps because Davis worked closely with former FBI Director Clarence Kelly in coauthoring *Kelly: The Story of an FBI Director*, he is content to regard COINTELPRO as a well-meaning law enforcement plan gone bad. Still, he may be a bit too kind in claiming, "The COINTELPRO operations were initially designed with all the good intentions in the world."

Davis makes frequent reference to internal FBI memoranda released more than twenty years ago, many of which were reproduced in their entirety in Blackstock's *COINTELPRO: The FBI's Secret War on Political Freedom*. Davis also leans heavily on Jayco's *FBI on Trial*, Donner's *Age of Surveillance*, and his own previous biography of Clarence Kelly.

Davis's opening chapter on the daring 1971 raid on the bureau's resident agency in Media, Pennsylvania, is a valuable introduction to the COINTELPRO story. The break-in at the Media office was conducted by a shadowy organization calling itself the Citizens' Commission to Investigate the FBI, and, despite one of the largest FBI investigations conducted up to that time, the bureau was never able to solve the case or identify the Citizens' Commission. The raid netted a treasure trove of about 1000 classified documents, which, to this day, represent much of the public's knowledge of COINTELPRO.

The official COINTELPRO programs ended in 1971, and Davis's book covers virtually all relevant, publicly available information from that period. Of the 13 programs eventually revealed by the FBI, however, this book addresses in detail only the major 5: the Communist Party of the USA, the Socialist Workers Party, White Hate, Black Nationalist, and New Left. These programs are movingly portrayed, often in the words of the FBI agents and the victims of their secret programs. Indeed, the most compelling and distinctive aspect of the book is its emphasis on personal anecdotes. Davis

also brings us up to date by documenting the FBI's recent neo-COINTELPRO activities against political groups like the Committee in Solidarity with the People of El Salvador, warning that society must remain vigilant against a recurrence of arbitrary state intrusion on the lives of citizens.

HERBERT N. FOERSTEL

University of Maryland
College Park

FOGARTY, ROBERT S. *All Things New: American Communes and Utopian Movements, 1860-1914*. Pp. vii, 286. Chicago: University of Chicago Press, 1990. $34.50.

Robert Fogarty's *All Things New* recounts the journeys of thousands of Americans who left their homes in the years after the Civil War to seek harmony and fulfillment in communal living. An impressive research feat, *All Things New* will quickly disabuse the reader of the notion that New Age is new, or that back-to-the-land communal fervor originated in the 1960s. This movement constitutes the most complete collection of militant vegetarians, religious cultists, spiritual architects, and exponents of liberation through sex this side of California in the 1970s. This book recasts our sense of late-nineteenth-century American culture, and it is supposed to. Fogarty's point is that the drive to create "enclaves of difference" is as American as, say, the devotion to "traditional family values." His book removes commune dwellers from the lunatic fringe and places them in a position much more useful to historians, as foils for the society they rejected but sought to change by example.

Fogarty divides the communards of the late nineteenth century into three categories, of which the most numerous were the charismatic perfectionists, who believed they could find paradise on earth. They espoused all sorts of beliefs, including vegetarianism, "complex marriage," celibacy, "structural, bisexual completeness above the plane of sin, of disease, or of natural mortality," and that the earth was a "hollow, concave sphere" with humans living on the inside. What these disparate sects shared was an almost messianic faith in their charismatic leaders. This faith fueled great loyalty to the communal experiment; however, it made most perfectionists so dependent on their leaders that their communities survived only as long as the founders remained vital.

That survival was still longer than the survival of the secular communities that are the subject of this book. Lacking the glue of religious faith, the other two kinds of communes that Fogarty discusses, reformist colonies and those based on socialist or anarchist principles, rarely stayed together more than a few years. These communards shared with the perfectionists a strong anti-urban feeling and the belief that the problems of nineteenth-century urban life could be solved by creating cooperative rural communities. Their attachment to the principles on which their communities were based was not strong enough, however, to sustain them through the travails of their errands into the wilderness. Even grand and well-planned schemes, such as the plot to link a series of cooperative colonies in Washington State into a socialist commonwealth, dissolved quickly and left few traces.

The book's greatest strength and weakness is Fogarty's refusal to flatten or simplify the differences between the many kinds of communes that mushroomed in the late-nineteenth-century United States. He gives each community a distinct identity and offers vivid sketches of charismatic leaders, but the result is a book more encyclopedic than coherent. Fogarty does not mine his rich

mininarratives for the insights into late-nineteenth-century American culture that they might provide, nor does he connect them as fully as he might to larger cultural and political movements of the time. Still, he provides a lively portrait of the countercultures of the post-Civil War era, and some food for thought in his characterization of a peculiarly American brand of utopian scheming. There is something encouraging and refreshing about this book. It leaves one feeling charmed and energized by the seemingly endless idealism, earnestness, even the kookiness of American commune builders.

ANNELISE ORLECK

Dartmouth College
Hanover
New Hampshire

GATES, JOHN B. *The Supreme Court and Partisan Realignment: A Macro- and Microlevel Perspective.* Pp. xvii, 253. Boulder, CO: Westview Press, 1992. $55.00.

Partisan realignments serve a number of critical functions in the political system. In addition to serving as a periodic "peaceful American revolution," a realignment is a window of opportunity for meaningful policy change and innovation. Analysts of voting behavior and political parties have rigorously examined these phenomena. Students of the Supreme Court have been less systematic in analyzing the role of the Court in the realignment process. In *The Supreme Court and Partisan Realignment*, John Gates undertakes the task of examining the institutional and individual-level effects of the realignment and the Court's role in the periods before and after the critical elections that serve as defining moments for partisan realignments.

Gates extends his analysis beyond previous studies of the Court and realignment by examining each of the recognized realignments, analyzing the individual behavior of justices, and including the Supreme Court's review of state cases involving issues that are central to the realignment. The inclusion of state cases is significant in that realignments are bottom-up phenomena that are evident below the federal election level. As a consequence, Gates is able to marshal the most compelling evidence to date to refute or at least qualify the "legitimizing" thesis advanced by Robert Dahl that the Court merely reinforces the position of the new majority. Gates determines that Supreme Court policymaking is much more complex and important to the course of national politics than Dahl argued (Robert A. Dahl, "Decision-Making in a Democracy: The Supreme Court as a National Policy-Maker," *Journal of Public Law*, 6:279-95 [Fall 1957]; Gates's analysis extends and buttresses arguments advanced in Jonathan D. Casper, "The Supreme Court and National Policy Making," *American Political Science Review*, 70:50-63 [Sept. 1976]).

Gates discusses two other possible roles for the Court in realignments: policy conflict following critical elections when the justices chosen by the old majority attempt to impede the power of the new majority (the "delegitimizing" role), and the Court's role in setting the agenda for the realignment, where the Court precipitates the critical election by making "salient and volatile decisions" that polarize the parties and hasten the realignment. Gates concluded that "the Supreme Court's policy decisions do not consistently demonstrate either an agenda-setting or a conflict role surrounding critical elections and realignment, albeit the data point more often to an agenda-setting role, rather than to the widely heralded policy conflict thesis."

The analysis of individual justices yields mixed results; expected divisions between justices along partisan lines do not materialize. Gates explains these findings by noting that sitting justices were selected prior to the emergence of the new crosscutting issue. This is particularly true in the transition from the New Deal period to the critical elections of 1960 and 1964. Hugo Black, William Douglas, and Felix Frankfurter, for instance, were selected by Franklin Roosevelt to uphold the New Deal, not for their values and attitudes concerning the civil rights and social issues of the post-*Brown* v. *Board of Education* period, the next set of crosscutting issues.

The book is a welcome edition to the literature on partisan realignments, judicial review, and the role of the Court in those periods of significant political change. Theoretically and methodologically, this is a sophisticated study that will be one of the core works of the field. Perhaps the only significant missing piece to the puzzle concerns the possibility that and the conditions under which the Court might block a potential realignment through its decisions.

RICHARD L. PACELLE, JR.

University of Missouri
St. Louis

GLICKSTEIN, JONATHAN A. *Concepts of Free Labor in Antebellum America.* Pp. 514. New Haven, CT: Yale University Press, 1991. $50.00.

The very first words of the introduction inform the reader of the major questions addressed in this scholarly product of a grant from the National Endowment for the Humanities:

How did Americans view the intrinsic character of manual labor during the three decades before the Civil War? What were the traditions of thought that helped shape these views? How did perceptions of the inherent rewards and pains of various forms of handwork figure in responses to key social and political developments of the period? And how did such perceptions contribute to mid-nineteenth-century agreement and disagreement over the nature of dignified, *truly free* labor? [Italics in original.]

Clearly, these are questions that have many dimensions, and even the major concepts resist easy definition. Given that the primary questions are addressed in little more than 300 narrative pages—endnotes total more than 188 pages—a remarkable amount of light is shed on the book's major queries. Subsidiary and related topics that are connected to these questions are appropriately addressed, including the mental aspect of the manual labor of the period—which obviously differs significantly from our own age of computers, gauges, premixed products, replacement components, and the like—and moral aspects of manual labor.

A number of interesting issues are raised and addressed by Glickstein. Do manual laborers see no dignity in their labor but see instead only the degradation or inferiority of their condition? Do professionals serve the end of locking laborers into their inferior status and condition by extolling the dignity, even the divinity, of the laborers' work? Do professionals who work with their minds earn nothing but only collect what manual laborers have earned? Is labor to be valued more than leisure? What of slave labor? These and many other interesting and knotty issues and questions are addressed by the author and by his sources, which stretch from the pre-Civil War era to later periods.

This well-written book should be of interest to many academicians who labor in various disciplines—chiefly, perhaps, philosophers, historians, sociologists, theologians, and academic social workers. It is a truly interdisciplinary work of a high level. This inquiry leaves few conceptual and philosophical stones unturned, and many will appreciate the detailed commentary contained in the endnotes, which adds considerable depth and subtlety to the main narrative. The introduction goes a long way toward providing the reader with context and with a reminder of certain of the difficulties of a study that examines a period of human existence that is vastly removed from our own. The reader is reminded, inter alia, that the pre-Civil War politicians, theologians, writers, and others whose ideas and words are cited and quoted do not necessarily speak for less privileged and powerful groups (principally, of course, but not solely, women and nonwhites); the reader also is warned that many of the commentators on manual labor at the time frequently spoke from self-interest, and the resulting hypocrisy likely colored many public pronouncements. Glickstein also offers aid to future researchers by commenting on the nature of research materials available to the serious student of the topic.

Glickstein mines a particularly rich era, an era in which slavery flourished in juxtaposition with a variety of trades and occupations that were being altered and replaced by occupations that were being altered or created by the industrial revolution that was then in its infancy. His sources are many, varied, and instructive, but a listing of them might have been of value to many, and in an age of the computer one would seem relatively easy to assemble. Because there is no separate listing of sources, readers must rely upon the index and the endnotes.

GEORGE R. SHARWELL

University of South Carolina
Columbia

GREIDER, WILLIAM. *Who Will Tell the People: The Betrayal of American Democracy.* Pp. 464. New York: Simon & Schuster, 1992. $25.00.

Who Will Tell the People is a trenchant account of a political system in which the people and the politicians hold one another in contempt, fewer and fewer people vote, government disparages popular values, and large corporations manipulate the policy process in their own interests at every step. "The corporations, together and separately, finance the parties and politicians," writes William Greider. "They sponsor the public-policy development needed to shape the governing debate. They mobilize public opinion around political agendas. . . . Above all, the formidable, ubiquitous presence of corporate political organizations persuades many citizens to retreat from the contest."

The stories in this book, some familiar, many not, are well told and well documented. Polls show overwhelming support for environmental protection, for example, but the government passes toothless laws, appoints safe administrators, and provides ticket fixing—under the aegis of the vice president in recent administrations—for corporations that, even so, find regulations burdensome. Republican executives and Democratic legislators keep a savings and loan scandal under wraps for years and, when it explodes, put the burden on the taxpayers, meanwhile reducing taxes on the rich at everyone else's expense. In each case, the government ignores the will of the people with impunity. In foreign and military affairs, the story is much the same but with more power in the White House and more secrecy.

The people have reason to be put off by electoral politics. Both parties are owned by the corporate interests, Greider concludes, and out of touch with the electorate. The Republicans, "the party of money," he says, have been able to win most presidential elections by posing as the party of the disaffected.

There is some hope, however, in nonelectoral participation, the day-by-day efforts of countless groups fighting the odds, raising a ruckus about problems of education, crime, taxes, pollution, utility rates, housing—in what he calls "irregular" politics, often negative and "crude and rude." He likes Václav Havel's vision of face-to-face democracy, expressed since as a land "crisscrossed by a network of local, regional, and state-wide clubs, organizations, and associations with a wide variety of aims and purposes"—a network in which, Havel says, "citizens will be more confident and proud, and will share a feeling of co-responsibility for public affairs."

Some of the most perceptive books on American politics these days are by journalists such as Kevin Phillips, E. J. Dionne, Jr., and William Greider, who understand the details and, to our benefit, how they fit together.

ROBERT J. SICKELS

University of New Mexico
Albuquerque

LINK, ARTHUR S. et al., eds. *The Papers of Woodrow Wilson*. Vol. 65. Pp. xxiv, 613. Princeton, NJ: Princeton University Press, 1991. $57.50.

At first glance, this volume might seem to be modifying old views of an all but incapacitated President, dominated by a wife who separated him from old friends and associates. Wilson seems all but in control of his office. He receives and answers letters. He walks, a reporter says, slowly to be sure, but is not confined to bed or a wheelchair. He would even like a third term as President and discusses strategy with close surrogates as the 1920 Democratic Convention nears. He is in complete charge of the fight for the Versailles Treaty.

A closer look at footnotes and surrounding data alters the picture. Senator Gilbert M. Hitchcock, leading Wilson's fight for the Peace Treaty, is shown to receive a letter signed by Wilson, but drafted by whom? The editors of the volume under review agree that Wilson's secretary, James P. Tumulty, was involved in its preparation and was conceivably its author, but in any case there is a revised first draft, an admitted Tumulty redraft, a Wilson redraft, a "penultimate" draft, and only then a final version. The President is not in full charge of his office.

He had already forced Secretary of State Robert Lansing's resignation, for having called a Cabinet meeting that Wilson interpreted as a power play. Although Wilson had permitted Colonel House to act freely in his name during the war, the President now stopped his access to the White House. Nonetheless, if anyone was an acting President, it was Tumulty, who maintained working contact with Cabinet members on vital issues: a threatened railroad strike, a threatened coal strike, problems with alleged seditionists. Tumulty was in constant contact with Wilson but mainly through Mrs. Wilson by correspondence, though they were both in Washington. Dr. Cary T. Grayson, Wilson's physician, kept close check on his patient. He gave positive reports of Wilson's condition to the press; he showed less conviction of progress in his private diaries.

The striking fact emerging from the documents is that Wilson, though impaired physically and even mentally, was not only determined to be President but was actually eager for and working for a third term. David F. Houston, of the Cabinet, offers an account of Wilson's own effort at a Cabinet meeting, supervised by Dr. Grayson. "The President looked old, worn, and haggard. . . . One of his arms was useless." Wilson's voice was weak and strained. When he so evidently could not focus on an issue before the Cabinet, the railroad crisis, Dr. Grayson looked pointedly at the door. Finally, Mrs. Wilson entered and said plainly, "We had better go."

This was the man, then, who pressed on his closest associates—Tumulty; new Secretary of State Bainbridge Colby; Home S. Cummings, chairman of the National Democratic Committee—his plan for a succession of events at the June 1920 Democratic Convention to have himself declared the Democratic nominee by acclamation. Wilson even prepared notes for an acceptance speech and for a new Cabinet. His friends, however, knew all this to be fantasy. They rejected his suggestions on the evasive grounds that reelection would kill him. His willingness to be a "martyr" to the cause of peace could not hide the fact that anything more than elaborately expressed praise—which Wilson received at the convention—would have subjected him to humiliation.

There are nuggets among these letters, papers, and collateral correspondence not to be found elsewhere. Wilson's undeliberated view of Herbert Hoover as a man without courage was doubtless prompted by jealousy. Wilson has been judged harsh toward such as Eugene V. Debs, in prison for opposing intervention in the late war. In fact, he would have freed those suffering in federal prisons for freedom of speech; it was such of his associates as A. Mitchell Palmer at the Department of Justice who would not permit him to show tolerance and compassion. In his last phase, Wilson was bereft of power.

LOUIS FILLER

The Belfry
Ovid
Michigan

LOWRY, WILLIAM R. *The Dimensions of Federalism: State Governments and Pollution Control Policies.* Pp. xii, 168. Durham, NC: Duke University Press, 1992. $29.95.

STOKER, ROBERT P. *Reluctant Partners: Implementing Federal Policy*.
Pp. xv, 213. Pittsburgh, PA: University
of Pittsburgh Press, 1992. $39.95.

Governmental efficacy, policy implementation, and American federalism are
the preoccupations of the two recent
books under review. Each assumes a different orientation to the topics; both are
valuable.

William Lowry's concern is with factors influencing state leadership behavior in implementing and supplementing
national policy. Rejecting equally the alternative characterizations of the states
as, on the one hand, wholly inept and
unresponsive and, on the other, the sole
bastion of current American policy leadership, Lowry seeks a more complex accounting of state policy performance in
the interplay between policy and intergovernmental concerns.

State leadership behavior, Lowry argues, is dependent upon two dimensions
of federalism: the horizontal dimension of
interstate competition and the vertical
dimension of strong top-down federal involvement. For any given policy area,
states may, in the aggregate, prove more
or less vulnerable to interstate competition—such as the threat of industry relocation—and more or less subject to the
prodding or facilitating efforts of national
government. Policies can thus be differentiated along these crosscutting intergovernmental dimensions. Lowry posits
that in policy areas where federal presence is high and horizontal competition
low, state responsiveness and leadership
will emerge. Where the converse applies,
states will falter. His analysis of four
cases of air and water pollution policy
affirms his views.

Readable, well-grounded, and interesting theoretically, the contributions of
this book remain modest, both because its
thesis seems somewhat logical and self-
evident and because its applicability may

be limited, inherently better adapted to
discussions of environmental or economic
regulation than to other domestic policies
—like education, drug treatment, home-
less policies—where the treatment of issues of horizontal federalism would be
less clear.

Very powerful contributions are evident, however, in Robert Stoker's ambitious, insightful book. Taking issue with
those who see diffusion of authority in the
American political system as the enemy
of national efficacy, Stoker seeks to forge
an approach that reconciles constitutional commitments to a liberal, federal
polity with the need for effective national
action. Along the way, he melds the literatures on power, governance, policy implementation, and federalism, and he
offers a compelling, long-overdue critique
of the implementation literature. While
aiming to extend beyond federalism to
address diffusion of authority between
market and government, his emphasis is
on the former.

The book's chief advances are embedded in Stoker's identification of "the implementation paradox"—that under a
system of diffuse authority, the act of
implementing national policy often empowers its own potential adversaries. The
central issue in implementation, then,
becomes how to contend with the "reluctant partners" that result. Here the implementation literature fails, he charges,
by confusing instrumental effectiveness
with governance.

While his argument is more complex
than I can do justice to here, Stoker accurately asserts that the implementation
literature tends to approach subnational
participants as implementation liabilities
and to promote strategies for contending
with them that emphasize conflict and
the use of federal authority—penalties,
sanctions—to force state or local confor-
mity to national will. Though this approach may ultimately prove instrumen-

tally effective from a policy standpoint, he argues, it fails as a strategy for governance. Governance, as he sees it, requires securing effective national action in a manner that respects and validates important constitutionally embedded values, such as federalism.

Building upon Clarence Stone's important observation that power is not only "power over" but "power to"—the assembling of the capacity to act—Stoker develops an alternative framework focused not on conflict and control but, novelly, on cooperative action and its potential for realization through construction of "implementation regimes." Despite some weaknesses and what seems to be an inherent bias toward conservative policy action, this book remains an important work.

Taken together, these books address a very timely and useful set of intergovernmental concerns. Differences in orientation and focus render them complementary, Lowry reminding us that federalism matters, Stoker's strong normative focus reminding us that it should.

DEBORAH A. AUGER

University of Delaware
Newark

MAYHEW, DAVID R. *Divided We Govern: Party Control, Lawmaking, and Investigations, 1946-1990.* Pp. viii, 228. New Haven, CT: Yale University Press, 1991. $25.00.

HERTZKE, ALLEN D. and RONALD M. PETERS, JR., eds. *The Atomistic Congress: An Interpretation of Congressional Change.* Pp. xvi, 342. Armonk, NY: M. E. Sharpe, 1992. $45.00. Paperbound, $18.50.

Public confidence in Congress hit record lows in 1991 and 1992. The legislature just does not seem to be able to get anything done. Why are things so much worse now than they used to be? Or are they?

David Mayhew's *Divided We Govern* tackles the most common explanation offered these days. The problem is divided government. For 20 of 24 years between 1969 and 1993 the Republicans held the White House and the Democrats at least one house of Congress. With immovable objects and irresistible forces, no wonder we have such problems. Yet Mayhew, Alfred Cowles Professor of Government at Yale University, debunks the myth that our problems are mainly institutional. Surveying 267 major laws enacted between 1947 and 1990 and 31 important investigations conducted during the same period, Mayhew exonerates divided government. The President and Congress have agreed on significant policy changes about as often under conditions of split control as during divided government. Investigations are more likely to occur under divided control, but only barely more frequently than expected.

Mayhew's book sets a standard to which all reform treatises will be held. One should not accept conventional wisdom on faith. We have come to expect painstaking research from Mayhew, and he lays it out here in great detail, including all of his data points and his myriad sources. While the particulars are sometimes overwhelming, they also produce a compelling case for his thesis. The White House and Congress can work together if they want to do so. Cooperation was most likely at the beginning of an administration and during the "activist mood" from 1961 through 1976, according to his statistical analysis. The public demand for innovation was high during this period, as it was during Progressivism and the New Deal.

This is a powerful thesis for what will clearly become a classic in American politics. Yet Mayhew's solution founders on what logicians call "affirming the consequent." The dummy variable for public activism is little more than a reflection of the dependent variable, legislative activism. Mayhew is right, but he misses what moves the public: not trust in government or the ideological tilt of the electorate but trust in other people. The activist mood is communitarian rather than ideological. When trust in other people is high, Congress and the President are more likely to be activist and willing to cooperate.

The volume by Allen Hertzke and Ronald Peters, Jr., political scientists at the University of Oklahoma, is a collection of essays on historical change in Congress. Two pieces are outstanding: Charles Stewart III's treatment of how party leaders, even at the supposed peak of their influence in the Reed and Cannon days, are at the mercy of their followers; and Barbara Sinclair's examination of the contextual factors leading to strong party leadership in the House—mostly the size and ideological homogeneity of the Democratic Party. All of the other essays are worthwhile. Randall Strahan challenges Stewart's assumption that context is more important to leadership style than personality in his examinations of Reed and Rostenkowski. While the comparisons are interesting, Strahan cannot quite show that Reed was such a transforming figure or that whatever successes Rostenkowski has achieved can be traced to his style rather than to context.

James E. Campbell shows how presidential coattails have declined over a 120-year period. David T. Canon traces the increasing competitiveness of southern Republicans as their legislative candidates have gained more experience in lower offices. L. Sandy Maisel traces patterns of quality candidates in House and Senate races; the material on the House is familiar, that on the Senate new and worthy of comparison. David Rohde does a very nice job in showing how partisanship in the contemporary House varies

with party and presidential strength and how the Democrats have increasingly shaped committee decisions to reflect liberal strength on the floor. Carol E. Swain and Donald C. Baumer provide workmanlike, if journalistic, accounts of African American representation in Congress and the contemporary Senate leadership.

The editors begin the volume with a lengthy essay that tries to integrate the diverse essays to follow, propose a framework for analyzing the "atomistic Congress" in which individualism rules, and send both a methodological and ideological message. They fail in their attempt. The ideological message is that Congress is composed of a bunch of self-interested politicians who cannot do more than raise their own salaries. Evidence? The methodological message is that "political science is torn between long-term trends that defy rigorous scientific explanation and short-term fluctuations that seem impossible to predict." Quantitative analyses are therefore banished to appendices, and the editors even take a passing potshot at what is arguably the best essay in the volume, Stewart's. How do these sophomoric statements add to our understanding?

I wish that the editors' introduction helped more. They are on the right track. American political culture has produced an "atomistic Congress." Yet their treatment of political culture is far too vague. What is American political culture? An answer would require a more systematic—dare I say "scientific"?—inquiry into value change over time, and this would reveal that conflict over core ideals is not new but has roughly followed the pattern of party alignments. Most frustrating is the editors' attempt to fit the nine essays into this framework. At least five of the pieces (Canon, Stewart, Rohde, Sinclair, and Baumer)—a clear majority—focus on the emergence of more coherent partisan cleavages in recent years rather than the atomism Hertzke and

Peters envisage. Both perspectives are correct, but this book gives no idea why.

ERIC M. USLANER

University of Maryland
College Park

MISCAMBLE, WILLIAM D. *George F. Kennan and the Making of American Foreign Policy, 1947-1950.* Pp. xvii, 419. Princeton, NJ: Princeton University Press, 1992. $35.00.

George Kennan has been the subject of three monographs—one by the reviewer—in the last couple of years; Miscamble's is the fourth, though in a way he can claim seniority since his work is based on a dissertation written more than a decade ago. This is a new work, however, with none of the thesis quality of the original. It is a solid overview of the decision period between 1947 and 1950, when the early Cold War came into being and Kennan headed the enormously influential Policy Planning Staff in the State Department. Miscamble is indeed chiefly interested in the policymaking side of things, namely, in Kennan's role and effectiveness in the formulation and execution of the many crucial American moves during the period. The subject is covered thoroughly and usefully. Thus, with the Policy Planning Staff as the vantage point, Miscamble surveys the major policy events, such as the Marshall Plan, the North Atlantic Treaty Organization, the division of Germany, the reconstruction of Japan, the development of the hydrogen bomb, and Korea. Nothing much in his account will surprise those familiar with Kennan or with this, after all, most familiar of moments in American foreign policy; nonetheless, it is good to have a detailed view of the bureaucratic ins and outs. The decisive role played by the historiographically neglected John D. Hickerson *contra* Kennan is commendably emphasized.

The weakness is in the analysis. Miscamble sets himself the Rankean task of letting the story emerge from "what actually happened" and so speak with "the authenticity of the past." He thinks this can and should be done without "some overarching interpretation" or "artificial methodological 'sophistication.'" Of "methodological 'sophistication'" there is indeed none. Nor is there much of an argument. Yet, as in all Rankean exercises, there is, of course, an "overarching interpretation" at work, and it is traditionalist through and through: the United States reacts to crises and developments abroad, and something concrete—and valuable—emerges piecemeal. Kennan was thus not an "architect" with a plan but "one of the on-site builders," notes Miscamble. At the same time, however, Kennan is said to have "possessed a coherent strategy designed to restore the balance of power." Miscamble's symptomatically lackluster conclusion never resolves this antinomy.

Kennan's policymaking texts from the late 1940s have become canonical in that they lend themselves to constant reinterpretation. Here, along the lines of John Lewis Gaddis, Miscamble makes Kennan into a much more mainstream American figure than he was. The sharp edges, the political peculiarities and contradictions, are largely ignored.

ANDERS STEPHANSON

Columbia University
New York City

NEWMAN, ROBERT P. *Owen Lattimore and the "Loss" of China* Pp. xvi, 669. Berkeley: University of California Press, 1992. $30.00.

Owen Lattimore was a principal victim of the anti-Communist hysteria generated by Senator Joseph McCarthy—and many others—after the "loss of China" to the Communists in 1949. Having had the exciting pleasure of meeting Owen Lattimore at the home of my Chinese history professor, Woodbridge Bingham of the University of California, Berkeley, in the midst of the McCarthy era, and subsequently being inspired to work to establish the Conference (now Council) on Peace Research in History after reading his *Ordeal by Slander* and seeing the results of government interference in academia during the 1950s, I found it fascinating indeed to read this book.

Younger generations will probably find the book far too long and detailed to be interesting reading, and it will gather dust in libraries as primary source material, but it is the great achievement of author Newman—a modern Boswell?—to have captured the life of a truly international scholar caught in the crossfire of that Cold War era and surviving—with many wounds. Utilizing Lattimore's personal papers and files—Lattimore was a great note taker on his travels and adventures—as well as the huge Federal Bureau of Investigation and other government files on Lattimore, the suspected Communist, Newman has reconstructed the poignant story of a life in very difficult times. The key facts that emerge are that Lattimore was never a Communist, even with a small *c*, and that the government agencies that attempted to prosecute—"persecute" would be a better word—him used all sorts of contrived evidence shamelessly. The truth that emerges is that Lattimore's first and second loves—the order may not be quite clear—were Central Asia and his wife, Eleanor, and both China and the USSR were obstacles not only to his studies of that Mongolian borderland but to visiting there with Eleanor as he loved to do, beginning with their honeymoon in 1927. On the honeymoon, Eleanor literally had to travel by dogsled because Owen could not get through Soviet red tape to meet her at their appointed Transiberian Railway

station as arranged. How could he have become "the top Russian espionage agent in the U.S."—Senator McCarthy's description—after that? And Lattimore survived financially by playing the stock market! Another interesting irony Newman uncovered is that John Melby, a Foreign Service officer, who was fired as a security risk for being friends with "pro-communist playwright" Lillian Hellman, considered McCarthy's accusation of Lattimore entirely accidental (p. 215 and note 23; cf. Robert P. Newman, *The Cold War Romance of Lillian Hellman and John Melby* [Chapel Hill: University of North Carolina Press, 1989]). Also, it is interesting, and sad, that Johns Hopkins University, where he was a tenured professor, treated Lattimore so shabbily, especially trustees and president Milton Eisenhower, even after he had been cleared.

In November 1962, he accepted a professorship at the University of Leeds, England. Newman calls this "starting over" and then "recovery and triumph" as Lattimore reemerged as a world-renowned scholar of Mongol-Central Asian history and customs. After Eleanor died in 1970, he had problems of readjustment, including a bout with alcoholism, but he was still working on books and papers when he died at age 88, in 1989.

While it could be said that the prosecutions and persecutions of the McCarthy era did no permanent, irrevocable harm to Lattimore, whose wit and wisdom sustained him, some of us may remember that this was not the case with another fine scholar who also became a target of our ultranationalist senators of that era. E. Herbert Norman committed suicide. (He may have attended a Marxist study group at Harvard.) This all seems like ancient history now!

HILARY CONROY

University of Pennsylvania
Philadelphia

SLOAN, JOHN W. *Eisenhower and the Management of Prosperity.* Pp. viii, 191. Lawrence: University Press of Kansas, 1991. $25.00.

BROADWATER, JEFF. *Eisenhower and the Anti-Communist Crusade.* Pp. xiii, 291. Chapel Hill: University of North Carolina Press, 1992. $34.95.

These two books offer conflicting views of Dwight D. Eisenhower's presidency. Historian Jeff Broadwater criticizes Eisenhower's rough treatment of the Bill of Rights during the McCarthy era, while political scientist John W. Sloan renders a favorable verdict on Ike's economic policies. While Sloan's work contributes to the revisionist literature that has dominated recent Eisenhower studies, Broadwater's monograph represents a significant departure from revisionist assessments that have vastly enhanced Ike's stature and reputation over the past twenty years.

Once scorned and ridiculed as an inept, bland, and unimaginative President led by his advisers and cabinet members, Ike is now positively viewed by most scholars as the leading man in his own administration, a strong and thoughtful executive who spoke softly but ruled with a firm yet "hidden" hand.

Along with Ike the leader has emerged Ike the doer. No longer are the Eisenhower years portrayed as "the great postponement" that merely served to interrupt the innovative work of more energetic and activist Democratic administrations. Instead, Eisenhower is now awarded high marks for achievement, especially in the fields of national defense and foreign policy.

In *Eisenhower and the Management of Prosperity,* John W. Sloan extends the revisionist view of Eisenhower into the realm of economic policymaking. Eisenhower, Sloan argues, "was the most significant player in determining his administration's macroeconomic policy" and was "constantly attentive and often assertive in this policy area" even though he "recognized his lack of expertise and experience."

Though heavily influenced by strong-willed advisers, the economic policies of the Eisenhower administration clearly reflected the President's deep personal commitments to cutting taxes, controlling inflation, and balancing the budget. These essentially conservative aims were offset by Ike's determination to protect New Deal welfare programs from right-wingers in his own party and by his willingness to balance the budget by making huge cuts in defense spending.

General prosperity, along with Eisenhower's ending of the Korean War, allowed Ike to have it both ways during his first term and to skillfully pull the United States out of a brief but sharp recession in 1954. Mounting fiscal pressures brought on by population growth, continued Cold War tensions, and an escalating balance-of-payment deficit reduced Ike's flexibility during his second term and forced him into an increasingly rigid and conservative posture. Overly fearful of unleashing inflation, Ike responded timidly to the election-year recessions of 1958 and 1960, with disastrous consequences for the Republican Party.

Nevertheless, Sloan rates Eisenhower's presidency as an economic success. Despite three brief recessions, Ike cut taxes in 1954, balanced three budgets, and kept inflation down to an annual rate of 1.5 percent. Though sluggish relative to that of Japan, Western Europe, and the Soviet Union, America's real gross national product enjoyed an average annual growth of 2.9 percent. Overall, says Sloan, Ike's performance in the modern presidential role of "manager of prosperity" surely "merits a much higher regard than it has previously received."

Jeff Broadwater is not so kind. In *Eisenhower and the Anti-Communist Cru-*

sade, Broadwater dissents from recent Eisenhower revisionism and provides a critical assessment of Ike's behavior during the Red Scare of the early 1950s. Broadwater explicitly rejects Fred Greenstein's contention that Ike systematically employed his behind-the-scenes "hidden hand" leadership to effectively topple Joe McCarthy in 1954. Instead, Broadwater returns to an earlier view that depicts Eisenhower as vacillating and retreating before McCarthy's reckless witch-hunting.

Though much of Eisenhower's reluctance to confront McCarthy stemmed from his fear of alienating the GOP Right, Broadwater argues that the main reason was simply that "Ike, for all his basic decency, shared with the McCarthyites much of their obsession with internal security and their unconcern for civil liberties." On those two issues, says Broadwater, "the administration stood closer to the McCarthyites than it did to the liberals."

Broadwater makes his case in convincing style by detailing Eisenhower's own witch-hunting activities. In April 1953, Eisenhower issued Executive Order 10450, which implemented an internal security program that gave executive-branch administrators sweeping powers to investigate and dismiss suspected "security risks." Grounds for dismissal were left dangerously vague, and affected personnel were denied the right to see the evidence used against them or to face their accusers. The ensuing purge, which claimed over 8000 federal employees during its first year alone, found enthusiastic henchmen in Attorney General Herbert Brownell, U.N. Ambassador Henry Cabot Lodge, and former Federal Bureau of Investigation (FBI) agent Scott McLeod, whom Secretary of State John Foster Dulles unleashed on the diplomatic corps. Enjoying Ike's hearty support, FBI Director J. Edgar Hoover flourished as never before. In addition to spying on the

American Communist Party and launching the notorious Counterintelligence Program (COINTELPRO), Hoover provided Ike with intelligence reports on Eleanor Roosevelt, Norman Thomas, William O. Douglas, and the National Association for the Advancement of Colored People.

In the final analysis, what emerges from Broadwater's detailed account is an Eisenhower who rather quietly yet dramatically out-McCarthied Joe McCarthy. For those readers who have been celebrating the Eisenhower renaissance, Broadwater's book will certainly spoil the party.

MICHAEL MAGLIARI

California State University
Chico

SOCIOLOGY

BROWN, KAREN McCARTHY. *Mama Lola: A Vodou Priestess in Brooklyn.* Pp. x, 405. Berkeley: University of California Press, 1991. $24.95.

Since the Herskovits-Frazier debate on the legitimacy of the African heritage in the Americas, scholars have learned to pay closer attention to the continuing and re-created relations between Africa and the New World. Pensioned-off West African soldiers settled in Trinidad, and free African migration continued during the nineteenth century. Not so in North America, for which Frazier maintained that African American culture was essentially a product of slavery, against Herskovits, who argued for the presence of "survivals" of Yoruba and Dahomean life. More recently, with the active re-creation of an Africa in such groups as Rastafari (Jamaica), the Earth People (Trinidad), and MOVE (United States), academics have become more sympathetic to the notion that each generation actively remakes its past, for "tradition" has constantly to be reenacted.

At first glance, the present volume is not promising. A glossy presentation, title, and subheadings ("Healing, the Vodou way") and a meager bibliography argue for some coffee-table exoticism. Seldom can a reader be more disconcerted, however, for this volume is superb: a poignant account of a Haitian migrant to New York and how she appropriates and reworks her family knowledge of voodoo healing and ritual. Intercutting the ethnographic chapters, each presided over by a figure from the voodoo pantheon, are a series of semi-fictionalized vignettes derived by Brown from family tales told to her by Alourdes, the priestess. In dense but readable narrative, the themes that Alourdes picks up recall and revise real, lived experiences situated in historical time. The *loas* (spirits), which possess her at formal ceremonies or at times of crisis, condense both historical memories and immediate daily life, "catalyst[s] who mobilize the will and energy of human beings." They are addressed in Port-au-Prince cemeteries and Brooklyn living rooms, through collective ceremonies and extemporized household altars, through corn meal and potato chips.

The *loas* manifest in transient thoughts and in dreams; they are formally supplicated or they suddenly descend to invest their human children. They are objectifications of parents, of personal memory, of anger and fantasy, of sexuality and poverty, of maternity or implacable natural power. In Brooklyn, Alourdes's clients come to her with sickness and misfortune, lost or sought jobs, erring partners and desired lovers, with all the problems of poor and marginalized immigrants in a new country. The *loas*, too, have to live in a new context: the Gede (trickster spirit) takes on American identities. The libations once poured onto the earth floor

of the Haitian house now are collected in bowls to be used in healing baths and thus to be returned into the bodies of the devotees.

A short review fails to do justice to this volume's richness. Voodoo is formal and informal, pluripotent, assimilating and appropriating, less concerned with belief or doctrine than with existing human relationships. Dr. Brown places a particular emphasis on the shallow matrilineages that emerge in Haitian society. As the reconstituted peasantry that formed after slavery breaks down under political corruption, droughts, and white imperialism, with migration to the towns and to the United States, the muted voice of the women becomes more salient. We have here tales of decisive women, economically active mothers and culture carriers who respond with exasperation to the feckless and violent men whose lives intersect with their own. Gently informed by her own life and by women's anthropology, Brown offers a sympathetic and vivid portrait of the lives of a group of women, a creolized world that, in its themes and in its apparent avoidance of polemic, justly stands comparison with Godfrey Lienhardt's *Divinity and Experience*.

ROLAND LITTLEWOOD

University College London
England

CHEN, HSIANG-SHUI. *Chinatown No More: Taiwan Immigrants in Contemporary New York.* Pp. xi, 281. Ithaca, NY: Cornell University Press, 1992. $37.95. Paperbound, $14.95.

ZHOU, MIN. *Chinatown: The Socioeconomic Potential of an Urban Enclave.* Pp. xxiv, 275. Philadelphia: Temple University Press, 1992. $44.95.

Until recently, as Alejandro Portes points out in his foreword to Min Zhou's book, Chinatown has received surprisingly little scholarly attention. The two books reviewed here are examples of a new and most welcome research interest, which has itself been encouraged and facilitated by changes inside and outside these extraordinary social entities in the past thirty years. Most important among these, the massive Chinese immigration after 1965, when the national-origin quota system that had severely restricted Chinese immigration was replaced by a system stressing family unification and economic considerations, has transformed Chinatown from a homogeneous (predominantly Cantonese peasants), closed society of sojourners whose economic activities were confined to laundries and restaurants to a heterogeneous (more urban immigrants coming from Taiwan as well as Hong Kong), less closed society of settlers engaged in a variety of business ventures and the professions, including social scientists.

While both books focus on these changes in New York City, they differ in terms of their theoretical sophistication and methodology. Hsiang-Shui Chen, an anthropologist teaching in Taiwan, focuses on the new Chinatown that developed in Queens in the 1980s. His primary methodology is participant observation. At the center are interviews with 100 households, representing the working class, the small-business class, and professionals, conducted between 1984 and 1987. Each class is represented by three in-depth portraits. Although these reports and the accounts of community and organizational life are interesting, Chinatown No More lacks theoretical sophistication. While the book provides interesting insights into the lives of new Chinese immigrants in Queens, it fails to make a connection with the ample literature on immigration and immigrant incorporation.

Min Zhou's Chinatown, which focuses on New York's Chinatown, more generally does not only make that connection,

but it also attempts to draw some practical implications. Its sources of information include documentary studies of historical data, fieldwork, and U.S. census statistics, the latter providing the primary source for the data analysis. The data are used skillfully to support the enclave model of immigrant incorporation. Following Portes and his associates, Zhou argues that the immigrant enclave provides alternative patterns of social mobility for Chinese immigrants, guarding against degradation, providing immigrants with opportunities in the enclave economy that are not available in the larger society. Zhou does a good job of tracing the development of Chinatown from a product of structural legal barriers imposed by American society and serving the needs of its sojourning, bachelor residents to a relatively heterogeneous, residentially more dispersed, economic and social entity. Zhou is to be commended for devoting a chapter to demonstrating that enclave economic opportunities are restricted to men. Women fail to benefit as individuals from enclave activity. While they may benefit as part of the family strategy, the enclave depends heavily on the availability of unpaid and low-paid female workers.

Both books outline the new Chinatown in the United States. Chinatown is more sophisticated and hence appeals more to the professional social scientist, but it lacks the rich ethnographic information that represents the strength of Chinatown No More.

BARBARA SCHMITTER HEISLER

Gettysburg College
Pennsylvania

CLIGNET, REMI. Death, Deeds, and Descendants: Inheritance in Modern America. Pp. xi, 236. Hawthorne, NY: Aldine de Gruyter, 1992. $43.95.

Social scientists have not given the subject of intergenerational transmission the attention it merits. It probably plays a role in the operation of the American economic and social structure. The study of inheritance also provides an interesting avenue into both the economic and the symbolic aspects of family life.

In this volume, Remi Clignet, a French-origin sociologist at the University of Maryland, provides brief commentaries on the literatures of a wide range of topics related to inheritance and, similarly, advances his opinions about diverse features of contemporary American society.

The heart of the study is a quantitative analysis of 232 federal estate tax returns of older, wealthy individuals in two years, 1920 and 1944, that were chosen for the availability of data in the files of the Internal Revenue Service. Of course, as Clignet recognizes, the transmission of property at death is only one aspect of intergenerational transmission. Inspired by the work of anthropologist Sonya Salamon on ethnic differences in inheritance practices of farmers in central Illinois, Clignet chose to study an unusual population of Americans. He sampled the estate records of individuals who had German or Irish forenames and surnames. He also attempted to balance the gender composition of the sample, and he excluded the wealthiest decedents and those under the age of 50. Statistical analyses of this idiosyncratic data set deal with such topics as the diversity of asset portfolios among the decedents, the incidence of intestacy, the choice of executor, and inequality of treatment of heirs.

Overall, the volume is disappointing. The results of the empirical work only tangentially relate to various points made in the terse snippets of commentary on theoretical issues. Not surprisingly, given the small sample sizes, few of the predictors of the indicators of estate composition and bequest patterns are statistically significant; differences between Irish and German Americans, the main issue incorporated into the design of the sample, are few and unremarkable. A more sharply focused presentation of the results in a journal article or two would have been a better format for Clignet and for students of American inheritance patterns.

Inheritance in America, by Carole Shammas, Marylynn Salmon, and Michel Dahlin (1987), is a more useful historical treatment, and On the Human Bond: Parent-Child Relations across the Life Course, by Alice S. Rossi and Peter H. Rossi (1990), provides a more developed sociological case study dealing with intergenerational issues.

DANIEL SCOTT SMITH

University of Illinois
Chicago

FLIGSTEIN, NEIL. The Transformation of Corporate Control. Pp. viii, 391. Cambridge, MA: Harvard University Press, 1990. $35.00.

Neil Fligstein's Transformation of Corporate Control offers an innovative sociological perspective for understanding the growth and prosperity of America's largest corporations through the evolution of four dominant conceptions of control from 1865 to the present. The four conceptions are direct control (1865-1904), manufacturing control (early 1900s to 1929), sales and marketing control (1920s-1940s), and finance control (1950s to the present).

The central thesis of the book is that the largest corporations in the United States survived and grew not according to economic views of capital efficiency, maximizing profits, and rational management practices but according to how firms adapted to the long-term shifts in their conception of control. Fligstein's contribution is the shift of the focus on the large corporations' success and growth

208

THE ANNALS OF THE AMERICAN ACADEMY

away from ahistorical and deterministic neoclassical economic theories of the firm to the institutional context of production, the complex interactions between the largest firms, and the state's effect on corporations through antitrust and other corporate boundary-setting laws.

Fligstein uses sociological theory and frameworks along with analytical tools of the historian and economist to make his arguments. The sociological theory of the firm that he employs is not new. As he recognizes, Alfred Chandler, Hannan and Freeman, Meyer and Rowan, Meyer and Scott, Perrow, and others also viewed organizations as fields, embedded in complex networks of interactions in which dominant coalitions created strategies and structures to exert their power over the internal organization as well as over their competition and environments. The legal and administrative constraints of the state also played a significant role in determining which firms survived and which did not. In 1986, I also presented a review of sociological literature and frameworks that showed how organizational actors use dominant coalitions and strategies to survive and compete (*The Management of Change, Administrative Logics and Action* [New York: Praeger, 1986]). However, it is Fligstein's creative, sweeping use and presentation of sociological theory supported by rigorous data analyses that give force to his arguments.

The first conception of control—in the late nineteenth century—was direct control of one's competitors. The strategies of price competition, cartelization, and the creation of monopolies were successfully used by corporations during this period. Since there were no rules to constrain competitors' behavior fields, these predatory forms of competition worked to control competition. Holding companies were the primary organizational form that worked well with this control conception and strategies to control large portions of product lines for larger companies.

The major goal of the second conception of control, manufacturing control, was to manufacture products without interference from competitors. The means used to accomplish this was predominantly defensive in nature. It was to control inputs and outputs through vertical and horizontal integration of production. The strategies used with this control conception were backward and forward integration of production, mergers for increasing market share, and oligopolistic product markets. Suppliers and marketing functions were absorbed into the organization by vertical integration. This strategy protected firms from their competitors' predatory strategies.

During the 1920s and in the post-World War II era, the third conception of control—sales and marketing control—evolved. The goal of this conception was to find, create, and maintain markets. The dominant strategies included differentiation in product quality and price, increased advertising to gain market share, new product development, and expanded domestic and overseas markets.

The fourth and current conception of corporate control is finance control. This conception seeks dominance over competition through the use of financial tools that measure short-run profits. Companies are understood as asset collections, not as producers of goods. The firm divests if the desired rate of return is not received. The key strategies that drive this form of control are "diversification through mergers and divestments (as opposed to internal expansion); financial ploys to increase the stockpile, indebtedness, and ability to absorb other firms; and the use of financial controls to make decisions about the internal allocation of capital." The organizational field under this control system shifts from one that is industrially based to one that is based on financial strategies, such as leveraged buy-outs, stock repurchases, and corporate restructuring. Short-run profit and rates of return are the keys to success, whereas, in the direct-control conception, price stability was the central motivation to dominate competition through external monopolies. Under manufacturing control, price stability through the internal control of the production process along with oligopolistic pricing was the main motivation. Under sales and marketing control, the ability to produce quality goods and maintain a mass market were the central motivators to compete.

The holding company was a major organizational form used under direct control; the unitary and functional form was used under manufacturing control; the multidivisional and multiproduct form was used under sales and marketing control and under finance control. The divisional form and the product center are also dominant forms used in the finance conception of control.

The major theme of Fligstein's book is made repeatedly, often to the point of redundancy: corporate interactions with political and legal forces internal and external to large firms were and are the basic determinants of control that help define markets and dominate competition. Nevertheless, this book is an important contribution to the history of business and to neoclassical theories that explain U.S. corporate growth and success. Fligstein has done a fine job of integrating several theoretical strains of sociology, history, and economics with historical data on corporations over a sweeping time frame. Critics may argue that his method is more descriptive and historical than predictive.

He concludes the book by looking into "the future of the large American corporation." This section is weak, and the topic really deserves more thought and space. Fligstein almost abandons his conceptual frame of control logics to speculate as a journalist. He notes that large U.S. firms face the current crisis of not meeting international challenges of competition. Since the financial conception of control still dominates U.S. firms, "any new view must overtake the power of the stock market and finance executives to dictate a concern with short-run profits." Two scenarios for the future are offered. The first holds that a long-run view of investment is required, accompanied by cooperation in structural changes between firms to create new technologies and aided by an industrial policy that permits joint ventures and discourages mergers; successful corporate examples will have to result for this scenario to be implemented and imitated. The second scenario suggests a continuation of the already existing corporate practices: "Smaller firms could continue to innovate and larger firms then purchase their assets." Even with this scenario, the author notes that "much depends on how the federal government changes the rules by which capital is depreciated, mergers are executed, and cooperation between firms is allowed."

JOSEPH W. WEISS

Bentley College
Waltham
Massachusetts

GREVEN, PHILIP. *Spare the Child: The Religious Roots of Punishment and the Psychological Impact of Physical Abuse*. Pp. xiv, 263. New York: Knopf, 1991. $22.95.

Social scientists are, by training and experience, rightfully skeptical of theses that ascribe varied and complex phenomena to a single source. Hence there are reasons to be wary of Philip Greven's attempt to designate the corporal punishment of children as the root cause of a panoply of social and psychological disorders. At the same time, Greven's lucid and provocative arguments deserve careful consideration; if he at times overstates his case and the evidence for it, he nonetheless raises critical issues concerning the way we rear our children, the foundations of our strategies, and the consequences of physical punishment in childhood for well-being as adults.

The book is divided into five sections. In part 1, Greven presents his dual objectives: to locate the roots of corporal punishment in Christian doctrine, especially fundamental Protestantism, and to explore the myriad psychopathologies that result from childhood discipline. Part 2 describes the experiences of prominent theologians, evangelists, and other religious figures with physical punishment during childhood, while part 3 reviews the biblical, judicial, and scientific sources advocating—or, in a few rare instances, condemning—the physical discipline of children. Greven's argument here is that society has been all too accepting of physical punishment in the name of parenting, applying standards to child rearing that would be considered abhorrent if applied to relationships between adults. Our uncritical acceptance and frequent misreading of Christian philosophy is the main culprit.

Part 4 of the book turns to the purported consequences of child punishment. The list of psychological and social afflictions, each receiving detailed treatment, is extensive, to say the least: anxiety and fear, anger and hate, empathy and apathy, melancholy and depression are joined by obsessiveness and rigidity, ambivalence, dissociation, and paranoia, to which are added sadomasochism (a particularly titillating discussion of T. E. Lawrence), domestic violence, aggression and delinquency, authoritarianism, and, finally, an apocalyptic impulse. Part 5 concludes the book with a plea for the abolition of child punishment and the widespread adoption of nonviolent methods of child training.

While Greven's themes are profound, they are, unfortunately, rarely matched by the weight of the evidence. Greven's primary methodology is psychobiography, in which he traces the life histories of eminent citizens to reveal, more often than not, a pattern of physical abuse as children and later maladaptations as adults. What this technique fails to provide, of course, is evidence that persons not abused as children fare any better. Further, Greven's indictment of Christianity as the instigator of violence toward children remains baseless without valid comparisons to other religions; certainly, one need not look very hard to find aggression, violence, fear, and hate in non-Christian societies. Moreover, some readers may find Greven's characterization of all forms of physical punishment—no matter how mild—as abuse too crude and unnuanced. These objections aside, Philip Greven has provided us with a stimulating and forceful discussion of a neglected and, quite likely, pathological aspect of our culture.

SCOTT J. SOUTH

State University of New York
Albany

IYENGAR, SHANTO. *Is Anyone Responsible? How Television Frames Political Issues*. Pp. viii, 195. Chicago: University of Chicago Press, 1991. $19.95.

SLATON, CHRISTA DARYL. *Televote: Expanding Citizen Participation in the Quantum Age*. Pp. 226. New York: Praeger, 1991. $47.95.

In *Is Anyone Responsible?* Shanto Iyengar examines television's subtle but important role in influencing how citizens understand the causes of social problems and whom the public holds accountable for solving these problems. The principal independent variable is whether or not news coverage on television places events in a political context. He studies a variety of social issues, including crime, poverty, and the Iran-contra affair.

Iyengar adroitly supplements his extensive laboratory experiments with both content and correlational analyses. Notwithstanding his calling them "field experiments" throughout the book, these are laboratory experiments. He concludes that newscasts fail to place social issues in a political context and that this makes public institutions less accountable to the American public.

Although the principal weakness of experimental studies typically lies in the generalization of findings, Iyengar's study has problems with internal as well as external validity. The experimental methods are not described well enough for me to discover if the subjects accepted the experimental manipulations. The samples are not representative: the subjects were too well paid and too well educated. Finally, the statistical methods should have been described more thoroughly. From what is presented, it is unclear if Iyengar recognizes that discussions between the subjects would act to reduce the effective sample size and thus increase the requirements for statistical significance.

Other than sharing the conviction that television plays an important role in American politics, Iyengar's book and Christa Slaton's *Televote* could hardly be more different. Where Iyengar's book presents an experimental study of television's influence on political perceptions, *Televote* describes an idealistic approach to using television to get alienated voters more involved in politics. In her book, Slaton claims that televote is an "unbiased, independent" way to circumvent "special-interest groups" and empower disinterested citizens. Televote involves following up information campaigns with a telephone poll.

As a remedy for the ills of modern democracy, televote is underwhelming.

Democratic participation involves much more than polls. I found patronizing Slaton's assumption that it is better for democracy to have university students distribute bowdlerized presentations of issues than to encourage citizens to form interest groups to advance their own goals. *Televote* would have been more interesting if Slaton had provided a balanced discussion of the issues raised in the *Federalist Papers* instead of wasting an entire chapter comparing "quantum" and "Newtonian" theories of politics. Finally, while it is crucial to evaluating the success of televote, Slaton never provides the data necessary for evaluating televote's participation rate.

GARY A. MAUSER

Simon Fraser University
Burnaby
British Columbia
Canada

KASINITZ, PHILIP. *Caribbean New York: Black Immigrants and the Politics of Race.* Pp. xv, 280. Ithaca, NY: Cornell University Press, 1992. Paperbound, $13.95.

Philip Kasinitz has written a timely and thorough book that brings into focus the large and influential Caribbean-origin community in New York City.

Although Kasinitz explores multiple aspects of the Caribbean immigrant experience in this well-researched book, a prominent theme throughout is the interaction of race and ethnicity. The author suggests that West Indians—as he reluctantly calls immigrants of African descent from the English-speaking Caribbean—achieve "economic upward mobility at the price of downward mobility in status" when they confront racial stratification in the United States. Assimilation and loss of cultural distinctiveness, in this situation, may lead to loss of social status. In response, Kasinitz argues that West Indians have played an active role in "making" ethnicity a public issue. Ethnic politics have increased with the growth of the West Indian community, development of ethnic institutions, shifts in New York's racial and ethnic composition, changes in the role of race in the United States, and New York politicians' increasing interest in the West Indian vote.

The first half of the book is a historical examination of some of these changes. Kasinitz identifies three waves of West Indian immigration beginning at the turn of the century. The most recent cohort, by far the largest, arrived in the wake of immigration legislation in 1965 that permitted more entrants from all social classes. Currently, there are between 500,000 and 1 million West Indians in New York City. Over the years, many of these immigrants have risen to positions of prominence in New York's black community.

As the West Indian population increased and more localities opened up to blacks, West Indian enclaves formed. Kasinitz makes an intriguing suggestion—which he unfortunately does not pursue—that these new West Indian neighborhoods provide opportunities for extensive home ownership, starting a "pattern of capital accumulation" that may help explain why these neighborhoods have not suffered the same kind of deterioration as other inner-city areas. West Indian ethnic institutions flourished; they included community organizations, local merchants, a community press, educational institutions, organized crime, self-help associations and networks, rotating credit associations, and informal "cottage industries." These developments, Kasinitz argues, solidified a sense of ethnic identity among West Indians.

The second half of the book addresses the creation of ethnic political identity. This is where Kasinitz's fieldwork becomes more evident and, in many ways, the book comes alive. Here the reader shares the excitement of the huge and relatively unknown West Indian Labor Day Carnival, when normal organizational life is suspended and ethnic identity can be reformulated. Key leaders in the West Indian community are profiled, based on information gleaned from personal interviews and secondary sources. Kasinitz details the emergence of "old guard leaders," "ethnicity entrepreneurs," and "militants." He observes that until recently, there was no unified West Indian vote despite the presence of West Indians in New York politics since the beginning of the century. In the 1980s, however, the Caribbean community began to play an increasingly important role in the political process.

Overall, the book is rich and informative. At times, the many themes introduced and the sometimes distracting citations of secondary sources make it a challenge to follow. Nonetheless, Kasinitz's observational skills and knowledge of the Caribbean community in New York City make this book an important addition to the growing body of work on immigration, race, and ethnicity in America.

MARGARET SHERRARD
SHERRADEN

University of Missouri
St. Louis

ECONOMICS

ELSENHANS, HARTMUT. *Development and Underdevelopment: The History, Economics and Politics of North-South Relations*. Pp. 176. Newbury Park, CA: Sage, 1991. $22.50.

GEORGE, SUSAN. *The Debt Boomerang: How Third World Debt Harms Us All*. Pp. xxi, 202. Boulder, CO: Westview Press, 1992. $34.95. Paperbound, $15.95.

In *Development and Underdevelopment*, Professor Hartmut Elsenhans, of the University of Konstanz, deals with a host of crucial changes in development aid and theory and their significance for the recent history of North-South economic relations, and he accomplishes this in a short but admirably comprehensive survey. He uses historical materials from early modern as well as recent times to show why nineteenth-century Western industrialization was not replicated in the Third World. A special value of this work is that it tackles, from a liberal point of view, both the historical changes and the social science concepts needed to explain why Third World social structures stand in the way of overcoming underdevelopment. Many of his expositions and analyses are set out in the "1., 2., 3." fashion dear to undergraduates, but his book was not written primarily as a text. His main purpose is to use history and theory to show that the way to avoid "downward equalization" in the Third World is to "form alliances" (unspecified) between Western advocates of more and better aid and certain elements of "State-classes" in poor countries, including those who by conviction or self-interest are inclined toward centralist or Marxian development policies.

This book is a 1991 English translation of the original 1984 German edition and does not take into account the shattering changes brought about by the recent collapse of the Soviet development model. Aside from a bibliography, it contains no scholarly apparatus, making it hard for readers to be sure of the source of some of his ideas and even of his figures. In his bibliography, the stars of neoconservative thinking on development are conspicuous by their absence.

The themes and commitments of Susan George's latest work will be familiar to those who have read her *Fate Worse than Debt* (1988). If only the North would cancel the Third World's terrible burden of international debt, what a wonderful world it would be! Environmental degradation would recede, the curse of addictive drugs would lift, northern jobs and markets would increase, and immigration into northern nations would diminish—as would the threat of international and civil wars. George is careful to say that she does not intend us to see in Third World indebtedness the sole cause of the global evils she treats, but she emphasizes repeatedly that debts are, "at the very least, aggravating factors."

The word "boomerang" in the title of this work is intended to convey the hope —now that appeals to the North based on moral and humanitarian grounds seem to have failed—that rich countries can be moved toward more rational action by understanding where their own self-interest lies. The book is, very forthrightly, a call to action: the last page invites readers to literally sign up for enrollment in the Transnational Institute's Debt Boomerang Project, aimed at solving the crisis through "popular participation in decision making, social equity, and ecological prudence." Each chapter in the book provides a wealth of carefully footnoted and otherwise good arguments for debt cancellation. The book's style is lively and engaging, as when George shows that reverse capital flows have equaled the value of "six Marshall Plans."

Given the book's objectives, it does not matter much that some claims are patently unfair, like the one that sees that the only reason for structural adjustment policies is to procure debt repayments. Phrases sneering at "our civilisation— such as it is . . . " seem to be meant more to keep the reader on his or her toes than to be taken in entire seriousness. And it is only to be expected that a book that, verging perilously close to conspiratorial theorizing, blasts proponents of debt repayment as agents of well-healed propagandists should on other pages complacently list the sources of funded support for the Transnational Institute, which sponsored this book.

There is, however, one blatant fault in this work that calls into question its author's willingness to abide by the rules of fair argument: nowhere is there the slightest consideration of the possibility that Third World misfortunes here addressed have anything to do with the crushing increases in Third World population.

MARTIN WOLFE

University of Pennsylvania
Philadelphia

TILMAN, RICK. *Thorstein Veblen and His Critics, 1891-1963*. Pp. xxi, 356. Princeton, NJ: Princeton University Press, 1992. $39.50.

Thorstein Veblen (1857-1929), arguably the leading U.S. dissenter in the history of American economic and social thought, held academic posts at Cornell, Chicago, Stanford, Missouri, and the New School for Social Research. He wrote such seminal works as *The Theory of the Leisure Class*; *The Theory of Business Enterprise*; *The Instinct of Workmanship*; *Absentee Ownership*; and *Imperial Germany and the Industrial Revolution*. His wide range of subjects included philosophy, anthropology, war and peace, and sociology, and his provocative thinking stimulated much analysis, both critical and supportive.

Rich Tilman's study of critical reactions to Veblen's economic and social views is the first of a projected three volumes, with the others to deal with Veblen's ideas in the context of European thought and "with sociological theories and methods in vogue in the West since 1945." In this volume, Tilman presents the reac-

tions of Veblen's conservative, liberal, and radical critics, mainly economists.

Tilman begins with conservatives, including "traditional" conservatives, the "Chicago school," and critics operating from a religious standpoint. He next examines liberal critics of all stripes—institutionalists, Keynesians, and so on. Turning to radicals, Tilman looks at some from the Frankfurt (Germany) school and then some American writers for *The Monthly Review* and from the ranks of Marxists, Trotskyites, and social democrats.

Included are such luminaries as conservatives Irving Fisher and Frank Knight; Lev Dobriansky, a religiously oriented economist; the progressive Richard Ely; and institutionalists Wesley C. Mitchell, John R. Commons, and J. M. Clark. Sociologists Talcott Parsons, David Riesman, Robert Merton, and Daniel Bell, too, are examined. Paul Sweezy and Paul Baran are among the radical economists cited.

Veblen's many assaults on establishment doctrines included his distinction between a real world of industry and a predatory world of finance, assaults on marginalism and neoclassical economics, and his idea of waste through conspicuous consumption, among others. He viewed depression as a result of lowered capital values associated with technological advances.

Critics denied the distinction between industry and finance, citing Veblen's failure to see the role of uncertainty, risk, and entrepreneurial foresight. They found exaggeration in his characterization of neoclassical economics, ideology-driven bias, amateur anthropology and psychology, lack of prescription for the economy, lack of coherent theory, and so on.

Tilman's is a valuable compendium on the work of an important historical figure whose analyses of some problems hold up today, perhaps most directly in the financial frenzy of the 1980s, when, for example, the leveraged buy-out craze led to disaster for many a solid business. Assembling in one place a critical study of Veblen's views should simplify life for the historian of economic thought. One possible criticism of Tilman is that he has some tendency to be too defensive about Veblen as he carefully analyzes the critics' views. Nevertheless, Tilman has done a masterful job.

ERVIN MILLER

University of Pennsylvania
Philadelphia

TURNER, LOWELL. *Democracy at Work: Changing World Markets and the Future of Labor Unions.* Pp. xviii, 279. Ithaca, NY: Cornell University Press, 1991. $24.95.

The central hypothesis of this volume is that certain institutions governing labor relations in advanced capitalist economies are principally responsible for the successes and failures that these economies experienced responding to the last decade's intensification of international industrial competition. Above all else, though not to the exclusion of all else, Turner argues that indigenous labor relations have dictated the ability of these economies to increase productivity and to adopt new technologies and new work organizations. He begins with an elucidation of the theoretical foundations of his position and then turns to a lengthier empirical argument.

Turner identifies two dimensions of labor relations central to his perspective. First is whether unions forged cooperative pacts with management to become integrated into the plant and firm decision processes, or are engaged in an adversarial, arm's-length relationship with management. The second dimension differentiates economies with a unified, national structure of labor relations from those with a decentralized and fragmented configuration that does not transcend individual firms or industries. Within this matrix, Turner suggests that nations such as West Germany, with management-labor integration, combined with a national labor relations structure, have experienced the most stable, adaptive economic response, have sustained robust organized labor, and have dealt most successfully with the turbulence of the 1980s. Economies such as Japan's, which have highly integrated management-labor cooperation but negligible national labor institutions, have fared well in this period—indeed, have been a driving force—but have suffered a decline in labor organization, to the point where labor leadership is literally indistinguishable from management. The next-best outcome includes economies such as Sweden's, where management and labor deal at arm's length but where a strong tradition of national labor relations exists. The worst outcome, both in terms of economic resilience and union vitality, has been economies with a decentralized, fragmented labor movement with adversarial, arm's-length management and labor relations, as in the economies of the United States, France, Britain, and Italy.

Turner primarily uses the automobile industries in these countries, particularly those of the United States and Germany, the polar cases in his matrix, to illustrate and substantiate his claim. For these two detailed cases, he develops insightful links between the relevant labor relations institutions and the recent trajectories of this industry, not only across national economies but also with respect to the dispersion of institutions and outcomes within the national economies. The only gaping hole in his treatment of the U.S. auto industry, for example, is the failure to discuss the recent Saturn initiative at General Motors. When Turner expands his view to embrace a few additional industries—telecommunications and apparel—or additional economies—Britain, Italy, Sweden, and Japan—the evidence is supportive but too sketchy to fully substantiate the remainder of his institutional matrix.

Presented with the carefully stated hypothesis and the marshaling of considerable evidence, the reader may still have unanswered questions. For example, should one not look at these institutions themselves as endogenous rather than exogenous? This would require a somewhat expanded historical context, as recent events have certainly moved more rapidly than the companion institutions, but does all this not truly unfold in an interactive and dynamic context, perhaps along the lines of the recent work on social structures of accumulation? And are Social Democratic nations, with their diminished cost of job loss, not more likely to tolerate greater latitude in the adoption of labor-saving technological change and changed work rules—or is this implicitly subsumed within the author's national labor relations institutions? Should one not also inquire into the institutional relationship between the core automobile industries and the peripheral sectors of these economies?

Despite these lingering questions, the reader will be impressed with Turner's command of most recent details of the U.S. and German automobile industries, as well as his familiarity with the highlighted labor relations institutions in these national industries, and will find this book a good place to gain a strong footing in these matters. Turner has compiled an extensive bibliography, which will be a welcome aid to scholars with similar pursuits.

ALEXANDER M. THOMPSON III

Vassar College
Poughkeepsie
New York

OTHER BOOKS

ANDERSON, WALTER TRUETT. *Reality Isn't What It Used to Be*. Pp. xiii, 288. San Francisco, CA: Harper & Row, 1990. $18.95.

BARTLETT, BEATRICE S. *Monarchs and Ministers: The Grand Council in Mid-Ch'ing China, 1723-1820*. Pp. xxi, 417. Berkeley: University of California Press, 1991. $45.00.

BEHN, ROBERT D., ed. *Governors on Governing*. Pp. vi, 184. Lanham, MD: University Press of America, 1991. Paperbound, $20.50.

BENDER, JOHN and DAVID E. WELLBERY. *Chronotypes: The Construction of Time*. Pp. xi, 257. Stanford, CA: Stanford University Press, 1991. $37.50. Paperbound, $12.95.

BENSMAN, JOSEPH and ROBERT LILIENFELD. *Craft and Consciousness: Occupational Technique and the Development of World Images*. 2d ed. Pp. xxiv, 395. Hawthorne, NY: Aldine de Gruyter, 1991. $49.95. Paperbound, $27.95.

BRAUNTHAL, GERARD. *Political Loyalty and Public Service in West Germany: The 1972 Decree against Radicals and Its Consequences*. Pp. xvi, 249. Amherst: University of Massachusetts Press, 1990. $27.50.

BREMBECK, COLE S. *Congress, Human Nature, and the Federal Debt: Essays on the Political Psychology of Deficit Spending*. Pp. xii, 176. New York: Praeger, 1991. $39.95.

BROGAN, MARTHA L., comp. *Research Guide to Libraries and Archives in the Low Countries*. Pp. x, 546. Westport, CT: Greenwood Press, 1991. $75.00.

CALINGAERT, DANIEL. *Soviet Nuclear Policy under Gorbachev: A Policy of Disarmament*. Pp. x, 180. New York: Praeger, 1991. $39.95.

CALVERT, ROBERT E., ed. *"The Constitution of the People": Reflections on Citizens and Civil Society*. Pp. xii, 168. Lawrence: University Press of Kansas, 1991. $27.50. Paperbound, $12.95.

CALVERT, SUSAN and PETER CALVERT. *Argentina: Political Culture and Instability*. Pp. xiv, 327. Pittsburgh, PA: University of Pittsburgh Press, 1989. $39.95.

CAMPBELL, COLIN and BERT A. ROCKMAN, eds. *The Bush Presidency: First Appraisals*. Pp. x, 308. Chatham, NJ: Chatham House, 1991. $25.00. Paperbound, $16.95.

CHILTON, STEPHEN. *Grounding Political Development*. Pp. viii, 134. Boulder, CO: Lynne Rienner, 1991. No price.

CITINO, ROBERT. *Germany and the Union of South Africa in the Nazi Period*. Pp. x, 245. Westport, CT: Greenwood Press, 1991. $45.00.

CLARK, BARRY. *Political Economy: A Comparative Approach*. Pp. xii, 313. New York: Praeger, 1991. $24.95.

CONSTABLE, PAMELA and ARTURO VALENZUELA. *Chile under Pinochet: A Nation of Enemies*. Pp. 367. New York: Norton, 1991. $24.95.

DAHL, ROBERT A. *Democracy and Its Critics*. Pp. viii, 397. New Haven, CT: Yale University Press, 1991. $35.00. Paperbound, $17.00.

DAMASKA, MIRJAN R. *The Faces of Justice and State Authority: A Comparative Approach to the Legal Process*. Pp. xi, 247. New Haven, CT: Yale University Press, 1991. $30.00. Paperbound, $16.00.

DAVIDSON, DONALD. *Regionalism and Nationalism in the United States: The Attack on Leviathan*. Pp. xxiii, 368. New Brunswick, NJ: Transaction, 1991. Paperbound, $19.95.

DEFRONZO, JAMES. *Revolutions and Revolutionary Movements*. Pp. xvi, 336. Boulder, CO: Westview Press, 1991. $59.95. Paperbound, $16.95.

DELL, SIDNEY. *International Develop-ment Policies: Perspectives for Indus-trial Countries.* Pp. x, 378. Durham, NC: Duke University Press, 1991. $49.95. Paperbound, $19.95.

DREXLER, ROBERT W. *Guilty of Mak-ing Peace: A Biography of Nicholas P. Trist.* Pp. ix, 152. Lanham, MD: Uni-versity Press of America, 1991. $37.50.

EASTON, DAVID et al., eds. *The Devel-opment of Political Science.* Pp. 296. New York: Routledge, Chapman & Hall, 1991. $49.95.

ELLSWORTH, EDWARD W. *Science and Social Science Research in British India, 1780-1880: The Role of Anglo-Indian Associations and Government.* Pp. xv, 220. Westport, CT: Greenwood Press, 1991. $47.95.

ELWELL, FRANK W. *The Evolution of the Future.* Pp. xii, 144. New York: Praeger, 1991. $37.95.

ENGLISH, JOHN A. *The Canadian Army and the Normandy Campaign: A Study of Failure in High Command.* Pp. xvii, 347. New York: Praeger, 1991. $47.95.

ENTRIKIN, J. NICHOLAS. *The Between-ness of Place: Towards a Geography of Modernity.* Pp. xii, 196. Baltimore, MD: Johns Hopkins University Press, 1991. $38.50. Paperbound, $13.95.

ERNST, WALTRAUD. *Mad Tales from the Raj: The European Insane in Brit-ish India 1800-1858.* Pp. xi, 196. New York: Routledge, Chapman & Hall, 1991. $74.00.

FALK, RICHARD A. et al., eds. *The United Nations and a Just World Order.* Pp. xvi, 589. Boulder, CO: Westview Press, 1991. $50.00. Paper-bound, $18.95.

FARRAR, MARJORIE MILBANK. *Prin-cipled Pragmatist: The Political Career of Alexandre Millerand.* Pp. xi, 432. Providence, RI: Berg, 1991. $80.00.

FISHER, LOUIS. *Constitutional Con-flicts between Congress and the Presi-dent.* 3d ed., revised. Pp. xv, 326. Law-rence: University Press of Kansas, 1991. $35.00. Paperbound, $14.95.

FISHMAN, ETHAN, ed. *Public Policy and the Public Good.* Pp. xxviii, 167. Westport, CT: Greenwood Press, 1991. $45.00.

FITZGERALD, DEBORAH. *The Busi-ness of Breeding: Hybrid Corn in Illi-nois, 1890-1940.* Pp. xi, 247. Ithaca, NY: Cornell University Press, 1990. $29.95.

FLORO, SAGRARIO L. and PAN A. YOTOPOULOS. *Informal Credit Mar-kets and the New Institutional Econo-mies.* Pp. xvi, 146. Boulder, CO: West-view Press, 1991. Paperbound, $23.50.

GRIECO, JOSEPH M. *Cooperation among Nations: Europe, America, and Non-Tariff Barriers to Trade.* Pp. xii, 255. Ithaca, NY: Cornell University Press, 1990. $39.95.

HALE, CHARLES A. *The Transforma-tion of Liberalism in Late Nineteenth-Century Mexico.* Pp. xi, 291. Prince-ton, NJ: Princeton University Press, 1990. $37.50.

HALLENBECK, RALPH A. *Military Force as an Instrument of U. S. Foreign Pol-icy: Intervention in Lebanon, August 1982-February 1984.* Pp. xv, 232. New York: Praeger, 1991. $47.95.

HEIMS, STEVE J. *The Cybernetics Group.* Pp. xii, 334. Cambridge: MIT Press, 1991. $25.00.

HELD, DAVID, ed. *Political Theory Today.* Pp. ix, 360. Stanford, CA: Stan-ford University Press, 1991. $39.50.

HELLINGER, DANIEL C. *Venezuela: Tarnished Democracy.* Pp. xx, 236. Boulder, CO: Westview Press, 1991. $34.00.

HOBBS, JOSEPH J. *Bedouin Life in the Egyptian Wilderness.* Pp. xix, 165. Aus-tin: University of Texas Press, 1990. $25.00.

HONNETH, AXEL. *The Critique of Power: Reflective Stages in a Critical Social Theory.* Pp. xxxii, 340. Cambridge: MIT Press, 1991. $35.00.

INKELES, ALEX, ed. *On Measuring Democracy: Its Consequences and Concomitants.* Pp. x, 234. New Brunswick, NJ: Transaction, 1991. $19.95. Paperbound, $14.95.

JACKSON, JAMES S., ed. *Life In Black America.* Pp. 311. Newbury Park, CA: Sage, 1991. $45.00. Paperbound, $19.95.

JERVIS, ROBERT and SEWERYN BIALER, eds. *Soviet-American Relations after the Cold War.* Pp. vi, 356. Durham, NC: Duke University Press, 1991. $45.00. Paperbound, $19.95.

JOHNSON, JOHN J. *A Hemisphere Apart: The Foundations of United States Policy toward Latin America.* Pp. x, 271. Baltimore, MD: Johns Hopkins University Press, 1990. $32.50.

KACHRU, BRAJ B. *The Alchemy of English: The Spread, Functions, and Models of Non-Native Englishes.* Pp. ix, 200. Champaign: University of Illinois Press, 1990. Paperbound, $12.95.

KASLER, DIRK. *Sociological Adventures: Earle Edward Eubank's Visits with European Sociologists.* Pp. xi, 195. New Brunswick, NJ: Transaction, 1991. No price.

KOBURGER, CHARLES W., JR. *The French Navy in Indochina: Riverine and Coastal Forces, 1945-54.* Pp. xxvi, 133. New York: Praeger, 1991. $39.95.

KOHL, WILFRID L., ed. *After the Oil Price Collapse: OPEC, the United States, and the World Oil Market.* Pp. xxii, 230. Baltimore, MD: Johns Hopkins University Press, 1991. $39.95.

KYMLICKA, WILL. *Liberalism Community and Culture.* Pp. 280. New York: Oxford University Press, 1991. Paperbound, $19.95.

LADD, HELEN F. and JOHN YINGER. *America's Ailing Cities: Fiscal Health and the Design of Urban Policy.* Pp. xiii, 348. Baltimore, MD: Johns Hopkins University Press, 1991. Paperbound, $14.95.

LAIDI, ZAKI. *The Superpowers and Africa: The Constraints of a Rivalry, 1960-1990.* Pp. xxv, 232. Chicago: University of Chicago Press, 1990. $45.00. Paperbound, $14.95.

LANE, JAN-ERIK and SVANTE O. ERSSON. *Politics and Society in Western Europe.* 2d ed. Pp. viii, 421. Newbury Park, CA: Sage, 1991. $55.00. Paperbound, $19.95.

LEMCO, JONATHAN. *Canada and the Crisis in Central America.* Pp. 199. New York: Praeger, 1991. $42.95.

LERNER, MAX. *Ideas Are Weapons: The History and Uses of Ideas.* Pp. xxi, 553. New Brunswick, NJ: Transaction, 1991. Paperbound, $18.95.

LEWIS, RAND C. *A Nazi Legacy: Right-Wing Extremism in Postwar Germany.* Pp. xvi, 184. New York: Praeger, 1991. $39.95.

MacKENZIE, JAMES J. and MOHAMED T. EL-ASHRY, eds. *Air Pollution's Toll on Forests and Crops.* Pp. ix, 376. New Haven, CT: Yale University Press, 1992. $45.00. Paperbound, $20.00.

MANGOLD, TOM. *Cold Warrior James Jesus Angleton: The CIA's Master Spy Hunter.* Pp. 462. New York: Simon & Schuster, 1991. $24.95.

MANSFIELD, HARVEY C., JR. *America's Constitutional Soul.* Pp. x, 236. Baltimore, MD: Johns Hopkins University Press, 1991. $25.95.

MARTIN, MALACHI. *The Keys of This Blood: Pope John Paul II versus Russia and the West for Control of the New World Order.* Pp. 734. New York: Touchstone Books, 1991. Paperbound, $15.00.

MARTINELLI, ALBERTO, ed. *International Markets and Global Firms: A Comparative Study of Organized Business in the Chemical Industry.* Pp. viii, 294. Newbury Park, CA: Sage, 1991. $60.00.

MILLER, JOSHUA. *The Rise and Fall of Democracy in Early America, 1630-1789.* Pp. xi, 154. University Park: Pennsylvania State University Press, 1991. $19.95.

MORELAND, LAURENCE W. et al., eds. *The 1988 Presidential Election in the South: Continuity amidst Change in Southern Party Politics.* Pp. xiv, 296. New York: Praeger, 1991. $47.95.

MULLER-ROMMEL, FERDINAND and GEOFFREY PRIDHAM, eds. *Small Parties in Western Europe: Comparative and National Perspectives.* Pp. 232. Newbury Park, CA: Sage, 1991. $55.00.

NAVARI, CORNELIA, ed. *The Condition of States.* Pp. vi, 238. Bristol, PA: Open University Press, 1991. Paperbound, no price.

NELSEN, BRENT F. *The State Offshore: Petroleum, Politics, and State Intervention on the British and Norwegian Continental Shelves.* Pp. xvi, 250. New York: Praeger, 1991. $47.95.

OAKESHOTT, MICHAEL. *Rationalism in Politics and Other Essays.* Pp. xxvi, 556. Indianapolis, IN: Liberty Press, 1991. $24.00.

OPELLO, WALTER C., JR. *Portugal: From Monarchy to Pluralist Democracy.* Pp. ix, 177. Boulder, CO: Westview Press, 1991. $34.95.

PARDO-MAURER, R. *The Contras, 1980-1989: A Special Kind of Politics.* Pp. xxii, 151. New York: Praeger, 1990. $35.00. Paperbound, $12.95.

PETERSMAN, ERNST-ULRICH. *Constitutional Functions and Constitutional Problems of International Economic Law.* Pp. li, 463. Boulder, CO: Westview Press, 1991. Paperbound, $45.00.

PITSVADA, BERNARD T. *The Senate, Treaties and National Security, 1945-1974.* Pp. 245. Lanham, MD: University Press of America, 1991. $39.50. Paperbound, $24.50.

PLANT, RAYMOND. *Modern Political Thought.* Pp. xi, 398. Cambridge, MA: Basil Blackwell, 1991. Paperbound, $18.95.

POLYCHRONIOU, CHRONIS. *Marxist Perspectives on Imperialism: A Theoretical Analysis.* Pp. xvii, 180. New York: Praeger, 1991. $39.95.

PRICE, ROBERT M. *The Apartheid State in Crisis: Political Transformation in South Africa, 1975-1990.* Pp. x, 309. New York: Oxford University Press, 1991. $55.00. Paperbound, $16.95.

RABAN, JONATHAN. *Arabia: A Journey through the Labyrinth.* Pp. 344. New York: Touchstone Books, 1991. Paperbound, $11.00.

RABINOWITCH, ALEXANDER. *Prelude to Revolution: The Petrograd Bolsheviks and the July 1917 Uprising.* Pp. 299. Bloomington: Indiana University Press, 1991. $35.00. Paperbound, $12.95.

ROSS, ANDREW L., ed. *The Political Economy of Defense: Issues and Perspectives.* Pp. x, 229. Westport, CT: Greenwood Press, 1991. $47.95.

SAUNDERS, HAROLD H. *The Other Walls: The Arab-Israeli Peace Process in a Global Perspective.* Pp. xliv, 240. Princeton, NJ: Princeton University Press, 1991. Paperbound, $14.95.

SCHLESINGER, PHILIP. *Media, State and Nation: Political Violence and Collective Identities.* Pp. ix, 202. Newbury Park, CA: Sage, 1991. $55.00. Paperbound, $22.50.

SEBBA, HELEN et al., eds. *The Collected Essays of Gregor Sebba: Truth, History, and the Imagination.* Pp. xxviii, 469. Baton Rouge: Louisiana State University Press, 1991. $45.00.

SOIFER, STEVEN. *The Socialist Mayor: Bernard Sanders in Burlington, Vermont.* Pp. xiv, 285. New York: Bergin & Garvey, 1991. $45.00.

TAAGEPERA, REIN and MATTHEW SOBERG SHUGART. *Seats and Votes: The Effects and Determinants of Electoral Systems.* Pp. xviii, 292. New Haven, CT: Yale University Press, 1991. $30.00. Paperbound, $16.00.

THOMPSON, KENNETH W. *Cold War Theories.* Vol. 1, *World Polarization, 1943-1953.* Pp. 216. Baton Rouge: Louisiana State University Press, 1991. Paperbound, $9.95.

TOCH, HANS and J. DOUGLAS GRANT. *Police as Problem Solvers.* Pp. xv, 303. New York: Plenum, 1991. $39.50.

TROYANSKY, DAVID G. et al., eds. *The French Revolution in Culture and Society.* Pp. xvii, 221. Westport, CT: Greenwood Press, 1991. $45.00.

TSIGANOU, HELEN A. *Worker's Participative Schemes: The Experience of Capitalist and Plan-Based Societies.* Pp. xiii, 254. Westport, CT: Greenwood Press, 1991. $49.95.

VALONE, STEPHEN J. *"A Policy Calculated to Benefit China": The United States and the China Arms Embargo, 1919-1929.* Pp. xxii, 155. Westport, CT: Greenwood Press, 1991. $39.95.

VAN CREVELD, MARTIN. *The Training of Officers: From Military Professionalism to Irrelevance.* Pp. ix, 134. New York: Free Press, 1990. $19.95.

WAGNER, MELINDA BOLLAR. *God's Schools: Choice and Compromise in American Society.* Pp. xiii, 270. New Brunswick, NJ: Rutgers University Press, 1990. Paperbound, no price.

WILLIAMS, MARC. *Third World Cooperation: The Group of 77 in UNCTAD.* Pp. ix, 182. New York: St Martin's Press, 1991. $55.00.

WILLIAMS, ROSALIND. *Notes on the Underground: An Essay on Technology, Society, and the Imagination.* Pp. xi, 265. Cambridge: MIT Press, 1990. $19.95.

WUTHNOW, ROBERT, ed. *Between States and Markets: The Voluntary Sector in Comparative Perspective.* Pp. 318. Princeton, NJ: Princeton University Press, 1991. $55.00. Paperbound, $11.95.

YARNOLD, BARBARA M. *International Fugitives: A New Role for the International Court of Justice.* Pp. xii, 149. New York: Praeger, 1991. $37.95.

YOHANNES, OKBAZGHI. *Eritrea, a Pawn in World Politics.* Pp. x, 331. Gainesville: University of Florida Press, 1991. $34.95.

ZIMMERMAN, DEIRDRE A. and JOSEPH F. ZIMMERMAN. *The Politics of Subnational Governance.* 2d ed. Pp. 311. Lanham, MD: University Press of America, 1991. $46.50. Paperbound, $27.50.

ZIZEK, SLAVOJ. *Looking Awry: An Introduction to Jacques Lacan through Popular Culture.* Pp. ix, 188. Cambridge: MIT Press, 1991. $22.50.

INDEX